Best In Hollywood

THE GOOD, THE BAD, AND THE BEAUTIFUL

James Best

WITH JIM CLARK

Published in the USA by:
BearManor Media
PO Box 71426
Albany, Georgia 31708
www.bearmanormedia.com

ISBN 1-59393-460-2

Printed in the United States of America.
Cover design by Scott Romine.
Book Design by Brian Pearce.

To my dear children, JoJami, Janeen, and Gary, all my grandchildren, future grandchildren, and the world. That should just about cover it.

TABLE OF CONTENTS

TABLE OF CONTENTS

ACKNOWLEDGMENTS

First and foremost, I offer a rose for Dorothy, my beautiful, precious wife, for her help and encouragement to write this book in the first place. She has a photographic mind and remembers dates and places. Without her help with research and proofreading, this book could very well have been in shambles because I have trouble remembering what I had for breakfast.

I especially want to thank Jim Clark, whose professional expertise and sensibility helped shape my dictated story into a readable form that still preserves the flavor of my personality, good or bad. Without his skill and perseverance, this book would never have been written.

I would also like to thank publisher Ben Ohmart at BearManor Media for believing in this project and wanting to help me share it with a larger audience of readers. I also thank Scott Romine, who designed the cover, Brian Pearce, the book designer, and David W. Menefee, our editor, for their talents and assistance.

I also want to thank you for reading my book. If you would like the latest information about what is going on in my world, I invite you to visit my web sites, *www.jamesbest.com* and *www.bestfriendfilms.com*. You might also want to check out some of my artwork. Most people do not yet know that I am one heck of a good artist, and I am also modest to a fault.

PREFACE

Writing this book serves several important purposes for me. One is to have a written record of some of my accomplishments. As in any life, there are some things about which I am not proud, but I hope this book can provide a factual record — at least as factual as an eighty-two-year-old memory can recall. I want to share my point of view about my life experiences with my children and their children. I want to give them some sense of what my life was all about.

I hope my family will not disown for me for the silly and sometimes dumb things I might have been involved in, especially during the days when I was hell-bent on being an actor in Hollywood. I hope they will remember me as a good ol' boy who tried to leave this world a little better than when I came into it. There were some very painful times along the way and sometimes tears, but most of all, there has been a heck of a lot of laughter in my humble attempt to be the best actor, artist, and person I can be. I can tell you one thing — I have enjoyed the ride and have been mightily blessed. The Good Lord has worked overtime for this old boy, and now I want to share some of that fun and blessed feeling with you — along with a little of the pepper and other spices of my life, too.

If by some chance my story pops the bubble of some preconceived ideas you might have had about Hollywood and all its glamour, then I am truly sorry. That is far from my intent. I loved Hollywood, and I still do. I love it not for what it has become, but for the glory that it once was. In the golden days, Hollywood was its own source of light and energy. The whole world basked in its wondrous glow.

Hollywood was always bigger than life. There was magic produced there like nowhere else on earth. Some greedy cusses and no-talents have shamefully taken over much of Hollywood and made it into a dim copy-cat industry that remakes older films that were made better and cheaper and with well-trained and original talent that was recognized the world over for being special. Hollywood produced glamour and untouchable stars that had names that everyone knew and adored.

Today, what passes for entertainment is often based on the so-called reality stars, which have their one shot, and then are forgotten in a matter of days or weeks, which is justifiable, in my opinion. Hollywood was once best at depicting excitement, mystery, and glittering, sexy glam-

Ready to speak my mind.

our, but I am the first to admit that Hollywood never was all sunglasses and autographs. The town had its seamy side. Its special blend of magic and illusion was created by some of the most artistic and fertile minds in America. Hollywood built and nurtured a wonderful fantasy world in which folks loved to believe.

Dimwits took over many studios, decided that the old movie moguls were doing it all wrong, and lost the thrill of the unknown. The spell has been broken, and the magic has been lost. No one can blame the public for turning away from attending movies in droves. Audiences can find other ways to spend their hard-earned money besides watching the girl or guy next door. People want to see the unattainable, real movie stars. If you cannot handle the hard truth, then let me gently suggest you buy a fiction book instead. On the other hand, if you want to know the good, the bad, and the beautiful that Hollywood can be, my story has it all.

Maybe this book will encourage some aspiring young actors, actresses, or writers to pull themselves up by their bootstraps and try for a better life. If some of what I have written is uplifting, provides a laugh, or causes a reader to smile, then my labor has not been in vain. This is not a shock for shock's sake type of book, nor is it meant to be. I am writing this book for those who might enjoy the experiences of a hopeful actor attempting to succeed in Hollywood during a time when it was the glamour capital of the world and the Hollywood of legend.

This book is also about surviving in a sometimes cruel town, where a dream can be fulfilled or broken in a heartbeat. Hollywood is a place where surviving an emotional rollercoaster is a constant battle. It is full of hungry tigers constantly on the prowl for fresh meat. For a newcomer, it is as scary as the devil, but for the few who manage to tame the tigers, Hollywood gives one heck of a rush. I wouldn't trade my Hollywood life for a year in an overpopulated harem of lovely women in Siam. Let me change that. I wouldn't trade my Hollywood life for *six months* in an overpopulated harem of lovely women in Siam. (And I'm showing my age. Make that Thailand.)

I invite you to sit back in your favorite armchair and join in the tale of my life. My writing is not Shakespeare, but whether you choose to read my book openly or hide in a bathroom or a closet to sneak a peek, you can rest assured that every last word is based, to the best of my knowledge, on hard facts. This book is the truth as I know it. Thanks for giving it a look.

CHAPTER 1

From the Top: Early Childhood

On July 26, 1926, playwright George Bernard Shaw turned seventy in England. That same day, Robert Todd Lincoln, the oldest and last surviving child of Abraham Lincoln, died in Vermont. And in the little town of Powderly, Kentucky, which is near Central City, a country boy named Jewel Franklin Guy was born to Larkin Jasper Guy and Lena Mae Everly Guy. That boy was me.

Like a canary in a coalmine, Powderly caught the hard times of the Great Depression before most the rest of the country. America in the era of Calvin

My birth mother, Lena Mae Everly.

Coolidge and the "Roaring '20s" was enchanted by F. Scott Fitzgerald's Gatsby and Charles Lindbergh's *Spirit of St. Louis*. Tennessee's Monkey Trial riled the country with a wrestling match between the ideas of evolution and Biblical creationism, but around Powderly, everybody was just poor. We all were the only people that any of us knew. Life was simply about survival. Whether we were fittest or un-fittest, it mattered little to us because we were all just as poor as Job's turkey.

I was the youngest of eight boys and a girl in the Guy family. My dad was a deep-shaft coalminer. My mother died when I was three. In those days, a lot of women died of black lung even if they did not actually work in the mines. The women breathed coal dust as they washed the miners' clothes. I am not sure that is what killed my mother, but she died from a respiratory disease.

After my mother died, my father was understandably overwhelmed with the prospect of trying to scratch out a living and raise all of us kids. There simply was not enough money to feed and clothe us. Not long after my mother died, two of my brothers and I were put into a home for orphans in Louisville, Kentucky. Years later, I wrote this poem, inspired in part by some of my feelings during that time:

A Little Child's Prayer

> *Please Lord, protect my little doggie,*
> *'Cause we're really lost, you know?*
> *And the night is so awfully dark,*
> *And there's no place for us to go.*
> *We both have lost our mommies;*
> *She has gone so far, far away,*
> *And from what the people tell us,*
> *She cannot come back this way.*
> *So's all we've got is each other,*
> *And we'll never, never part,*
> *Till we find another mommy,*
> *Who will take us to her heart.*
> *She'll hold us close so we will not cry,*
> *And keep us safe from harm,*
> *And tuck us in our own wee beds,*
> *And snuggle us nice and warm.*
> *And even tell us funny stories,*
> *So we can smile and laugh and then,*
> *She'll kiss away all our troubles,*
> *And take us home again.*

Maudie, my sister, was fourteen at the time my brothers and I were put in the orphanage. She had done her very best to keep me with the family, but at her young age, there was only so much she could do. All her life, she refused to call me Jimmie, but reverted to my birth name, Jewel. I got to meet her one time, and I must say that her sense of humor was very much like mine. I corresponded with her from time to time, but we really never got together again. Until the day of her death, she always carried terrible guilt that she had to be the one to give me up to the orphanage.

My adoptive mother and father, Essa Knowland Best and Armen Neely Best.

Despite the trauma of being separated from my original family and home, being sent to the orphanage ended up one of the most fortunate things that ever happened to me. I came to be adopted when Essa Best, my future mother, was a social worker volunteering in conjunction with a nurse from Louisville. One blessed day, they came over to the orphans' home to do some charitable work. My mother told me later that when they were finished and started to leave, I walked up to the fence next to where she stood, looked up at her, and then pleaded, "Take me home with you"— and she did. Strangely, years later I received a picture of my birth mother. She had a similar stature and the sweet, kind, angelic face of my adoptive mother. When I was at that orphanage and saw this sweet lady, I more than likely mistook her for my birth mother and just wanted her to take me home.

When we arrived in what was to be my new home in Corydon, Indiana, I was amazed at the lovely house that I was to be blessed to live in for several years. I am sure that adorable small house in Indiana that my mama took me to live in was a heck of a lot different than the rundown coalmining shack in Kentucky. My adoptive mother's husband did not know he was going to get a son that day. Mama and I walked in the

Left: An early photo of me and my mother, Essa Best, after I was adopted. (Others in the picture are unknown.) Right: Eight years old as a member of the drum and bugle corps in Corydon, Indiana.

house, and she said to her husband, "Armen, this is your son." I immediately went over and jumped up in his lap and hugged him. It was love at first sight. She was a kind, little Irish lady, and he was a proud man of German descent. They were wonderful parents, who instantly took me in as part of their family.

My adoptive mother asked me what name I would like to be called. I said, "Jimmie." I think I must have remembered Jimmie, my older blood brother. Years later in World War II, he was attacking the Germans while crossing the Rhine River. A sniper shot him through the head and he was killed.

Our family lived in a little house in Corydon, a quiet little farm town just across the Ohio River from Louisville. In the early 19th century,

Corydon was the state capital. We lived right on the town's edge across from the west bridge, an old iron overpass that had an ugly history. During the Civil War, three men were hanged from its girders. Several years ago, it was replaced and its sordid past was forgotten. Today, Corydon has a population of about 5,000, and the town still possesses its loveliness.

My dad had a garage where he serviced cars. There was always a bunch

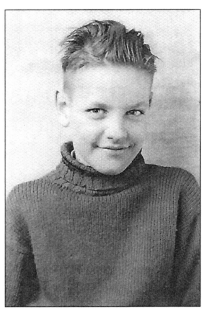

Left: An angel at eight. Right: Age eleven with girls on my mind.

of junk cars out back behind the garage, which resembled Cooter's Garage from *The Dukes of Hazzard*. We lived right next to a honky-tonk, which looked a lot like the Boar's Nest from *The Dukes of Hazzard*. Prohibition ended in 1933, but during the last half of that era, the ban on liquor sales was ignored by the honky-tonk owner. He often hid liquor bottles in a fencerow that separated my dad's garage and his roadhouse. He did this because government revenuers would drop by unannounced and search the premises for illegal booze. We often woke up to find guys sleeping in our backyard after a rough night at the honky-tonk. If they were lucky enough to find our outhouse, they helped themselves to it, too.

I loved living outside of town. At times, it was a bit lonely, but Walter and Brook Wiseman, two of my best playmates, lived about a quarter mile down the road. Harriet, a cute little blonde heartbreaker, lived across a field another quarter mile away. Even at my young age, I was very much enamored of Harriet. I remember that we boys used to climb up some cherry trees behind her house. She occasionally shared the cherry tree with us. Walter, Brook, and I very quickly ate the cherries from the bottom limbs whether they were ripe or not. Harriet climbed to the treetop to pick the cherries, which allowed us an unintentional glimpse of her panties. We nearly killed ourselves eating all the cherries from those bottom limbs. As you may know from experience, green cherries give you the runs, and sometimes we questioned whether our discomfort was worth getting a peek at Harriet's pink panties.

After a lot of looks up her dress, I fell madly in love with Harriet, but I never told her, so she never knew. Later in life, I learned that if you love or even like someone, you should tell him or her. Had I done that as a little boy in that cherry tree, maybe Harriet would have shown me her panties without my having to eat so many of those damn green cherries. Perhaps in later years, when I had a little more experience and we were both much older, she just might have shown even more. Gazing up cherry trees was an innocent enough start, but focusing on girls at such a young age meant trouble. Pursuing pretty ladies in pretty panties got me into trouble all through my life.

My childhood years were not just a tree of cherries. By the time I was adopted, the Great Depression was in full force. My dad had always allowed people to pay on credit for the work he did on their cars. That policy was fine when times were good. He did the work, and people paid steadily as they could over time. During the Great Depression, nobody could pay for anything, and consequently, my dad lost his business. If he was worried, he never let his feelings show. He always had a wonderful sense of humor.

In order to provide for his family, my dad went to work up north for the Work Project Administration, the U.S. government program that created work on various government projects during the Depression. The program helped sustain those willing to do any kind of work for a small wage. It was better than nothing. There was no government welfare in those days. If you were not willing to at least try and work, you went hungry. That seemed fair enough. During those years, I did not see much of my father. At the same time, my mother worked as a telephone operator back in those days when telephone operators stuck the plugs into switchboard holes and telephones had a crank that you had to turn to make a call.

I think men and women take up the acting profession in order to overcome or escape some of their real life fears. As a young boy, I was very shy. I remember the first time they got me up in front of my grade school class to recite something. I was so scared that I wet my pants. I went running home. Even though my mother knew I was terribly embarrassed, she made me change my pants, go right back to school, and then face my schoolhouse audience, snickers and all. Even though my recitation had been all wet, at least it was not followed by a soggy repeat performance.

How's that for a day's catch!

Some people develop determination and self-discipline that allows them to overcome their fears. In my case, I simply avoided situations requiring me to be the center of attention in front of groups of people. Years later, it took an urge of a different sort to draw me onto the stage.

I was not a terribly good student. I would much rather have looked out the window and daydreamed about the weather getting warm enough for me to go swimming in the creek. The creek was a wonderful place for me. I remember that there were two gullies that led down the muddy banks to the creek. We slithered into the gullies and threw mud at each other, and then we went skinny diving. The most significant memories I have of grade school are climbing cherry trees, wetting my pants, throwing mud, and skinny diving in the creek.

About the time I finished grade school, we moved to a little three-room, wood house up on top of a hill. We still had an outhouse. Some of my strongest memories about the house on the hill were the ice storms that hit during winter. Slipping and sliding down the icy hill to school was treacherous fun, but the climb back home was a chilly chore.

I do not remember us ever seeming poor because everybody associated with us was also poor. We just took it for granted that everybody was in the same fix that we were in and that we had no reason to complain. We developed a sense of humor about those sorts of situations. I quickly discovered that a few belly laughs helped us to forget that our bellies had not been getting as much food as we liked.

Fond memories of fishing with my dad.

Back then, being adopted was not like today. After I was adopted, I found out that adopting parents could keep a child for a year, and then if they did not like him, they could send him back. A lot of people adopted kids, made them work, and then turned them back in as if they were cattle. There was always a fear of that in the back of my mind because my mom and dad had some friends who adopted a boy at the same time that I was adopted. Later on, his parents sent him back, but I do not know for what reason because I was young. My folks never spoke to those people again. I knew my parents loved me, and I really had nothing to worry about, but even in such a loving home, it was hard to completely shake the awareness that I was returnable. As it turned out, my mom wanted to go back and adopt one of my brothers, but because of the Great Depression, my parents simply did not have enough money. I was blessed that they were even able to take me.

My dad worked six days a week. On Sunday, we went fly-fishing or hunting, which were wonderful experiences for me. We caught bass and brim, and then we cooked them up. When I was little, Dad and I waded in the streams. He waded in front of me to check for holes to make sure that I would not step into one and go in over my head. I developed a wonderful love for fishing, which I have to this day.

A lot of times, we also hunted quails, rabbits, and squirrels for food, but there were few deer in Southern Indiana at that time. I think some of the most pleasant moments of my childhood were when we went squirrel hunting. I followed behind my father. He had big feet, and I always followed by stepping in his footprints. He was as quiet as an elephant silently stalking through a jungle, and I have never seen a man who could walk through a brush pile like he did and never make a single limb pop.

My father's sideline to make additional money was as a gunsmith, and he was a tremendous shot. He taught me a lot of what he knew about guns, and that knowledge became useful throughout my life in movies and on several occasions when I served in the military as an MP. In basic training, I was an expert shot with all the weapons and even shot better than my instructor. Before I got to that point, I first had to take my shot at high school.

CHAPTER 2

The Lowdown on High School

I went to high school in Corydon, Indiana. I was painfully shy until I reached my sophomore year. Then, I was fortunate enough to be voted the class president. I do not really know why I was elected. I was a lousy student. The students did the voting, and they did not care if I was an intellect or not. I had dark hair and blue eyes, and I was a self-confessed ladies' man.

I was also one of the biggest klutzes that ever tied on a basketball sneaker, which is what they called tennis shoes in those days. I could not hit the basket nor dribble very well. I was able to memorize all the plays, but only by the time the basketball season was over. The one thing in basketball that I was good at was playing rough. I intimidated the opposing team with all sorts of creative tricks that went unnoticed by the referees. I was not at all above starting a fight, which was easy, because I was skinny as a rail. Nearly all the players on any opposing team thought they could run all over me. They were wrong. My dad had taught me how to box when I was barely old enough to hold up a set of horsehair boxing gloves. Those were deadly weapons. They got water-logged in one of our floods and then dried out harder than a mother-in-law's heart.

I came very close to having a few knockouts with my little playmates before they were aware of the hardness of the receiving end of those gloves. Needless to say, there were not too many of my little friends who cared to box with me. I had developed quick reflexes and lightning-fast hands. Even though I could not hit as hard as some of my heavier opponents, I managed to hit them so many more times that the barrages took a toll and they either gave up or were forced to lie down in major pain. I was well respected by all my schoolmates. I was not picked on, except by new kids on the block or the exceptionally stupid old-timers. Those who did pick on me for some reason and wanted to fight me soon found out that the fight did not end that day or the next. Sooner or later, I got even.

I remember one mean kid who was several years older than I. He insisted on using his strength and size to try and enhance his stature as a bona fide bully and all-around jerk. Since I had a pretty good reputation of being able to handle myself, I guess he figured that beating the crap out of me every day — if he could catch me — would keep him in shape and build up his reputation as a tough guy. He probably figured a track record as a bully would be in his favor in the unlikely event that he was ever called on to fight someone his own size. This particular bully was a big kid and dumb as a brick. He had remained in the same grade for at least three years. He was well muscled for his age and grade. I think he had muscles in his eyebrows. He really enjoyed waiting for me after school just to use me for a punching bag. He just loved to beat me up.

I tried every way I knew to avoid a confrontation. I shared my candy, when I had any, and tried to be as friendly as possible at all times, which was all to no avail. The big bully was well aware that I had but one choice of a route that I had to traverse to be able to reach the office where my mother worked as a telephone operator. I decided I had enough of his tomfoolery, and it was downright embarrassing trying to explain my bloody noses to my very concerned mother. Since dad was up north working on the WPA, I was on my own. To try and equalize the forthcoming conflict that I knew would occur the next day, I found a club just the right size and I laid it along side the wall in the alley behind the bank. I always had to go that way, and the brick-headed jerk knew it.

Sure enough, when I got out of school and was on my way to report to my mother, there he was waiting for me. He took out after me. I ran like the devil to keep far enough ahead of him and still have time to reach the alley and the surprise I had waiting for him. I barely made the alley and grabbed the club, as he came around the corner. I hit him between the eyes and he stopped mid-stride, as his body flew straight out, parallel to the ground. I had hit him so hard that I heard him sigh like a child seeking the comfort of his mother's arms, as he melted into the sidewalk.

I took off running with a certain unexplainable, mixed emotion. It was a great relief that I could not contain. I feared that I had killed him, but I had a great satisfaction that I had permanently eliminated the threat. I was thrilled that I no longer had to walk home in fear, and I was doubly thrilled at the prospect of having just killed his bullying ass once and for all. Of course, I had not, but he did not come to school for several days. When he did return, he had the greatest pair of black eyes I have ever seen on a human being. I hardly ever saw that boy again, even though we had quite a few classes together. He just seemed to disappear when-

During high school.

ever I came near him or even looked his way. This may sound like I was a mean little kid. I guess I was to a certain degree, but not unfairly mean. I was taught to stand up for myself and what I thought was right, and I did. I am proud to say that I still do to this very day.

Ever ready to rumble, I very much wanted to play high school basketball, but unfortunately, during my freshman year, I got undulant fever, which was also called Malta fever. I got it from drinking cow's milk that was not pasteurized. I remember hearing the doctor tell my parents that I had about three days to live. The doctor's news did not set well with me. I have to say that it really did give me a quiver in my liver, but I was just ornery enough to prove him wrong. I recovered, but I did miss most of my freshman year. I made up the missed work in the summer and did not lose pace as far as going through high school in four years.

While I was in high school, I rarely got to practice basketball, and therefore, I was not very good. Even though basketball should have been second nature to a boy born in Kentucky and raised in Indiana, I never advanced past the second string except on one occasion when I did make enough points to earn a first-string sweater. When I was a senior, a boy named Frank O'Bannon was a freshman. He was from a relatively promi-nent family, but he was smaller than many of the other players, partly just because he was younger. If others started picking on him, I immediately stepped in and told them to pick on somebody their own size — me. I loved a good scrap in those days.

Frank and I sacked groceries together at the Kroger store. At one time or another during my school years, I also dated both of his sisters, Jane and Rosemond. After high school, Frank and I went our separate ways. I became the pretend "Sheriff of Hazzard County," and in 1996, after many years as a leader in the state Senate and terms as lieutenant governor, Frank became the real governor of Indiana. He was elected to a second term in 2000, but in 2003, he tragically died in office.

While governor, Frank surprised me by bestowing the 2002 Sagamore of the Wabash award upon me. The award is the highest honor that the governors of Indiana present. It is similar to the Kentucky Colonel honor issued by the governors of Kentucky. I am proud to say that I am also every bit as much of a Kentucky Colonel as Colonel Sanders, although he did parlay his Kentucky Colonel-ality into a bit more notoriety and prosperity than most of the others who received the distinction. I was greatly honored to be a recipient of the Sagamore of the Wabash even if I did have trouble spelling it. I received it while appearing at an event for *The Andy Griffith Show* called Mayberry in the Midwest in the charming little town of New Castle, Indiana. The award was a nice nod from one old Kroger sack boy to another.

I attended that Mayberry event two years in a row. The first year, members of the local police SWAT team provided my security at the event. They were a great bunch of guys. We laughed, giggled, and had a good time that whole weekend. At one point, I asked if I could go out to their range and fire their weapons. They said that would be fine. I do not think they expected me to be able to shoot. I went out to the range with the SWAT team. I must have done pretty well. They made me an honorary member of their SWAT team. They said I was a better shot than eighty percent of their guys.

The second year that I went to New Castle for the Mayberry event, I again went to the firing range. I was out there shooting on the range when all of a sudden a tow truck came up with a car and dragged it out there.

One of the SWAT team members said, "Mr. Best, you can shoot the hell out of that car."

I said, "But that is a good car. What do you want to shoot it up for?"

He said, "Well, we confiscated it on a drug raid a while back."

So we proceeded to open on it with machine guns and shot that car all to pieces. It was good therapy and it helped prepare that car for recycling.

That second trip to New Castle was when representatives of the Frank O'Bannon's office presented me the Sagamore of the Wabash. That really caused me to pause and reflect on the winding path my life had taken since the time I had to be given up for adoption. The odds were stacked against me, but I was lucky to have been raised by good parents in Indiana and to have some good breaks along life's way.

In Powderly, Kentucky, around the same time that I got the Sagamore of the Wabash, community leaders arranged for a highway to be named James Best Way. They put up a twelve-foot sign with a picture of Rosco and Flash on it. The sign reads, "Former Home of James Best." The sign was later moved because it was nearly causing accidents from people gawking at it as they drove by. High winds took it out another time. I do not know if it has ever been put back or not.

In my adopted hometown of Corydon, while I was working on the *The Dukes of Hazzard*, I donated my family's home for the local historical society to restore. Because the house was more than 150 years old, I thought it would be something worth preserving, regardless of who had lived there in the past, but six months later, some low-life officials of the town sold my home. I never could find out who instigated that sham because no one ever took the blame. Someone stole everything from my home that they could possibly take — silverware, furniture, paintings, books, and everything else. They even scavenged everything from my dad's gunsmith shop, which definitely was a unique place and worth preserving. It was full of antique guns. Then they just sold the house and took the money. They did put up a little plaque that tells that the location is the Former Home of James Best. Powderly, where I was born but only lived a few short years, treated me better than Corydon, where I was raised.

In high school, I was in only one play. It was our senior class play, Mark Twain's *A Connecticut Yankee in King Arthur's Court*. Although my fellow students voted for me to play the part of Hank Morgan in the play, the Principal's son got the lead instead of me. He had been runner-up for the lead after I eked out a win for the role when our fellow students voted for me to play the part. The Principal said that I needed to study more on my mathematics. There may have been a great deal of truth to that, but everyone knew that citing my math skills was just a ruse to allow his son to play the lead. It was my first lesson in a dog-eat-dog existence that was lying in wait for me in my future in show business. Nepotism is a way of life in Hollywood. You are either in the loop or you are out. I ended up playing the much smaller part of Sir Lancelot in that play. I think I had only three or four lines. I guess it was just as well because we all sucked as actors in those days.

Fast-forward many years later. When I returned to my hometown, there was a basketball tournament going on at my old high school. When I arrived, the bleachers emptied and the game halted, as the students swarmed the hometown boy for autographs. The police took me outside in order to allow the game to resume. I was thrilled to sign autographs for so many of my dear friends of the past, and lo and behold, I looked down the long line of autograph seekers and there was my old Principal standing in the line waiting for an autograph. I went over to him and said, "You don't have to stand in line for an autograph from me." I may remember his knocking me out of my first experience on the stage as an actor, but I laughed about it even at the time it happened. I am not vindictive like that. My math never improved, but I was blessed later in life to be able to make enough money to hire people to come up with the right numbers for me.

When I was a freshman in high school, I worked at a five-and-dime store, as well as the Kroger store. At the five-and-dime, I worked for 99¢ a day. I went in around 5:30 or 6:00 in the morning on a Saturday. I scrubbed and mopped down the floors of the two-story building and waited for customers to arrive. The farmers would come in on a Saturday and shop for the whole week. The store sold everything from ice cream, which was a rare treat in those days, to linoleum. One of my jobs was to cut the linoleum. I was soon taken off that job because I could not cut the darn stuff straight.

My boss wisely also kept me away from the ice cream as much as possible. We were never allowed to sample the candy or ice cream, but I loved ice cream, and I was always eager to carry the nearly empty container to the backroom because there was always a little of the ice cream clinging to the bottom, which I eagerly took the liberty of removing with my spoon.

When I worked at the Kroger store, I sacked groceries and worked as an assistant butcher. I still will not eat weenies or certain cuts of meat. I know what they are and where they came from. It is a good thing I have always liked to catch and eat fish.

My love of the outdoors was a natural basis for becoming a Boy Scout. I really enjoyed Scouting. I was honored to be awarded one of the highest Scouting awards given, the Order of the Arrow. It was given to me in part for saving the lives of two boys at Tunnel Mill Reservation, which was used as a Boy Scout camp at Charlestown, Indiana. We were playing a game of watermelon polo. The leaders threw a watermelon in the creek.

After a hug from my mother, I was off to war in 1944.

Two opposing teams swam toward it and then tried to push or toss the watermelon across the other team's boundary line. They were allowed to do anything to the opposing team, short of drowning them. They could hold them underwater until they let go of the watermelon, and then they tried to take possession of the watermelon and shove it over the goal line. The exertion and lengthy time in the water was strenuous.

One of those strenuous times, I noticed a boy in trouble. He had strangled and was fighting for air. I pushed him to the shore even though he was hanging on to me for dear life and making it difficult to get him to the shoreline. No one else noticed that the boy was in trouble. Not five minutes passed before the same thing happened to another boy, who once again nearly drowned both of us as I shoved him to the safety of the shore. That time, several council members were present to help pull the boy up the bank. It was difficult because he was fighting for air. They all said that I saved those two kids. I think that was the main reason I was bestowed the Order of the Arrow. It was a prestigious award that was given to only about five Scouts during that jamboree. There must have been five or six hundred Scouts attending the event.

If your team won at watermelon polo, you got to eat the watermelon. Our team lost. I love watermelon, and when I was kid, Walter Wiseman, Brooks, his brother, and I raided their grandfather's watermelon patch. We were caught, and old granddad shot at us with a shotgun loaded with rock salt. A rear end full of rock salt stung like crazy and sure did emphasize our bad mistake of stealing watermelons. We never stole watermelons or anything else from him again.

As I was preparing to graduate from high school, World War II was raging, and we were eager to fight for our country. I signed up for the Army Air Corps because all the guys in my class wanted to do it. We decided that we would be pilots. We envisioned the girls' reaction when we won our silver wings. We just wanted to fly and shoot down a bunch of Germans, but we never considered that we might be shot down by equally eager German country boys.

Before the war, I had never thought deeply about what I wanted to do with my life after I graduated. Dad wanted me to be an electrical engineer or something along those lines. Dad took care of the electrical work, the steam engine, and other equipment working at Keller Manufacturing Company, an international furniture factory that later made war materials for the Army. During my teens, I had gone to work in that factory with my dad to help bring in a little extra income for our family. My intention was to get a job working with Dad showing me the ropes, so I figured it would be easy.

Then, I discovered that the work was not easy and the money sucked. My dad said, "No, you'll work your way up from the bottom." The only job I could get was slinging lumber that came out of a kiln and dried at well over 100°. We put them in big stacks and then rolled them into a shed covered with a tin roof. It was my job to throw the hot wood down to my uncle, who ran them through a planer. That planer made a tremendous amount of noise. In those days, we did not have the luxury of high-tech earplugs. We stuffed our ears with cotton, but that did little to keep our ears from taking an awful beating. The screeching sound bounced off the tin roof at a decibel level that even Caruso could not reach. On top of that, I worked mostly in the summertime, so it was as hot as Africa in there. There I was, a skinny young man slinging that lumber and making 20¢ an hour.

I guess I did my 20¢ worth because they graduated me up to wrapping chairs and other furniture for shipping. That was what they called piece-work. If your quota was 100 chairs and you wrapped ten extra chairs, then you got extra points for working hard, which meant extra money. A lot of times, I worked another hour or two to make extra money. I may not have known what I wanted to do with my life, but I did know that I did not want to work in a factory. In fact, when I joined the service and got my call to report to basic training, I wrote on the ceiling of the building where I had slung lumber, "I quit — hot as hell," and signed my name. The funny thing is that they have renovated that building several times since I worked there those many years ago, but they have always left my signature on the ceiling. They just built around it. I am very proud of that.

In 1944, I graduated from high school. I had already signed up for the Army Air Corps to train as an air cadet with some of my high school buddies. It was a great thrill when we went to a local recruitment office to enlist and had to pass three days of hard physical and mental tests. I had not been the greatest student, but I was amazed to find out that my test scores were higher than those of some of my friends. Passing those air cadet tests enabled me to train as a pilot in the Air Corps. It was very prestigious to wear the little silver wings on my lapel. It seemed to impress all my pretty little classmates. Unfortunately, I soon learned that enlisting in the military involved more than hanging out with my buddies and impressing pretty girls.

CHAPTER 3

Over Yonder: Military Service and Intrigue in Europe

As soon as school was out, I was shipped out to Camp Atterbury in Indiana, and from there, I was taken to Keesler Field in Biloxi, Mississippi. I was there at the same time as Neil Simon, who got his inspiration for *Biloxi Blues* while stationed there. I can confirm that he painted the picture of that experience exactly right.

Walter Winchell, the most prominent newscaster of that day, said, "If you have a boy fighting overseas, write to him. If you have a boy at Keesler Field, pray for him." It was tough, and some of the men could not take it. Even our bar-

In 1944, I wore my first full uniform.

racks leader took his own life by hanging himself with a bag rope. I was the one who found him twisting with the rope around his neck. I lifted him up and another soldier cut him down, but we were too late, and he died. Another man shot his brains out with a .45, and one distraught soldier jumped from the water tower.

I never understood why we had to go on twenty-mile, forced marches with full field packs, when we were supposed to be training to fly in airplanes. I joined the Air Corps because my greatest dream was to be a fighter pilot. Unfortunately, the service did not need pilots as much as it needed waist gunners and radio gunners for all the big B-17 bombers. The Germans dived down in their planes and fired shots to take out the big bombers' motors. By doing this, they killed a lot of our waist gunners. They did not kill the pilots as often. That was a little more information than I cared to know. The tail gunners were the most vulnerable, and it

Left: Driving a supply truck at Keesler Field. Right: Proud member of the military police.

was a fact that a tail gunner in combat on a B-17 averaged only four missions before being killed.

The Air Corps put me into radio gunnery school and shipped me out to Sioux Falls, South Dakota. Then, I was shipped overseas on a Liberty ship, which was a cargo and troop transporter built in large quantities for the war. On our way across the Atlantic, we hit a mine. I guess it was defective or corroded because when it went off, the explosion caused little or no damage to the ship. A lot of us had to change our underwear after we felt the blast shake the ship.

When our group arrived in La Havre, France, the war in Europe had ended, and there was no longer a need for waist gunners. If any Germans still wanted to fight, they did not have any planes. From France, I was sent to an airfield in Fürstenfeldbruck, Germany, which had been an air-field for the Luftwaffe until allied forces captured it. The former pilots were our prisoners, and they were used as waiters for the tables in our mess hall. Since the German Air Corps was nearly extinct at this point, the Army Air Corps did not need us for flying.

Some of my buddies and I were transferred to the military police in Wiesbaden, Germany, to serve as an occupational force to help clean up the city and get rid of the German deserters, black market dealers, and what they called "werewolf gangs." We actually had quite a few skirmishes with these gangs. They were very well trained — mostly by German offi-cers — and they were extremely dangerous. Many of them were punks armed to the teeth and would rather kill you than let you move in on their black market dealings. Most of them had actually been in combat at the front lines during the war. They were known for their courage and toughness.

During the last days of the war, these kids were given bicycles and bazookas, and they bravely set out to tackle invading Russian tanks. Many of those gang members were actually just young men and boys, some as young as twelve or thirteen years old. A lot of them still held strong resentments toward all U.S. soldiers, which we understood. After all, we had just kicked the crap out of their armies and flattened nearly every building in Germany. We were also dating their girlfriends and confiscat-ing the few hotels and houses left standing for officers' quarters.

There was a lot of black market activity going on with these were-wolf gangs. German money was worthless, and so cigarettes were used as money. In Wiesbaden where I was an MP, a carton of cigarettes was worth about $300 in American currency, and a couple of cigarettes got your laundry done for a week or two. If the gal doing the laundry was pretty, a soldier could get a lot more than his laundry done for a few more cigarettes.

Trying to police Wiesbaden was extremely dangerous and not some-thing that I was at all excited about doing. I did not like shooting at people, and I surely did not cotton to having people shooting at me. Our commanding officer was a former paratrooper, who had jumped behind the German lines during the invasion of Normandy. His unit had scat-tered after their landing, and surrounded by Germans, he had to fight his way out. He did not have much regard for the Germans, no matter what their ages.

We lost three of our military police buddies when they made the mistake of going in on a raid and standing in front of the door and knocking to gain entrance. Unfortunately, the room contained members of black-market werewolf gang. It was a fatal mistake for them because the gang shot through the door and blew the door fragments into their bodies, killing them instantly. Those gangs had no intention of being captured.

I had a very bad experience with three werewolf gang members. We had been warned not to walk alone on the streets at night, but I was dating a young lady on the outskirts of Wiesbaden, and I violated this rule, which was a bad mistake. At a late hour, I walked back to my hotel after my date with the *fräulein*. I saw three young men approaching me down the street. Sidewalks in Germany were very narrow. Even when I was not on duty, I always carried a .45 automatic in a shoulder holster under my Eisenhower jacket. That night, I had a weird feeling that these young men were not going to relinquish the sidewalk to a G.I., and I was not going to back off from the young punks. I placed my hand inside the jacket and gripped the .45. I was fortunate to have the premonition of danger. As we got close together, I saw the flash of a knife in one of the men's hands. He made a lunging swipe at me, and I felt the knife strike my neck, which was a very bad mistake on his part. I was terrified to feel blood from the wound. I took him and one of his buddies down. I left the last of the three men alive only because I was in bad shape and knew I needed his help.

I forced the man to help me get into a house so I could call for help. I was told later by the doctors that if the knife had gone in just a little deeper, I would have bled to death. I was very shaken by the experience. I kept the knife and brought it home with me from Europe. I later loaned it to a friend and never got it back again. Even today, I sometimes have nightmares reliving that traumatic experience. I still cannot allow anyone behind me in public. I really freak out if they touch me, especially when I am not prepared for it.

Our commanding officer was unsympathetic about my experience, and he chastised me in no uncertain terms for walking the streets alone at night. He said he was tired of losing MPs through stupidity, and he told us that if any of us were found dead with our pistols still in our holsters, he would court-martial our bodies before sending them home to our mothers. That really put the fear in us. We knew we had a truly fearless leader. I strongly believe the whole MP outfit would have fol-

Watch out, werewolf gangs! I'm ready with the trusty .45 that would save my life.

lowed that man into hell, and sometimes, we were not too sure that we had not.

Many times when we were on a raid, our commanding officer was the first one up the steps. We never once heard him say, "All right, you men go on up there. I'll be right behind you." We were always assured that he would lead the way.

Being an MP was not my greatest desire, but it was my job, and the Army does not generally ask you what you like. Just because I was in Germany did not mean that I had lost my focus on what had always interested me the most. There were many eager young ladies who did not hate American soldiers. I dated some of these German ladies, which was supposed to be *verboten* for American military.

One lady I dated had been a model and movie actress before the war, or at least that is what she told me. From her lovely features, I did not doubt it for one minute. Let us say that, figuratively speaking, I liked to watch her climb cherry trees. She kept telling me about this German man in her neighborhood who owned a jewelry store. She said he had been an SS officer during the war and had worked in a hospital. There were rumors that a lot of people had been taken to that hospital and never heard from again. Some thought that maybe the patients were prisoners of war or Jews who were being experimented on, or maybe they were simply being killed.

I also kept hearing stories about this same man from my lady friend's neighbors. No one seemed to know all the facts for sure. I told my commanding officer that a lot of the Germans I knew were talking about this man's work at the hospital. My commanding officer said that after the war it was common for Germans who got mad at each other to claim that another was a war criminal. He felt that was probably the case with the jeweler.

Red, my friend, rode shotgun in a jeep with me. He joined my chorus of pleas to bring in the German jeweler. Our commanding officer finally agreed to let us bring the man in, mostly just to get us to shut up about it, I am sure. I told Red that we had permission to get the guy. The next Sunday morning after I made my rounds, I picked up Red and we went to the man's apartment. We kicked the door down, and Red, who had spent three years on the front lines and was as tough as anybody, found the guy still in bed in the bedroom. He stuck his .45 in the guy's ear and forcefully told him to get dressed.

I was standing in the center of the other room when a young German girl dressed in a business suit came into the room. She had her purse hanging down and she started crying. I tried to tell her in the best broken German that I could speak that we were just going to take him in, and that if he checked out all right, we would bring him back in an hour or so. She reached in her purse to get a handkerchief, but then I saw the glint of a gun. I had a baton in my hand and had to use it quickly to put her down. We had the ambulance come and get her. I never asked what happened to her. I did what I had to do to save my life. Now and then, I still have nightmares about the incident, but I know in my heart that she fully intended to kill me.

Red and I took the guy in. Our commanding officer said for us to take him into his office and ask him some questions. Red obviously knew the right questions to ask and how to ask them. He had lost a lot of friends to the Germans, and he was not squeamish about scuffing somebody up a little bit. We found out through questioning the man that he had indeed been an SS officer. He even had an SS tattoo below his armpit as proof of his past.

Later, when I was no longer in the MPs, I found out that someone had read in *Stars and Stripes* that the man Red and I captured was a real badass and a most-wanted war criminal. Through him, the MPs caught another war criminal. My old MP unit got a presidential citation and I got a sergeant's stripe.

One day during the period when that sort of thing was going on, I was off duty and went up to a Red Cross station to get some free doughnuts and coffee. Coming down the steps was a pretty, young lady dressed in a green uniform that had an American flag on one side and a patch that read "CAT" on the other.

"Come here, please," I said in German.

She said in English, "I beg your pardon?"

"Are you an American?" I asked.

She said, "Yes," and I kissed her right on the mouth.

You crazy son of a bitch!" she exclaimed. "I'll call the police."

"I *am* the police," I said. "What can I do for you?"

With the ice effectively broken, she told me her name was Mimi Kelly. (She went on to a fine career as a performer on stage, including stints on Broadway in *South Pacific*, *Finian's Rainbow*, and other productions.)

"What is that uniform you're wearing with the shoulder patch with "CAT" embroidered on it?"

"I'm a Civilian Actress Technician."

"What's that?" I asked.

She said, "Well, I act. We tour all over the French, British, and American zones in plays, and we're performing tonight at the opera house."

I said, "Why don't I pick you up after the show, and we'll go out and go to a pub and have a few drinks and see what develops?"

"Okay," she agreed, "but you have to come and see the play, too."

I said, "Well, I really don't want to see the play." My one and only experience with a play on either side of the stage was still *A Connecticut Yankee in King Arthur's Court*, and I wanted no part of anything like that again.

She said, "The only way I'll go out with you is if you come to the play first."

I could not have cared less about the play, but she was a mighty pretty girl. If the only route to a good night with this Lady Genevieve was to attend her play, then I decided to suck it up and be Sir Lancelot one more time. I went to see the play. I forget what the name of it was, but as I sat in the audience and the curtain went up, I was transported into a different world. It was like discovering a new planet or a child's first glimpse of Disney World. I went backstage afterwards to see Mimi, who it turned out was the play's leading lady.

While back there, I saw GIs changing out of wardrobe and into Army uniforms.

I said to Mimi, "Wait a minute. Those guys are privates and corporals, and I'm a sergeant. Do you mean to tell me that they're acting in this play, touring around, getting treated like officers, and staying at the very finest hotels?"

"That's right," she replied.

"With you pretty girls?" I asked.

"That's right."

I said, "I'm in the wrong damn outfit. Here I am getting shot at every night by the werewolf gangs."

Right then and there, I realized that I should become an actor. I went to talk about my new calling with my commanding officer. Having helped capture the jeweler-war criminal, I had gold goo-goos with the outfit, so my C.O. sent me over to see a Russian actress, who interviewed me to see whether I could go into Special Service.

I went in, and she asked, "Have you ever acted before?"

I said, "Are you kidding?"

Of course this old country boy was lying through his teeth. She laughed at my chutzpah, and played along by having me do an improvisation of a man down in a coal mine talking on the phone to his mother up at the top of the mine. She told me to do the scene and then go to tears. Lo and behold, I did it, tears and all. I had never had any training whatsoever, but I cried right on cue. It seemed relatively easy when all I had to do was think of my choices: being an actor with pretty girls around a swimming pool or being an MP battling with those werewolf gangs who wanted to cut off my goo-goo.

The drama coach said, "You're probably one of the biggest liars I have ever met, but I'm going to approve your transfer."

Army administrators walked my orders through in twenty-four hours. The next thing I knew, I was in the resort town of Assmanhousen, just down from Wiesbaden on the Rhine River, with Hitler's yacht sitting out front for us to use if we wanted. In between rehearsals, there I would be on a regular basis lounging around a swimming pool looking at pretty legs and drinking fine Rhine wine. When I got tired of lounging at the pool, I had a beautiful room with a great big four-poster bed complete with a down mattress and pillows. I thought I had died and gone to heaven.

I was with Arthur Penn's theatrical company. Arthur was casting *My Sister Eileen*. Frank Aletter and I played the two drunks. We had about three lines apiece, but by golly, we were actors — with full pool privileges and plenty of actress passes. Our life of touring on the road was not all umbrella drinks by the pool. There was some hard work involved. We traveled in two or three old ambulances that we took the insides out of and replaced with sofas and chairs. We had six big trucks for transporting our sets, costumes, and props. The sets were all color-coded to help us quickly put them together. The men in our company had to be jacks-of-all-trades. We built the sets, carried the girls' luggage to the hotels, and acted in the plays. Whatever was needed, we did it.

Once I was driving with my leading lady in a jeep to one of our shows. We entered a particular zone where the Russians were in charge of security. There I was, armed with nothing but my .45 and driving into a checkpoint guarded by a Russian soldier with a machine gun. I drove up and he stopped us. He walked up and saw the pretty girl sitting next to me. He signaled for her to get out of the car.

I said, *"Nyet, nyet."* I knew he spoke German, and I proceeded to tell him *"Nein"* and *"Nyet"* in my broken Hoosier German-Russian accent and to get away from the vehicle because the girl was with me.

The Russian guard continued motioning for my lady friend to get out of the car.

I told her, "Don't you dare get out of this car."

When the Russian came over closer to the vehicle, I whipped out my .45, stuck it in his face, and commanded, in German, "Get away! Get away, you shit you!"

Performing in a 1946 soldier show production of My Sister Eileen *that started my career.*

He smiled and said, "Yah-yah," and then waved us on through the checkpoint.

There was no doubt in my mind that he was going to open fire on the back of our car when we got into his territory. We both tensed up waiting for the bullets to come tearing through the back end, but he did not shoot. I guess he liked the fact that I was brave enough to make him back off. Nevertheless, it almost felt like it was time to run home and change my underwear again.

I re-enlisted for another six months or a year — I do not remember which. I do remember that I was having too much fun touring with *My Sister Eileen* to stop. Besides, I was getting a very interesting education in the wonderful art of romance from one of the leading ladies in the company. She was about ten years older than I and a heck of a lot more experienced in acting and other good things. I was young and eager to learn all I could from such a multi-talented lady.

When the GIs in our troupe gradually rotated back to the United States, I got increasingly better parts. I finished up the tour in the role of Frank Lippincott, one of the leads. Because the play was being performed before thousands of GIs during the course of our tour, Arthur Penn and others routinely checked up on us to make sure that the play was being performed up to snuff. During one of his checkups, Arthur said to me, "Jimmie, you have good potential for being a good actor. I think you should go to New York when you go back to the states and study at the Neighborhood Playhouse."

That was all the encouragement I needed. I said, "I think I'll do that."

I never made it to the Neighborhood Playhouse, but I did firm my resolve to continue acting.

CHAPTER 4

Back Home Again in Indiana

After World War II, I finished up my military service, and the government gave me what they called a "52-20," which meant they gave me $20 a week for fifty-two weeks to help get me on my feet. I did not have any money and my folks were poor, so $20 a week sounded pretty good to me. Since my dad's work with the WPA had ended, he had been working at the lumber factory back home, just as I had done previously. I can only hope that he made more than the 20¢ an hour I had made, but it probably was not much more.

I went back home for a while. I had an Army buddy in Jacksonville, Florida, and I decided to hitchhike there to visit him. When I arrived, he happened to mention that they were doing a play called *Stardust*. I went to the theater, auditioned, and got the part. I did *Stardust* and then, yada-yada-yada, I hitchhiked back home.

When I arrived home, I received a telegram that I had won the Best Acting award for 1946-47 at that little theater. That news was especially exciting to me because there had been some Broadway actors in the play with me. I had actually competed with some fine professional actors from Broadway and won. I was beside myself with excitement, and I just knew I would become successful as an actor.

But I've almost "yada-yada'd" over the most dramatic part of the story. As I was hitchhiking back from Florida, I decided to swing by and visit another Army buddy up in Americus, Georgia. While I was there, he got me a date with a very pretty telephone operator, a Southern belle at Southern Bell, you might say. I spent a few days up there with her, and even though I hated to leave such beauty, I was on a quest. I decided to hitchhike back home again to inform my folks that I was on my way to New York and the Broadway stage.

One night while I was still in Georgia, there was not much traffic on the highway. I built a little fire just to keep warm, as I waited for dawn and some cars to start coming through again. Unfortunately, the first car that came by before the sunrise was a local sheriff's car. It pulled up, and two pot-bellied deputies got out.

"What are you doing there?"

Starring in a 1947 production of Stardust *in Jacksonville, Florida (actress unknown).*

"I'm just passing through," I told them.

"Did you know you've built a fire in our city park?"

"I didn't even know there was a town here," I said, which was one heck of a big mistake and exactly the wrong thing to say.

"Not only do we have a town here, but we also have a jail for vagrants who build fires in our park," one of them said, grabbing me roughly. "Get in the squad car!"

I said, "Look, don't go grabbing on me. I was in the military police. I know how to conduct myself. I will do whatever you want me to do, but just don't manhandle me."

One of the deputies grabbed me again, and then I decked him. That was an even bigger mistake than the one I had made a few seconds before. Both deputies pounced on me, gave me a very good pounding, and then shoved the much more cooperative me into the patrol car.

They took me to their jail and put me in a little room, where they handcuffed me to a chair.

"We'll get your head straight," one of the deputies said.

They then proceeded to really ring my bell by putting a telephone book up beside my head and then hitting it with a baton. That way, they did not make any marks on me, but you can believe they sure got my attention. For a guy who just a few days earlier had such a good connection with a telephone operator, I was definitely dialing up some painfully wrong numbers now.

The next morning, I was taken before a less than softhearted judge and was charged with vagrancy and resisting arrest. I was sentenced to thirty days on a work gang, also called a "shovel gang" because the gangs worked on the roads shoveling gravel. Some of the guys on the gang were hard-rock losers, who had been in jail for a long time. Some were lifers, and some had worked the hard-core chain gangs in the old days in Florida. I had heard horror stories about young men who were put on the work gangs and used by these killers in many ways that I did not want to even think about.

Taking preventive measures, I immediately went into telling jokes and stories. I am sure that my being the gang's jester saved me, to put it in crude jailhouse terms, from being made someone's bitch. My fellow prisoners seemed to like me and they would tell me stories about the old days and their experiences on different chain gangs. I asked all sorts of questions about how the gangs worked and what you had to do just to get through the experience. In some ways, I guess hearing about the incredible harshness of the extreme chain gangs made my thirty days on the work gang seem like paradise in comparison. I also planted the knowledge I soaked up about chain gangs in my brain. Years later, it bore fruit in very important ways when I wrote *Sweatin' Blood and Doin' Time,* a movie script about life and death on a Southern chain gang.

CHAPTER 5

My Midwestern Route from Indiana to New York

When I had completed my involuntary work on the road gang in Georgia, I went straight back to Corydon. I did not build a single fire along the way. I told my folks that I was going to hitchhike to New York to become an actor. They were supportive, but they asked if it was really something I was determined to do. I know they thought I perhaps had gotten shell-shocked in the Army and was not really thinking straight. I know the townspeople of Corydon had a very definite reaction to the gossip that the Best boy had gone bonkers and was going to try to be an actor. With most of my friends and neighbors, my notion went over like a French kiss at a family reunion, but I was determined to make it in show business

I ended up hitchhiking to Chicago because I had run out of money and needed to pump up for the final leg of my quest for stardom in the Big Apple. On the way, I met a young man who was also hitchhiking. He invited me to meet some of his buddies, and I was surprised to find out that they were all members of a gang. There I was in Chicago in the 1940s hanging out with these tough-guy gangsters and their girlfriends, and even though some of the girls were really cute and friendly, I knew they were not for me, so I got the first legitimate job I could find, which was working as a busboy at a Thompson's Cafeteria.

At that time, Thompson's was a big restaurant chain in the Chicago area with two or three dozen locations. They were open late, sometimes all night. They had decent, cheap food that was served quickly. Because they were open at all hours, I could work as many hours as I wanted in order to get overtime. I went down in the basement and slept for a little while on piles of dirty aprons. Then, I went back upstairs and worked some more. I wanted to go to New York as fast as possible, but at least I had enough sense to know that I needed to save up a little scratch before blazing into New York.

For a while, I was not in too big of a hurry to leave Chicago because the cashier was a pretty, young Italian lady. She had an apartment, and she invited me to stay there with her for a little bit. The downside was that she was a very jealous sort. Working as a busboy, I was busy out among the tables, and I naturally flirted with every woman who came into the restaurant. Thompson's cafeterias were very popular with women doing their shopping and going to the theater. I had lots of opportunities to flirt while working.

My fiery cashier witnessed my behavior. One day, she had finally seen enough, and she pinned me against a wall with a knife.

"If I catch you doing that again, I'll slice you up until you're too short to hang!" she told me.

Looking at that long, sharp knife, I had no other choice but to believe her. I stopped flirting at work. I stayed at her place, which was very convenient, because I did not have to pay rent. The only trouble was that her place had been infected with bedbugs. I remember waking up scratching. I decided I was not in the best long-term situation. In the middle of the night, I wisely packed my few things and slipped away, never bothering to wake her or to say goodbye because she might have had that long, sharp knife under her pillow. I have always wondered how she could sleep so sound with all those bedbugs chomping on her lovely body. The night manager of the restaurant was a wimpy little guy, who was enamored of the pretty cashier and very jealous of the fact that she and I were more than friends.

I went to him and said, "You owe me $80. Pay me. I'm quitting."

He was determined to make my life as miserable as possible. "I can't pay you for a day or so," he said.

I threatened to make his life even more miserable in the next few minutes if he did not cough up the money he owed me. I got my money and hit the road to tackle my dreams. I was about half mean in those days because of having been in the military police, not to mention my hanging around with gangsters and knife-wielding Italian cashiers, and I did not take any crap from anybody. I got my $80, and I suppose he got the gal — and the bedbugs.

I hitchhiked part of the way on a truck about the size of a milk truck. For such a long ride, my wallet was uncomfortable against my skinny little butt, so I put the wallet filled with $80 in my shirt pocket. The next thing I knew, the driver knocked me in the head, stole my wallet, and left me lying against an abandoned gasoline station wall with a bloody head. There was nothing in my luggage but dirty laundry and maybe a few bedbugs, so he threw it on top of me. I picked myself up, cleaned up as best I could, and continued hitchhiking on into New York.

On the last leg of the trip, the driver asked, "Where in New York do you want to be dropped off?"

I said, "Let me off on Broadway."

"Where on Broadway?"

"Where the theaters are," I replied. "I'm going to be an actor."

That is how brash and stupid I was. He dropped me off on Broadway. My head was hurting, and I was hungry, poor, tired, and a huddled mass all by myself. I needed a good wash, too. I sat down in a doorway and fell asleep against my suitcase. The next thing I knew, I was being poked at. I looked up to see a cop nudging me in the ribs with his baton. I immediately flashed back to Georgia and thought, *"Oh no, not again."*

The cop asked, "What are you doing here?"

Ever ready with the smart-aleck remark, I said, "I'm trying to sleep if you'll quit gouging me with that stick."

Maybe because the cop noticed that I was already injured, or maybe he did not beat the living tar out of me for that remark because there were many people around.

"What happened to your head?" he asked.

I told him the story. He was somewhat compassionate for a New York cop. He said, "Well, you're a vagrant if you don't have $5. I can run you in as a vagrant."

"I'm not a vagrant," I insisted, showing pure cockiness and stupidity. "I'm here. I am going to be an actor. Someday, you'll see my name up in lights."

There was a well-dressed gentleman in the crowd watching my run-in with the cop. He said, "Here, I'll give him the $5, and then he won't be a vagrant anymore. So you can leave him alone."

I said to him, "No sir. That's very nice of you, mister, but I don't take charity."

I opened my suitcase and found a poem that I had written about my dad. The piece of paper the poem was written on had the address for my dad's gunsmith shop on it.

I said, "What I'll do is sell you this poem for $5. If you ever want your money back, you just write to this address and you'll get double your money back."

The man gave me the $5, I gave him the poem, and the policeman let me go. The man never returned the poem, and I was sort of flattered that he wanted to keep it.

This isn't the poem I gave that man, but it is from about the same period and sums up how close to the bottom of the heap I was:

Short Time

Through this world of vice and crime,
I have lost one thing and that is time.
The most precious thing since the world was dust.
It eats at our lives with a vicious lust.
Why can't it pass and leave us alone,
To reap the harvest we have sown.
But it's not as simple as it seems,
And it passes us by and takes our dreams.
But it leaves us one thing, when we're weathered and old,
A handful of memories and a heart growing cold.
It seems time is always passing and always too late,
And death hovers near and will not wait.
It swoops to enfold us with its icy wings,
Leaving us wishing we hadn't done all those
meaningless things.
But if we were again placed on this earth,
And swept back to the date of our birth...
Attempting with good the success ladder to climb,
We find once again there is so little time.
For happiness is not bought with the money you pay,
But is found in each second of each hour of each day.

I found my way to the YMCA nearest to the Theater District. I assumed it would be a cheap and safe place to stay. It cost about $3 a night. I figured my $5 was good for at least one night and a chance to clean up. I checked in, and then I went to take a shower. Unfortunately, as a naïve country boy, I did not know much about homosexuality, and

the place was full of homosexuals carefully looking over the new arrival —
too carefully to suit me. I checked out of there very quickly.

I did not know where else to go. I just started to walk the streets until
I came across an Italian restaurant. I was starving, but with only a buck
or two, I did not have enough money for a meal. That did not stop me
from ordering a really nice big Italian meal for myself.

I ate like the Russians were in Pasadena. When I finished, I asked the
waiter, "Would you be so kind as to send the manager over?"

The waiter asked, "What's wrong? Wasn't the food any good? You
scarfed it down pretty quickly."

I replied, "The food was marvelous. Simply delicious, but I have got
to talk to the manager."

The waiter summoned the manager, a nice Italian gentleman, who
came over.

"Sir, I've eaten your meal, but I can't pay for it," I told him. "Now, you've
got two choices: you can call the police and have me arrested, but you
still won't get paid. Or, you can let me work for you because I worked at
Thompson's restaurants in Chicago and I'm a very good worker. I'll do
three times more work than that meal is worth."

He handed me an apron and put me to work. I immediately started
cleaning dirty old pans. I had never seen so much sticky spaghetti in my
life. I was in no position to complain. I was just happy to be in New York
with a full stomach. The manager eventually made me a waiter, and I got
to where I was actually making a few bucks.

On my feet again and springing somewhat back into form, I got
pumped up a little bit and called Mattie Engelberg, an actress I had
known from my time in Germany. She had been a replacement in our
touring company of *My Sister Eileen*, and she was then living in Brook-
lyn with her parents.

Mattie told me about auditions being held in town for a summer stock
production in Milford, Pennsylvania. I did not have clothes to wear for
an interview, so I went to a hockshop and bought a jacket and a pair of
pants with what little money I had left. The pants did not have any cuffs,
so I rolled the pants legs up and put some little gold pins in the folds to
make cuffs. I must have been an odd sight when I walked in, but they
auditioned me. Since I had a good background with acting, they overlooked the fact that my clothes were not presentable and they gave me a
job in summer stock, which led to more jobs in winter stock.

Meanwhile, Mattie landed a role starring in *Marinka*, a Broadway musical comedy that was going on the road. It was a Russian operetta, a period piece sort of thing. Mattie was a wonderful actress, and she had enough clout to get me an audition with The Penthouse Players. I could not sing or dance, but I looked pretty good in a uniform. Fortunately, with my experience overseas stage managing and working behind the stage, I was hired.

In the dance sequences, I kept stepping on the girls' long dresses and ripping their hems off, which prompted the director to make me stand over in a corner just as a prop. Prop or not, I was thrilled to be on the road with a professional Broadway show. I drove the truck for the company, which meant another $50 a week for me. For over a year, we toured all over the country. We did children's shows in the afternoon, and then the Broadway show at night. In the entire company, I think there were only three men who were straight. That was great for me. With all the girls in the show, it was like having a harem to pick from. In fact, I was invited to share a hotel room with some of the girls at different times, and I saved a lot of money on hotel room rent. I also had free romance. Life just did not get any better than that.

When I came back to New York, I stayed in the Palace Hotel between Broadway and Sixth Avenue, not to be confused with the luxurious New York Palace Hotel on Madison Avenue. I was paying $11 a week for my room. The hotel was full of hookers, dope-heads, would-be actors, and some folks who were a little bit of all three. I had a tiny room on the bottom floor next to an alley with the typical New York ambiance of whiskey bottles flying down from the top floors and crashing down onto the alley walls just outside my window.

Between winter and summer stock work, I did some modeling for the Thompson Modeling Agency. I did not realize until later how big the Thompson agency was. I was very fortunate to have been accepted into that group, but I never cared for modeling because I was a modest country boy. When I went on a modeling job, men and women changed clothes in the same room. I did not mind watching the women change, and I did not mind taking my clothes off in front of the ladies, but I did feel uncomfortable taking my clothes off in front of some of the more sensitive-acting men. With my temperament, I guess I just felt that accepted model behavior was not acceptable to me.

I hit the streets each day and walked six to eight miles, making the rounds to get an acting job. At the Palace Hotel, I met Joe Mell, an actor

Modeling in New York for Thompson Modeling Agency.

Modeling was not my thing, but it paid the bills.

who was set to direct plays at a summer stock theater in Monticello, New York.

"I'd like to be in the summer stock show," I told Joe.

"The play isn't opening for another month," he said, "but you can go on up and clean the place up. There's a cot you can sleep on for free."

To a struggling actor, "free" is one of the sweetest words in the English language.

I went up there and started cleaning the theater. I got a day job caddying at a nearby golf resort, and I also picked up a one-time job driving a truck back to New York. It paid a handsome $10. When I drove the truck back, I stopped by the old Palace Hotel just to say hello to some of my actor, actress, model, hooker, and dope-head friends. I did not mess with the hookers and I was not a doper, but I did mess with some of the more attractive actresses and models. We were all very friendly. We were pathetic friends linked together through similar circumstances. We were tied in a time and place with each of us in our own desperate search for something better.

At the hotel, there was a guy who had contacts at Universal Studios and claimed to be an actor. He was an older man, and he had what he called a "companion," whom he also claimed was his nephew. I always wondered about that relationship. At that hotel, the strict, unwritten rule was "Don't Ask, Don't Tell." He had seen some of my modeling pictures, and he asked if he could send them to an agent friend of his in Hollywood. Of course, I said yes, and those pictures were somehow seen by someone at Universal Studios.

Later, when I dropped by the hotel, my friends told me that some people from Universal in New York were looking for me. I thought they were putting me on. They insisted that Bob Goldstein, the head of casting, was trying to reach me. I was wearing just an old pair of Levis, I had a two-day beard, and I was all dirty from driving the truck, but I went on up to the Universal offices on one of the big fancy streets. The receptionist said, "Oh yes, Mr. Best. Mr. Goldstein wants to see you."

She opened the door and I walked down a hall where I had to practically wade through carpet so plush that it was as high as saw grass. I was led through another doorway, and there sat a man behind a big desk. I had never seen such a fancy office in my life. I had usually been only on the outside and never got to see the interiors of most big agents' offices. On his desk were all sorts of baseball trophies. He was owner of one of the big Major League baseball teams and had a tremendous interest in the sport. I introduced myself, and immediately went to my fastball.

"These are really nice trophies," I proclaimed.

He responded, "Do you like baseball?"

I was not a big baseball fan, so I got around the question by saying, "Well, baseball is the greatest sport in America."

We started talking a little bit, mostly small talk, and all the while he was eye-balling me up and down, which made me a little nervous. He looked at me as if I was a prize stallion on an auction block.

"So, can you act?" he asked.

I was tired from my day driving that dirty old truck, and that question irked me.

"I'll be honest with you, Mr. Goldstein," I said. "If you can get anybody my age in here who can out-act me, I suggest you get him."

He said, "Boy, you've really got a chip on your shoulder."

I said, "No sir, I have been thrown out of the best of offices — maybe not this fancy, but I have been thrown out of a lot of offices — all over New York. I have the experience, courage, drive, and the desire, and I am going to be an actor."

He said, "I don't doubt that. How would you like to go to Hollywood for $125 a week? How does that sound?"

Well, that was the shocker of all time. I got tears in my eyes and said, "Don't kid with me. Please don't kid."

He said, "I am not kidding." He picked up the phone and told his secretary, "Get Mr. Best a one-way ticket to Hollywood."

I said, "Mr. Goldstein, is it possible that I could go through my hometown of Corydon, Indiana, and tell my folks? I told them I could make it, and I'd like to go back and say, 'Hey, I'm on my way to Hollywood.'"

He smiled and said, "Yeah, that would be fine. I think Hollywood can last another couple of days without you."

I was being called up to the big league in my chosen profession. That was all the baseball I needed to know. I went back home and I told my folks. Of course, they were very proud. I did not stay long, and then I was off to capture Hollywood.

CHAPTER 6

Early Days in Hollywood

In 1949, I arrived in Hollywood during its Golden Era. Hollywood was like a queen with sparkly jewels. Universal Studios had arranged for me to stay at the Universal Hotel, which was across from the studio gates. A nice lady ran the place with her very pretty granddaughter. I did not have a car, so the only place for me to go each morning — and the only place I wanted to go — was the studio.

I went out there with a contract to work at Universal. They geared me up to be a leading man. In those days, I suppose I was not too bad looking, so I was given a lot of parts for the young leading man. I finally told the studio that I did not want to be a leading man because leading men come and go, but a character actor can work until the day he dies.

I went down to the casting office to read for a role in one of their Westerns. I was still very thin, weighing about 155 pounds, which was scrawny for a six-foot-tall man. In my early days in Hollywood, the wardrobe people sometimes had to put a body suit on me to beef up my arms and shoulders.

I told this particular casting agent, "I want to play the mean guy in the film."

The casting agent laughed. "Who would be afraid of you?"

That infuriated me. I jumped across his desk, grabbed his shirt, and said, "You son of a bitch. If I had a switchblade, you'd be scared of me."

His eyes looked like saucers because he could tell I was extremely mad. He said, "You've got the part! You've got the part!"

After that, I went on to play mostly heavies. While I was under contract, the studio was always after me to perfect my speech. They even went so far as to hire a speech teacher to train some of us actors to speak without an accent. I do not think it helped Tony Curtis or me. The teacher actually used to have us say that old cliché, "The rain in Spain falls mainly on the plain." It was funny that the studio wanted to correct my speech, and yet in nearly all the movies that I did at Universal, the studio wanted me with a Southern accent.

A critic or columnist in a newspaper could make or break an actor's career. The future for young aspiring actors was determined by what these critics

In 1950, some of the contract players for Universal Studios included (left to right) Joyce Holden, Rock Hudson, unknown, Richard Long, unknown, me, and unknown.

wrote in the industry trade papers, whether their comments were good or bad. In those days, *The Hollywood Reporter* and *Variety* were the bibles for actors. These were the little magazines that gave all the news and dirt about Hollywood. They listed all the movies being shot and those that were in pre-production, and they had news about who was casting and at what studio.

Hollywood Reporter and *Variety* reviewed recently released movies, which was what most actors looked for if they had participated in one of the films being reviewed by a critic. Actors scanned those trade papers every day just to see if they were in favor with the columnist or critic at the time. A bad review from those self-proclaimed judges and critics sounded a death knell for many an actor.

The Universal publicity department's idea of a cowboy. What a pose!

As Cole Younger in Kansas Raiders *(1950), my first Western with Audie Murphy.*

Critics often were just frustrated would-be actors, who could not make it as actors, but were good at convincing a lot of moviegoers that they knew who was good, bad, or mediocre in the motion picture industry. Granted, some critics are good and fair, but there are others who are less than knowledgeable about what the movie-going public likes. In my humble opinion, most critics are these jokers who wait for a war to start,

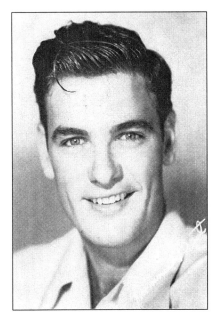 

Left: One of my first headshots while under contract to Universal Studios. Right: This photo was sent out by Universal's publicity department in response to fan mail the studio received for me.

run and hide in the hills until the battle is over, and then come down and shoot the dead. They expect a medal for their bravery. That is my definition of most Hollywood critics.

There was a wonderful mystique around the motion picture industry, which at that time did not give away all the secrets of the making of a movie nor tell all the sordid details of some of the more unsavory characters in the business. I am sure there was a lot of immorality that was going on in Hollywood then, just like any other place else in the world. In those days, the motion picture industry frowned upon bad behavior rather than encouraged it. You had to at least appear to follow a certain amount of ethics, or else you could not be successful in the movie business.

Back then, Hollywood was a place where genuine talent and persever-ance eventually lead to success. I am living proof, and I sincerely believe that to be true.

In Hollywood, I was considered a rebel because I always told the truth. That did not always go over like gangbusters because Hollywood was a world built on fantasy and often just plain lies. I was an old coun-try boy who called things the way I saw them and told the truth. It made me stand out, and it also helped to make me successful. If I told someone that I was going to do something or handle some-thing a certain way, they could bet their sweet ass and your grandma's housecat that was the truth.

I was different than a lot of actors, but I was not more talented than them. Nearly all the major stu-dios put actors and actresses under seven-year contracts with six-month options. That meant that if the studio could not build you into their predetermined mold for star-dom in as little as six months, your butt was gone. You were judged by the reactions of fans who wrote let-ters to the new actors featured in the movies and movie magazines.

I preferred this early headshot because I thought I looked dramatic.

During the 1930s to the early 1960s, contract players at the major studios were quite common. Actors were blessed to be working under contract and trained in all sorts of interesting and beneficial skills.

A columnist such as Hedda Hopper or Walter Winchell could make or break a young actor's career with just a few words spoken on radio or a blurb in a fan magazine or newspaper. The well-kept secrets of some of the actors or actresses who were having extramarital sexual affairs were very closely guarded by the studios. They could not afford to have their actors' bad behavior become public knowledge. A great deal of money was spent by the studio publicity departments to keep secrets. In those days, fans did not want to be disillusioned by their favorite stars' amoral behavior. They did not even want their favorites to get married. I think it was because they all had the false illusion that they might have a chance to one day meet and marry their heartthrob.

When I was under contract at Universal Studios, Rock Hudson was the perfect example. Rock Hudson was a homosexual. In my whole career, I was never more surprised than finding out that Rock preferred men to women. Rock and I had both dated the same girls, such as Susan Cabot and Vera-Ellen. At that time, I had never heard anything about Rock being gay. Rock seemed to be nothing but a ladies' man. The studio went to great lengths to squelch all rumors to the contrary, even going so far as to have Rock marry his agent, whom I had heard from many sources was a lesbian.

When I was under contract, I was unaware of any contract player abusing dope. Later, I was shocked to find that it was fairly common. I just recently read Tony Curtis' autobiography, where he admitted to having had a dope problem later in life. Tony and I were friends and did quite a few movies together, but we were not social friends. He had his group of friends, and I had mine. Still, Tony was godfather to my son Gary.

CHAPTER 7

Horsing Around at Universal Studios

When I was under contract to Universal in those glorious days, most of the productions were Westerns and what were crassly called "tits and sand." The latter were swashbuckling action pictures or desert epics set in Arabia. Tony Curtis and Piper Laurie did a lot of these. Universal signed an entire year's crop of Miss Universe beauty contestants for use in these types of movies. Of course, once the studio had finished using these beauties as glorified extras, they were ruthlessly dropped and replaced by the next year's crop of contestants.

With the Midwestern accent I had at the time, I was sort of typed as an actor who was right for Westerns. I had never really ridden horses other than at the circus when I was a little kid and rode on the little ponies that walked around in a circle three times for a dime. Fortunately, the studio kept a stable full of horses on the back lot to use in movies and to try to train non-riders like me to ride.

My future as a cowboy depended on my ability to ride well enough to not look like a complete novice. I learned quickly, but only after falling off a lot and eating half the dirt on the back lot. The wranglers were very patient with me and knew how much I wanted to learn. They showed me tricks to fool the studio front office enough so that they would use me in many Westerns. The wranglers also trained me to keep from getting killed in the wild chase scenes that I had to engage in many times.

During the early 1940s, Universal shot a full length feature in thirty days and they were called "thirty-day wonders." A movie shot that quickly was not considered a top-of-the-line A picture. All Universal contract players were considered B players, the exception being stars such as Marlon Brando, James Stewart, and Burt Lancaster. When these stars were in a movie, it was considered a class A production. Other studios had the likes of Gregory Peck, Joseph Cotten, Janet Leigh, Vera-Ellen, and Spencer Tracy. The major studios shot extravaganzas and big musicals with big-name stars. These were the big boys and girls, and it was in the hearts of all of us contract players to someday join the ranks of the big stars of the major class A studios such as MGM, Paramount, and Warner Bros.

Unfortunately, my roles were in films made at the minor league studios for the majority of my career. If I had appeared in some famous and well-respected movies with a major role, I would have gained more prestige and recognition. It is imperative for an actor to have the right part in the right movie, and it has to be exploited in the right way for that actor to become a major superstar. I never attained that status.

Although I have appeared in close to ninety features and worked with some of the greatest stars ever to grace

One of my first cowboy publicity shots. Draw!

the silver screen, I have never in my heart believed that my full potential as an actor has been shown to the world. It is my true hope and dream to put my *Hell-Bent for Good Times* on the screen to prove to Hollywood and movie-going audiences that I am capable of much more than just Rosco P. Coltrane.

Perhaps another reason my career did not take off like some others is that I did not socialize in the same way as a lot of the actors. I was not a schmoozer. I tried to keep my private life private. I worked hard, and then I went home.

Dick Clayton, who was a big-time manager for Burt Reynolds and others, told Dorothy, my wife, "You know, Jimmie could have been a major movie star except he would not play the game."

I am proud that I was not a game player. I was not going to drink and schmooze and do the things that a lot of people did to obtain success. If I could not do it with my talent, then I was not going to do it.

I am not saying that everybody was a game player. There were many wonderful people — Jimmy Stewart and James Garner, for example — who were family men. A lot of guys not only had fantastic talent, but also morals that I respected. I am not saying I was a prude. Lord knows I cut my own swath in Hollywood. I was a little naughty, and maybe sometimes more than a little naughty, but I was never cruel and never indecent.

I dated some of the most beautiful women in the world. In fact, I am not sure that I did not date Marilyn Monroe. There was a place called the Hollywood Studio Club that took in young girls to protect them from men of prey. It was run by the Los Angeles YWCA, and it began when Mrs. Cecil B. DeMille spearheaded its establishment during the 1920s. The studios put blossoming actresses under contract and arranged for their housing in the Hollywood Studio Club for safekeeping.

The Hollywood Studio Club was like a honey pot for a bear like me. I dated a lot of the girls there. I generally dated a girl a couple of times. I guess I was fickle, but I loved variety. When you work in a candy store, you do not eat just gumdrops all the time. When I dated a girl from the Hollywood Studio Club, I was not allowed to go above the first floor. The girls had to sign out when they left, and they had to tell the gatekeeper where they were going and when they were going to be back. They could also get an overnight permit. I always tried to talk them into the overnight permit.

When any man arrived to pick up his date, he had to wait in the lobby for the girl to come down. All the girls walked through the lobby to go up to their rooms, and they invariably came over and flirted with me. A lot of times, they gave me their telephone numbers. Later, I found out that Marilyn Monroe was living there at that time. I do remember this one blonde girl, but I dated quite a few blonde girls.

The reason I think I might have dated Marilyn Monroe is because of Jeanne Carmen. Jeanne was an actress who made a personal appearance at a Western film festival I was attending a few years back. She was Mari-

A boy-next-door shot from Universal, but I wanted the tough-guy roles.

lyn Monroe's friend at the Hollywood Studio Club. She said to my wife Dorothy, "You know, I used to date your husband."

Always quick on the draw, Dorothy responded, "You and quite a few other people."

Jeanne got on the dais at the film festival and talked about how she and Marilyn used to date the Kennedy brothers. Then, she started selling pictures of herself wearing fewer clothes than the Western film festival would have liked. The festival organizers later found out that they had mistakenly invited the wrong actress to the festival. They had intended to invite Jean Carson, one of the "fun girls" from Mt. Pilot on *The Andy Griffith Show*. I thought the pictures were very interesting, not appropriate for that particular festival, but very interesting.

In 2007, Jeanne Carmen died. She was one of the actresses I had dated. The way she talked made me think that I had actually dated Marilyn Monroe around that same time. If so, either I did not make much of an impression on Marilyn, or she did not make much of an impression on me. Either way, I do not earn a good score.

Nightlife aside, as soon as the sun came up each morning, I was through that front gate at Universal because I wanted to learn and be a part of the exciting business that I loved. Fortunately, the studio made it extremely easy for someone as eager and ambitious as I was to learn as much as I could soak up. The studio provided professional training for all aspects of performing in movies. For example, Hal Belfer, Donald O'Connor's choreographer, gave us dance lessons. I was a total klutz and settled on tap dance as my area of dance concentration. I did not want any part of ballet and "make pretty toes" stuff.

The speech coach worked to get the Southern accent out of my speech. He used to fall asleep during our sessions, which was all right with me. He snoozed, and I kept my sleepy Southern accent. I ended up being cast mostly in Southern parts during my career.

I don't know about y'all, but I don't believe more attentive speech training can change that.

Actors under contract were allowed to go down to the soundstages and watch some of the superstars and character actors working on different movies. We were lucky to do this whenever we wanted, and I did every chance I got. When I arrived at Universal, Sophie Rosenstein was my main drama coach. She was a very good instructor, and she gave me a good foundation for the type of acting required for the camera versus

Publicity headshot for Universal's Ma and Pa Kettle at the Fair *(1951)*.

the stage. At the time she was teaching me, she was dating Gig Young. In 1951, they married, but unfortunately she died of cancer just a year or so later. Tony Curtis was under contract with the studio at the same time, along with Shelley Winters, Rock Hudson, Jeff Chandler, Audie Murphy, Abbott and Costello, and Marjorie Main and Percy Kilbride from the "Ma and Pa Kettle" film series. I was fortunate to work with all of them.

In two years, I appeared in thirteen pictures for Universal. I did a one-line walk-on one day, and then I appeared in a feature lead the next. That was quite an experience because I got to go on the set and watch Marlon Brando and Teresa Wright appear in *The Men*. I got to see Jimmy Stewart create Harvey. In *Abbott & Costello Meet the Invisible Man*, I played the Invisible Man. On the video box, that is my outline. Of course, that was a nothing, unaccredited part, but it was good experience to be involved with Bud Abbott and Lou Costello and others.

I also was the temporary voice for Francis the talking mule in some of the "Francis" pictures. I went on location and spoke for the mule, and then Chill Wills arrived in a limousine at the air-conditioned soundstage. He dubbed over my voice and picked up all the money, while I was making my $125 a week — and glad to get it.

Around this time, my love life developed a complication. I had been warned by actors with more experience than I about the Hollywood game. I was told not to mess around with the contract actresses because no one knew who they were dating or who they someday might be dating. I took that advice and still managed to have a satisfying romantic life. I kept a low profile and stayed out of trouble by dating secretaries and the grand-daughter of the woman who ran the hotel where I was staying. Then, I made my big dating mistake.

Beginning with the first year of the Miss Universe Pageant, Universal Studios signed each Miss Universe to a contract. Well, I assumed that dating Miss Universe was not quite the same as dating a regular contract actress. I thought they were fair game, so I dated one of them. She had been on the cover of *Look* magazine, and she was a gorgeous girl. She had one brown eye and one green eye. She was a beautiful lady, but she was also a blabbermouth. For my part, I never kissed and told anybody, and I did not expect anything less from my dating partners. We had a few drinks and a lovely evening of creative activities. The next day, I went on the studio lot only to hear that people were saying, "Oh, Mr. Best, we hear you dated Miss Universe."

"How did you know that?" I asked.

"Oh, she was in here and was telling everybody."

The next thing I knew, my option, which was coming up for renewal every six months, was not picked up. I had been there for two years. I had three features still unreleased. I had made three feature pictures with Audie Murphy, appeared in *Winchester '73* with Jimmy Stewart, and acted

I'm ready to charge with Greg Martel (left) and Tony Curtis in Winchester '73, *my first movie with Jimmy Stewart.*

with Anthony Quinn and Rock Hudson in *Seminole*. I starred in *Ma and Pa Kettle at the Fair*. All that did not seem to make a difference.

Bob Palmer, casting director for Universal, said, "Jimmie, we want to keep you on at the same salary."

I said, "You're kidding. I have three unreleased films. I went on tour with Audie Murphy, and the girls were tearing my clothes off. I am going to ask for a raise."

He said, "No, we're not kidding. You stay on at the same salary, or you're gone."

I cannot repeat what I told him to do with his contract. I was black-balled for a year in the industry. I did not learn the reason until about fifteen years later when a director told me. I was not on the outs like so

I had this shot taken in hopes that Universal would see me more as a character actor.

many who were blacklisted because they had been "named" as a Communist. I had simply dated the wrong girl. I eventually realized the woman I really wanted to be with was Mattie.

Almost immediately upon my arrival in Hollywood, I had worked on *Comanche Territory* on location in Arizona. While there, I roomed with the great character actors Ed Cobb and Glenn Strange. I would hear them talking about how much they missed their wives while we were on location. I studied on that for a while, and then I decided to fly back to New York. One reason was to see Mattie, but the other reason was to go by and see the owner of a Greek restaurant that I used to go to in New York.

When I was a skinny, starving actor, I had gone to this man's restaurant and ordered a cup of coffee and slice of pie, which was all I could afford. The next thing I knew, there was a whole plate of food in front of me. I was not the only actor treated so generously by this kind restaurant owner. After I had been in Hollywood for a while and was making some decent money, I went back to New York to thank the man and give him some money. He was reluctant to accept my money.

I told him, "You were kind to me when I was struggling, and you're still helping other actors who are coming along now. I want to thank you for what you've done for me. I want to help you a little with others you're helping."

While I was in New York, I called Mattie and arranged to meet her at the theater where she was appearing in winter stock. I will never forget seeing her reflection in the cracked mirror in the dressing room after a performance that night. She looked so sad.

I said to her, "Why don't you marry me and let me take you away from all this?"

She said, "Okay."

All of a sudden, I was caught up in this swirl of sentimental feelings. I did not want Mattie to be lonely, and since I was lonely, we were married. Our marriage displeased her mom and dad, who preferred their princess to marry a man of means, or at least a man with a steady job, certainly not a would-be actor making just $125 a week. I am also sure they would have preferred that she marry a man of the Jewish faith.

We went to California. We were not actually trying to start a family, but in 1950, we did have a blessed son. We named him Gary Allen. By that time, our marriage was already beginning to fray. We were too young

After I left Universal, Cort Best, my uncle, took this shot. I guess I'm wondering where I'd go from there.

for marriage, and we tried to work things out and stay together because of our son. I did not know what real love was. I was selfishly in love with my career, and I needed space and time to succeed in such a competitive industry. Mattie said that I was not a good husband, but I was not the ogre that she made me out to be to my son. I was a good father.

Our marriage simply did not work, so we split. Mattie kept Gary,

Left: With Mattie and our son, Gary Allen Best. Right: In 1954, I enjoyed a visit with my mother after I came back home from Hollywood. That's a photo of Gary on top of the television.

and I paid alimony and child support, which in those days was even more substantial than today because divorce was discouraged much more. Mattie was bitter about the divorce and blamed me. As a consequence, Gary grew up thinking badly of me. We did not have a relationship for many years, but things eventually healed.

At that point in my career, the only person who would hire me was Gene Autry. Gene was richer than Wells Fargo. He didn't care about what I might have done to offend some studio honcho by stealing his girl. Gene had the television series *Annie Oakley, The Range Rider, The Gene Autry Show, Death Valley Days,* and several others all running at various times.

I worked for Gene Autry for $350 per show. I did my own stunts, unless the character I portrayed was to be killed, and then a stuntman doubled for me. If I fell off a horse by accident, then Gene got a free stunt, which he always found a way to use. Those television shows were produced so quickly that sometimes the directors failed to read the script carefully. Once, they had me fire a shot, change hats, gun belts, and boots, and then appear in another shot taking a bullet. Later, they realized that they had mistakenly filmed me shooting myself. Makeup consisted of about three pads of Max Factor Pancake Makeup, depending on how light or dark I needed to be. I was given just one sponge to apply the makeup and a cracked mirror in a cloth-walled dressing room that was full of rips and tears. I had to rinse out the sponge several times before I used it because everybody else used it, too, and it was saturated with makeup.

Gene Autry was cheap, but he was very rich. Being thrifty was part of why he was very rich. Gene Autry was also a true Western icon. I had grown up watching him in all of his early cowboy pictures. On the first day when I went to work on a soundstage, I saw a very chubby man getting on his horse with a ladder. The man was Gene Autry. Chubby cowboy or not, he was still an icon to me and millions of others. He was a kind man, and he did hire me. Sometimes, I did two of those shows a week, which meant I was making good money — certainly better than the $125 a week I made at Universal.

Working for Gene was great training, especially because of the scripts we used. We had to put a lot of intensity into our performances to make up for the drama and suspense that the scripts lacked. I became good at snarling. When all else failed, we staged a fight or shootout to get the action revved up, but we never had to resort to foul four-letter words to get our point across.

When a character was shot, it was unnecessary to have body parts flying all over. A little dab of chocolate syrup on the front of the victim's shirt was enough for the audience to understand that was where the bullet went in. If I fell off a horse or a big rock, everybody knew I was dead. In those tough Westerns, real injuries naturally occurred. They went with the job. We did not have the luxury of wires to hold us up or big cushy shock pads to break our falls.

After being blackballed for a year, I started working all the time, eventually appearing in about 600 television episodes and more than seven dozen major feature pictures. I appeared in many Westerns because they were extremely popular during the 1960s.

Gunsmoke was fun because Jim Arness was such a good sport. I did one episode in which Matt Dillon shoots me down in a dirty, dusty street. I had done so many Westerns by that time, and gotten killed in most of them, that I had a well-established reputation for performing great dying scenes. The director asked me how I wanted to die.

I said, "Have the grips dig a hole in the street about six feet wide and fill it with water. Then when Matt Dillon shoots me, I'll fall to my knees and then fall forward face down into that puddle of dirty water, but I am not yet dead. Then, I will try to rise up and lift my gun to shoot at Matt. Then Jim will shoot me the second time and I will really die and proceed to collapse in the water."

I thought the director was going to have a stroke right there on the spot. He said, "What the hell are you telling me? Matt Dillon never has to shoot anyone twice. That's a ridiculous suggestion."

As you might know by now, I do not easily give up. I still thought it was a good idea, so I went to Jim Arness and told him what I had wanted to do in the shootout.

He laughed and said, "Hell, Jim, I'll empty the damn gun into you if you want me to. I don't care." In the scene, he ended up shooting me twice, and I made quite a splash.

I was offered the lead in *Wanted Dead or Alive*, but I was under contract to do another series at the same time with Jack Chertok. He would not let me out of the contract, even though I could have done *Wanted* without even testing for the part. I later asked who got the part, and my agent said, "Some New York actor named Steve McQueen."

The same thing happened with *The Real McCoys*. I had made a movie called *Come Next Spring* with Walter Brennan. He liked me and said he was going to do a series called *The Real McCoys*. He asked if I would like to play his grandson in the series. Again, Chertok would not release me from my contract, which was a real bummer. I would have given anything to have worked with Mr. Brennan because he was another one of my icons. That part ended up going to Richard Crenna.

I worked with Charlton Heston and Susan Hayward in *The President's Lady*, a 1953 feature for 20th Century-Fox. I aged from eighteen to eighty-two in the role of Samuel Donelson. Charlton was less than friendly to me. I think he had an idea that his stature was quite a bit

above mine, even though he was yet to play Moses. He was merely playing President Andrew Jackson to Susan Hayward's Rachel Jackson, and
I was playing Susan Hayward's brother. One morning on the set, Charlton was sitting under a tree reading a book.

I said, "Good morning, Mr. Heston."

He just looked up at me and returned to reading his book.

With Walter Brennan in a Guns of Will Sonnett *episode called "Meeting at
Devil's Fork" (1967).*

The next day, I came through the same area, and there he was under
the tree again with his book.

I said, "Good morning, Mr. Heston."

He looked up at me and again returned to reading his book.

I walked over and I said, "You son of a bitch, when I speak to you, you'd
better at least acknowledge my presence."

From then on, he said "Good morning" to me and treated me very
nicely. I think Moses found out that day that there is an Eleventh Com-
mandment: Thou shalt not snub thy fellow actor.

In 1954, another legend I had the privilege of working with was Humphrey Bogart in *The Caine Mutiny,* which was made for Columbia Studios. I played one of Bogey's lieutenants in one of the film's many unaccredited roles. Especially at this fairly early point in my career, it was fun just to be part of a film with Bogey, and it was a great movie.

When we shot *The Caine Mutiny,* just about everybody in the produc-

I didn't have much of a role in The Caine Mutiny *(1954), but what an honor it was to work with that cast, including Humphrey Bogart.*

tion except me got to go to Hawaii for the parts filmed at Pearl Harbor. I was just one of many Navy lieutenants. Most of my scenes were aboard a big, fake ship on a giant soundstage. The crew had built this large sluice-like thing out of wood. It held back thousands of gallons of water. They tripped that thing and a huge wall of water hit us and knocked us plum silly against the metal plates of the fake ship. It was rough but exciting, and it got me immersed in the part in a hurry. I was eager to do anything for Bogey, who somehow managed to stay drier than the rest of us.

In the early 1950s, Rock Hudson, Tony Curtis, and I worked in several movies together. I did six pictures with Rock and three with Tony. We were all basically in the same boat — each of us under contract to Universal and fighting to be recognized and get ahead. We started out playing bit parts, usually in Westerns. At that time, a lot of notable, young actors were in the same career scramble to establish our positions in Tinseltown. In 1953 when we made *Seminole*, Rock was playing an Army lieutenant, which was the lead role, and I was a corporal. Rock began hitting his full stride about that time, and for the next fifteen years, he went on to play leading men in top box-office features and became a true Hollywood star.

Strawberries anyone? Seated with me are Humphrey Bogart and Van Johnson. Among those standing are Jerry Paris, Fred MacMurray, and Robert Francis.

Tony Curtis was not far behind. For the next twenty years, he generally played lead roles in his films.

Seminole with Rock was an interesting picture. It had a good cast that included Anthony Quinn, Barbara Hale, and Lee Marvin. The director was Budd Boetticher, who was a former boxer and football player at Ohio State and a former American bullfighter in Mexico. Budd was nicknamed "the bloody director" because he loved to create drama by showing blood on camera, and he did not care how he went about getting it. Budd and I were good friends, and during the 1950s, we made three pictures together.

In *Seminole*, I played a soldier drowning in quicksand. Rock Hudson was to swim and rescue me. They used ground-up burnt cork for the sand, which floated on water and looked like quicksand. The crew had rigged an elevator-type device that rolled me down and sank me below the quicksand surface. I was supposed to stay under water until Rock rescued me by tying a rope on himself and doing other preparations. While I was under water, I sucked air through a rigged-up hose. Budd called for action. The elevator lowered me down, as I did my drowning scene and went under water. Blub-blub-blub. I panicked and quickly put my hand up, which of course ruined the shot. Crew members jumped in to help me.

Budd hollered, "What's going on?"

I said, "You didn't give me any air. I can't breathe down there. I've got to have some air."

So they got an aqualung and put it underneath me, and we tried again.

The elevator lowered me down. I performed my tremendous drowning scene and went under. I stuck the hose in my mouth, but the crew had forgotten to turn the air on. In panic, I raised my hand again.

"Cut!"

By this time, Budd was tearing out what hair he had left. He screamed, "Let's do it again and get the man some damn air this time!"

Take three. I went under again. Blub-blub-blub. When I first sucked on the hose, I drew a mouthful of cork and had to put my thumb in the hose to keep the cork out. I spit the cork out and put the hose back in my mouth. Meanwhile, Rock was on the shore acting up a storm, tying a rope around his waist, and sloshing in the water to rescue me. All of a sudden, I heard the crew sloshing through the muck to retrieve me again.

Budd hollered, "Best, what are you doing?"

"What do you mean, what am I doing?"

"Your ass was sticking out of the damn water about three feet."

"The aqualung shoved me up," I told him. "I can't help it. It's full of air and it shoves my body up."

They tied the aqualung down and lowered me again. Blub-blub-blub. I did the drowning scene and was down there for what seemed like hours. I heard Rock sloshing, but he could not see what he was doing because of the cork in the water. He went underwater, grabbing around trying to find me, and took hold of me by my private parts, and I started laughing. I nearly drowned for real, as he dragged me out.

"Cut! Cut! CUT!" Budd yelled. "Best, you're supposed to be drowning. You're not supposed to laugh hysterically!"

We finally succeeded in getting the shot on the next take.

In 1959, one of the other films I made with Budd was *Ride Lonesome*, which was one of my favorite pictures on which to work. It was James Coburn's first movie. Randolph Scott played the male lead and Karen Steele was the leading lady. She was beautiful in all respects. She wore a white blouse that was so revealing that the desert sand nearly turned to

All eyes are on Randolph Scott in this scene from Ride Lonesome *(1959), but I'm sure that's not the direction I wanted to be looking. Pictured (left to right) are Karen Steele, me, Randolph Scott, Pernell Roberts, and James Coburn.*

glass. Lee Van Cleef played a small role as my brother. Pernell Roberts, another fine actor, was also in the picture.

One scene in *Ride Lonesome* called for Randolph Scott to hang me on an old gnarled tree. A steel cable ran down through the center of the hanging rope that was attached to a harness I wore. I had just gotten married to Jobee, my second wife, and she was on location with me at Lone Pine, California. I gave her a camera and said, "Take a picture of this. They're going to hang me here. I won't really hang unless the steel cable breaks. If it does break, then you'll have my picture and a good lawsuit."

The scene called for Lee Van Cleef to fire his pistol at Randolph Scott, at which point my horse was to jump out from under me. I was to hang until Scott shot the rope in two and I dropped to the ground.

I said to Budd, "This is a pretty rough scene. When that horse jumps out, I'm going to go banging against that damned old gnarled tree."

Budd said, "I've got to use you, Jimmie. You'll be in a close-up, so I

Off the cuff with Randolph in Ride Lonesome.

can't use a stuntman. I want to see pain as you hang. From an eager actor's point of view, that sounded like one hell of a way to get noticed. Like a fool, I agreed.

"And…action!" Budd shouted.

Lee Van Cleef shot, the horse jumped out from under me, and I kicked and acted as though I was really being hanged. All of a sudden, some the crew members rushed in, grabbed me, and lift me up. They thought I was really dying. Budd had a fit.

"You damn fools!" he screamed. "Can't you see he's just acting?!" Budd then said to me, "Well, now you'll just have to do it again."

"No, sir," I said. "That's a stunt, and besides that, it hurt. Get a stuntman."

He said, "I can't. I've got to shoot it close enough so that I recognize your face."

"Well then," I said, "It's $500 if I do it again."

I got the money.

In most cases, I would never take a job away from a stuntman. It irks me to hear a lot of these would-be macho actors claiming that they do all their own stunts, when I know they perform against a green screen. Not long ago, I heard a couple of these young guns talking in an interview

Ready to draw in Ride Lonesome.

about how they did all these mountain climbing scenes themselves. I talked to the stuntmen. They laughed, "Yeah, they did it in front of a green screen. It's all special effects."

In the old days, I did Westerns with some top stuntmen such as Buddy Van Horn, who doubled for Clint Eastwood, coordinated stunts for most of Clint's movies, and directed several films for Clint. He used to be my double when I was under contract at Universal Studios.

Hal Needham is another legendary stuntman who doubled for me, as well as Clint Walker, Burt Reynolds, Richard Boone, and countless others. Hal directed the *Smokey and the Bandit* pictures, *Hooper*, and many others. Hal did much more than double for actors. He became a leading stunt coordinator and key collaborator with Burt Reynolds. He was especially well known for his elaborate car crashes. He also has landed quite a few roles as an actor. His credited and unaccredited contributions to movie stunts left their mark on the industry. Hal once jumped from a low-flying Piper Cub plane onto a cowboy riding on a running horse. Although he did the stunt perfectly the first time, he went ahead and did it a second time because his mother, who was visiting the set that day, missed seeing him do it.

Hollywood stuntmen are among the most interesting people to be around. One of the most interesting in this fascinating group was Jimmy Van Horn, Buddy's brother. Jimmy was one of the top stuntmen, but he was also a very heavy drinker. Jimmy was not afraid of the devil himself. He feared only one thing: dialogue. If he was given a line to speak, he just got in his car and went home, but he did exceedingly dangerous stunts without blinking.

One time when we were doing a Western, *The Battle at Apache Pass*, there was a chase scene where Jimmy got shot off his horse. I heard something pop as he hit the ground. While Jimmy lay there, George Sherman, the director, said, "Oh, no. I need that again. I didn't get a good shot of that. We need you to do it again."

Jimmy started to mount his horse again, and I said, "Jimmy, I thought I heard something pop."

He said, "Yeah, you did. I broke my leg."

"And you're going to do the stunt again?" I asked with amazement.

He said, "I have to. We can't get insurance for stuntmen. I've got to pay for the hospital bill."

He performed that stunt again with a broken leg, which took guts. Jimmy died before he was fifty, which was young even by the standards of his rugged profession. I regret that the repeated one-two punch of stunts and heavy drinking finally took their ultimate toll, and we lost Jimmy Van Horn, a legend in the stunt field.

Another legend is Stan Barrett, "Stan the Man," as we call him for good reason. Stan Barrett is simply one of the finest and most versatile stuntmen in Hollywood history. He can do it all, and has done so many times. He

Passing time with the crew on Shenandoah *on location in Eugene, Oregon.*

has the scars and poorly healed bones to prove it. In my estimation, Stan is also one of the finest human beings I have ever had the privilege to call my friend.

In 1965, Stan was in his early twenties, and I met him while I was shooting *Shenandoah* in Eugene, Oregon. He was visiting his brother and was not actually involved in the movie industry. I had finished a day of shooting, and I was tired and dirty. I stopped in the hotel after work to have a beer, and Stan walked up to me and said, "Mr. Best, I hear you study karate."

"That's right," I said.

He smiled and told me, "I'm a black belt myself."

We got to talking and quickly became friends. Jimmy Stewart was having a private birthday party for some of the cast. I invited Stan to join the group, and he was thrilled. Later, I got him a job on the movie, and he actually had a line of dialogue with Mr. Stewart. Stan did a good job on the picture, and he was hooked.

At the time, I was teaching motion picture technique in North Hollywood, and Stan asked if he could study acting with me. I invited him to stay in my guesthouse while he was studying and until he got a job

The Budweiser rocket car going 739.666 mph with my buddy Stan Barrett inside.

and could pay rent.

Stan studied acting for a while, but then came to me and said he wanted to be a stuntman. I got him an interview with Hal Needham. Hal tested Stan by having him fall off a high platform onto a thin mat. Stan missed the mat and landed on the hard soundstage floor, but he never complained, and he passed the test. He immediately got a doubling job for Burt Reynolds in the detective series *Hawk*, which was being shot in New York in 1966.

Stan was on his way. He proved over and over that he had everything it took to be a top-notch stuntman. In 1979, Stan broke the world speed record with a jet-propelled car at 739.666 mph. I refused to go watch him do the stunt for fear of watching my best friend being killed in what I thought was surely a death attempt. Stan did the run several times, but they failed to turn his car around in the specified time for the return run. Thus, the record was not official. I have pictures of the car at full throttle and it is literally flying off the ground.

Over the years, Stan and I grew to be like brothers, and we worked together in many movies and television shows. Some of his most dangerous stunts that I have ever seen in my career were in *Hooper*, the Burt Reynolds movie on which we both worked. Stan was to drive a car under two huge brick smokestacks that were collapsing. If he drove too slowly, he would crash into it, but if he drove too fast, he would mess up the timing and the second falling smokestack would crush him to death. I don't think death or serious injury was ever in Stan's mind when he accepted this potentially deadly stunt. He just said a little prayer and headed straight for the wall. To this day, I would head for the wall for Stan and he would do the same for me.

CHAPTER 8

The Hollywood Fight Scene

Though my star was not rising on the same trajectory as Rock Hudson's and Tony Curtis's, I was staying plenty busy during the 1950s. I made an average of about four features a year, and after my release from Universal and my year of being blackballed, I was busy, especially with episodic television shows. I got to work with many terrific and talented people, including superstars such as Maureen O'Hara, Paul Newman, Lee Marvin, Jimmy Stewart, Henry Fonda, Humphrey Bogart, Barbara Stanwick, Anne Francis, Walter Brennan, Burt Reynolds, Andy Griffith, Ronny Howard, and many more. There was also a grand cadre of superb character actors, such as Jack Elam, Leslie Nielsen, Strother Martin, Morgan Woodward, and R. G. Armstrong. I was busier working in television than in feature films.

The popular *Bat Masterson* series ran from 1958 to 1961 starring Gene Barry. I worked in two episodes, one in the first season and one in the last season. Gene and I conflicted in personality and our particular approaches to life. Gene was a star, and he took himself very seriously. I believe he thought that he was above everybody else. On one location shoot, a stuntman and I had been out on location riding horses all day, while Gene had spent the day in an air-conditioned dressing room twirling his cane or something. At the end of the day, the three of us were riding in the back of a limousine and I invited a stuntman to ride with us. He and I were covered with sweat and sand, and Gene did not care for that. Our day had been hard and long, and both the stuntman and I wanted a beer.

I am not a big drinker, but I said to the driver, "If you don't mind, could we stop and get a beer?"

Gene did not like that idea at all, but I told him that we would just stop for a second, get a quick beer, and then hop right back into the vehicle with them. We pulled over, and the stuntman and I hopped out.

This stuntman and I were always teasing each other and horsing around. I did not know that he had shaken up my beer can before we got back in the limo. I popped that beer and it spewed on the movie star in the front seat. He turned around and slapped me. I had been through military combat training, and I was studying karate. I was tough and not inclined to take any crap from anybody.

Cutting up with Walter Brennan in the 1960s.

"Pull it over to the curb," I told the driver.

He asked, "Why?"

"Just pull it over." When he still hesitated, I reached over his shoulder and grabbed the steering wheel. "I said pull it over." He did, and then I jumped out and opened the door for Gene Barry.

"Get out here. I'm going to kick your butt," I told him, but he refused to climb out. "Listen, you get out and fight me like a man. If you're going to hit me, then you hit me with a fist, but don't slap at me like a woman." He still refused to get out of the car.

We have to fast-forward about four years for this story's payoff. Gene did not know it, but I had been hired to play a heavy against him in an episode of *Honey West*, which was a 1965 spin-off from Gene's very popular *Burke's Law* series. The title role was played by Anne Francis, with whom I had worked in *Forbidden Planet*, the sci-fi classic from a decade earlier, and in a *Twilight Zone* episode a couple of years earlier. I liked Anne very much, and I admired her beauty and her talent.

There was a fight sequence with Gene and me in the episode, and I knew where Gene was supposed to hit me. I told the wardrobe person, "I want an Eisenhower jacket that will cover my belt buckle, but I want a

A scene from Forbidden Planet *(1956). Left to right: Me, Leslie Nielsen, Anne Francis, Earl Holliman, unknown, Warren Stevens, Morgan Jones, and unknown.*

big steel belt buckle — the biggest one you can find made with extremely heavy metal. It won't show. It is not going to mess up your wardrobe."

We began shooting the episode. When we came to the fight scene, I walked over to Gene, who would hardly speak to me. I said, "Listen, we've got this fight sequence. I study karate, so I can take a punch. Just bury your fist in me and really stick it to me. It'll look great."

Gene lit up like a Christmas tree because he just knew how satisfying that was going to be for him. He could not wait to let me have it. We got into the scene, and following the brilliant direction he was given, Gene hauled off and threw a punch right toward my beltline. Just as it was about to land, I lifted the jacket and he hit that belt buckle square with his knuckles — enough to tear the skin off. I thought he was going to cry like a baby. The crew took him down to the hospital and bandaged his little hand.

Somebody asked, "Best, what did you do?"

Innocent as a lamb, I replied, "I didn't do anything to him. He hit my belt buckle."

I had a few run-ins like that. I once appeared in a television Western in which Robert Vaughn played my brother, a man who wanted to be a gunfighter, but could not because of his crippled right arm. He tried to entice me to be a gunfighter, and during an argument, he was to hit me. Robert Vaughn actually hit me.

I said, "Robert, you could miss me just a little and I can snap my head back, and it will look like you took my head off."

Take two. He hit me again.

I again told him, "You don't have to actually hit me."

By that time, the muscle in my jaw was having spasms and I could barely speak. The production broke for lunch. The medics shot some muscle relaxant into my cheek so that I could at least say my lines.

I came back from lunch and went to Robert's dressing room. I pinned him against the wall and said, "If you come within eight inches of my chin this time, I'm gonna kick your butt."

Take three. He threw his punches so far from me that the director said to him, "You've got to swing closer than that."

I like to think that I never looked for a fight. I took karate, not because I wanted to learn self-defense, but because my wife was a dance teacher. I tried to take dance from her, but I was such a klutz that she threw me out of her jazz dance class three times. I interrupted the students' concentration with my silly antics, which I did to cover up my embarrassment at not being able to keep up with the other dancers.

I decided to take up karate because the movements are strong yet graceful. I also thought karate would help my reflexes so that I would not get hit as much by overzealous actors, who get carried away with their acting while performing a fight scene.

I was about thirty-five years old when I went to my first karate class. The class was filled with seventeen-year-old and eighteen-year-old kids who had been taking karate for a while and could not wait for a chance to whip the novice actor. Johnny Leone, the instructor, was a seasoned forty-year-old, who would knock me down with one punch if I was not braced right. His students were trained the hard way. At first, the more experienced students ran me off the mat with plenty of bruises and lost pride.

I thought, "The heck with that."

I went to Johnny and asked him to give me some private lessons. I trained with him privately and worked out in my swimming pool. I increased my speed and technique so I could compete with the younger and more experienced students. I was determined to go back and kick some butt, but I was still just a white belt. I had not had a chance to go before the karate judging panel for an increase in rank. The hotshots in the class were waiting on the mat for their pigeon to return, but they made a mistake. This time, the bruises were on the other foot, as well as their hands, arms, and body. This "old" actor was able to give them all they wanted and more.

Professor Lu was a master kung fu instructor, an Asian gentleman who trained for eighteen years in a Chinese monastery. At that time, nobody in Hollywood knew about kung fu because it was a closely-guarded secret. Many Asians did not even want kung fu to come to America where they presumed the art would be bastardized. Professor Lu chose only three Caucasians out of our karate class to study with him; the rest had to be at least half Asian. I was one of the chosen three, and it was a great honor to be selected.

Professor Lu came to my house once. Jobee had a little white poodle that walked up to greet him when he arrived. Professor Lu took his hand about two feet above the dog and stroked the air as if stroking the dog. The dog reacted as though it were being touched. My hair stood on end when I watched this.

Professor Lu could also sit in the lotus position on the floor and let me attack him for real. He popped me three times in the chest before I could get to him. He did not seem to have a muscle on him. He weighed only about 120 pounds, and yet he could generate enough force to slap through a cement block.

The only problem studying with him was that I could not attend all the classes because of acting jobs. After being accepted by the professor, I could not just up and quit due to the dishonor that act entailed, as well as the risk of being seriously reprimanded with genuine hurt and pain.

Professor Lu spoke very little English, so I went to his right-hand man and said, "I must ask to leave. It's a great honor to be allowed to participate, but I'm not worthy because of my professional demands and my need to provide for my family. My spot should go to somebody with more time." Fortunately, I was allowed to leave without permanent injury.

After being around Professor Lu and the martial arts, I was convinced that kung fu would be an interesting basis for a movie or television series. I tried my best to convince the studio big shots that karate and kung fu would be the next wave of action movies. When I mentioned this to people at the studios, they rejected the idea. They just laughed and said, "Kung fu? What is it, some kind of Chinese disease?" That is how stupid some of the studio heads were.

Within ten years, Bruce Lee and others kicked down the door to Hollywood, and many movies that have come out during the last thirty years have had some sort of marital arts used in them.

CHAPTER 9

Audie Murphy

One of the nice benefits of my being under contract to Universal Studios during the early 1950s was that I was cast to work in three pictures with Audie Murphy. He was the most-decorated soldier in World War II, earning nearly thirty medals plus medals from other nations. I do not know exactly how many battles he was in, but he fought extensively.

Audie won the Congressional Medal of Honor for fighting off Germans while he was standing on a burning tank. When Germans were

Audie Murphy and me skeet-shooting on the Universal back lot in 1951.

overpowering his squad, Audie jumped on the tank and the Germans would not come near because they thought it was going to blow up. Audie grabbed a machine gun atop the tank, and although he was wounded in the hip, he fired away at the German soldiers that had his squad pinned down. When it was over, more than 200 German soldiers lay dead around the tank.

Audie and I became friends, but few people got close to him. I asked him about that one time.

I said, "Audie, you don't let anybody get really close to you as a friend."

He said, "Jimmie, I lost too many friends in the war. I can't allow that kind of closeness. I can't go through that again."

I understood and respected that. I know that Audie hurt inside because of his war experiences. He had a lot of nightmares, and I know he had a temper. Doctors today would have diagnosed him as having post-traumatic stress disorder. Despite all of his internal battles, he

Audie Murphy and I have a captive audience in Kansas Raiders.

became a formidable Hollywood star and an even more successful businessman.

My first picture with Audie was *Kansas Raiders*, which was released in 1950. It was a good movie and one of the first pictures that Tony Curtis and I did together while under contract with Universal. Audie played Jesse James and I played Cole Younger. In one scene, Audie and I came out of the bank that we were robbing. Scott Brady, another Universal contract player, hit Audie with a whip or piece of rope, and Audie shot him down. I looked at this World War II veteran, who had killed many people, and as I saw him pull a gun and kill Scott Brady, I knew I was getting a glimpse of what he must have looked like when he really killed the Germans. He always had a "baby face," but the rage in his eyes was frightening.

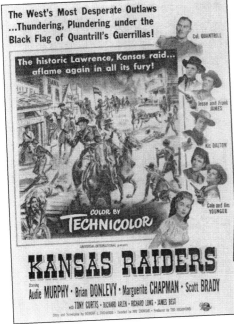

Above: *Coming in handy with
Yvette Dugay and Frank Silvera in*
The Cimarron Kid *(1951). Below:
Posters for* Kansas Raiders *and* The
Cimarron Kid.

Another time, Audie and I were doing a personal appearance in Texas for *The Cimarron Kid*, our second picture together. Audie had just recently gotten married to Pam, his second wife, and she was with us on this trip. Audie was behind the wheel as we were driving when a carload of guys who looked like Texas-sized football players approached from the opposite direction. They yelled something derogatory at Audie, who

A scene from The Quick Gun *(1964). Left to right: Audie Murphy, me, unknown, Ted de Corsia, William Fawcett, and unknown.*

was a hothead and took guff from no one.

He told Pam, "Get out."

She asked, "What?"

"Audie again ordered, "Get out." He opened the passenger door, politely shoved her out, and shut the door as we took off back down the street.

"What's going on?" I asked.

He said, "We're gonna go get 'em."

In a rare moment as the voice of reason, I said, "Audie, did you see who they were? There were five guys in that car, and they all looked like football players."

He said, "That's all right. I've got an equalizer."

He reached up and grabbed a .45 from the visor. Thank goodness we did not find those guys because Audie could have killed all five of them, and in Texas, they would have given him a medal because he was such a revered hero and movie star in his native state.

In 1971, Audie died tragically in a plane crash. In 1969, his last picture was ironically entitled *A Time for Dying,* in which he played Jesse James, the same role he played in *Kansas Raiders* with me. *A Time for Dying* was directed by Budd Boetticher, who had also directed Audie and me in *The Cimarron Kid. A Time for Dying* marked Budd's return to directing after a sadness-filled decade away from Hollywood. He and Audie had planned to make several movies together, but it was not to be.

CHAPTER 10

More Hollywood Razzmatazz

Hollywood was never my home, but just a place where I worked. I am proud that my early years were during the "Golden Era" before Hollywood became severely tarnished by bad attitudes, dope, and the hippy culture, all of which largely turned the city from sparkling jewels to dirty pebbles.

There are a few, hopeful signs that maybe some of the young kids today have the potential to avoid Hollywood's trapdoors and put some real quality back on the screen. I was in my share of schlock, but schlock done with heart and style.

I regularly go out on personal appearances for *The Dukes of Hazzard* and talk to fans. They tell me that they like to go to movies, but not to view the predominance of trash coming out of Hollywood. Even movies intended for kids are filled with bathroom humor, sexual innuendo, and graphic violence beyond anything that Wile E. Coyote ever suffered. I am not a prude, but I certainly do not think that every other word has to be four letters. I think that the use of harsh language in movies is, more often than not, merely a substitute for creative, thoughtful writing.

I also do not believe that a good movie should show some guy's brains violently blown out. I enjoy a good action movie as much as the next guy. I have been in my share, but I do not think graphic material is good for young people. I believe that young minds can become numb at seeing blood, guts, and extreme violence. That kind of entertainment is not our best export to other countries, whose citizens often come to regard Americans as the most violent, terrible people in the world.

Fifty years ago, I worked with Gene Autry, Hopalong Cassidy, and other cowboy legends. We substituted chocolate syrup for blood. One shot to the chest usually finished a character off. If I got hit with a bullet, I fell down, closed my eyes, and somebody said, "Well, ol' Snake Eyes is dead." Audiences knew who was good or bad by the color of his hat.

Nowadays, you go to a movie and see the hero shoot for twenty minutes with sparks flying everywhere, but no shots actually hit the bad guy until the very end. Directors allow special effects men to go crazy using hundred of squibs and explosions to liven up an action picture that suffers from dull acting and a pitiful script. I never saw a bullet make a spark when it hit a human being. A tracer bullet glows, but it was never used in small arms fire. Most bullets are lead, and lead does not spark off anything or anybody. Most directors have no clue as to what a bullet looks like in a real firefight since most of them have never experienced genuine combat action.

In some modern-day films, the hero brags to his girlfriend that he can hit a gnat with a pistol fired from 500 yards away. When he gets around to fighting the bad guys, they enter a bar to have a showdown and shoot the building to pieces, but nobody gets hurt. After the gunfight, the hero fights the bad guy with karate or kung fu kicks and punches that would kill any ordinary man, and all they have to show for it is a single trickle of blood from a bruised lip. After studying karate for years, I know that if you do not win in the first few seconds, you are not going to win.

I do not mean to sound bitter. I thank God for the opportunity I have had to participate in a wonderful, creative industry, but it hurts me to see all the mystery and glamour of Hollywood spoiled by greedy producers and directors making a buck with foul language, nudity, and graphic violence.

Thousands of people have more talent than I, but they never get a chance to perform or experience the wonderful pleasures that I have. I have dined with kings and homeless people. I have run the gamut of emotions with the rich, the poor, the in-between, the good, the beautiful, the bad, and the ugly. I have had more than my share of wonderful and not so wonderful experiences because of my film work.

In 1958, I played a character named Rhidges in *The Naked and the Dead*, which was based on the best-selling novel by Norman Mailer, who also co-wrote the screenplay with brothers Denis and Terry Sanders. The movie starred Aldo Ray and Cliff Robertson.

Raoul Walsh was the director. Walsh was a man's man. Back in 1915, he played John Wilkes Booth in D. W. Griffith's *The Birth of a Nation*. In 1929, he lost an eye while filming *In Old Arizona*, a Cisco Kid picture. A bird flew through the windshield of an airplane in which he was flying, and the broken glass put his eye out. Nevertheless, he maintained a great vision as a director. He was also one of the founders of The Academy of Motion Picture Arts and Sciences.

Walsh was a tough director with deep, gritty roots. He defined the old school, and he had a habit of not closely watching the action he was directing.

Diane McBain, Philip Carey, and me in Black Gold *(1962).*

He turned to his assistant, who was always right beside him, and asked, "Did they get their words out?"

If the assistant said "yes," then Walsh replied, "Print it."

I actually saw him do that while we worked on *The Naked and the Dead* in Panama, the only time I ever worked outside the United States. On the way down to the location, we were at a Panamanian airport near the border where armed guards were posted. Officials told us not to cross because this one particular area was rife with unrest. Student protests about poor schools had escalated into widespread violence against the government. An undertone of tension surrounded us even before we began to shoot the picture.

All of our crew sat around on rickety benches, fighting boredom and waiting for our plane to arrive at an unusually quiet, nearly deserted, crummy old airport. I decided to fight the tedium with entertainment. In the dead silence, I began to hit my Adam's apple with the side of my hand and make bagpipe sounds. Raoul Walsh looked down the row of benches and locked his one good eye on me. I instantly quit playing. Walsh slowly rose and walked toward me in an intimidating way.

"Do that again," he commanded.

I thought he was about to hit me, but instead he wanted me to play my Adam's apple again. I did just as he directed.

"I want to put that in the movie" he said.

I thought, *"The studio spent a million dollars on the script, and the director wants to put my makeshift bagpipes in the movie?"*

Walsh continued. "Write a little scene where you do that bagpipe thing, and we'll put it in the movie."

His request got this old country boy's engine revved up. I always wanted to be a writer and was confident that if given the chance, I could do it as well as anybody. I went right to work and came up with a five-page scene with my bagpipe display at the center. I proudly took what I wrote to Walsh.

He squinted at me with his eye and cussed. Then, he screamed, "I just want you to say "da-da-da" and do the bagpipes. I don't want the damn *Gettysburg Address*! You've got me five pages here. It would take another month to shoot this."

"Yes sir."

In the final movie we shot, I sat in a truck talking about how it used to rain back home and how the racket on the tin roof made my old pappy get out his bagpipes and wail away. Then, I played make-believe bagpipes on my Adam's apple.

This picture also had an invasion scene using landing barges. The special effects crew set out explosives on the beach to create shell blast effects. They told us not to worry and just stay away from spots with little red flags stuck in the sand marking the explosives.

We proceeded to stage the invasion on the shore. As we were running up the beach, I saw a shell hole where explosives had already gone off, and thinking that it was a safe spot, I jumped in.

"Move forward! Move forward!" the crew yelled.

I got up, and then I saw a red flag about eight feet away. I ducked just as a whole barrage of explosives blasted off and blew our helmets skyward. Walsh observed the unplanned comedy and doubled over laughing.

While shooting another battle sequence in the middle of a jungle, Walsh was unhappy with the special effects. He wanted red flames to make the scene fiery, and so he ordered the entire jungle set on fire. The jungle was overrun with all manner of critters, and while special effects men soaked the whole area with gasoline, I began to worry about the fleeing animals.

"Let me know when they're going to shoot that thing," I said to one of the crew.

"Why?" he asked.

"I'm going to get on top of the truck because everything in the world is going to come out of that swamp when that fire starts. I don't want to be on the ground having them crawl up my pant leg."

Sure enough, when the crew set off the explosives and the ensuing fires started raging, the place covered up with every imaginable critter running from all directions.

One day while the cast lounged on the ground waiting for the cameras to set up, I noticed a scorpion crawling up Cliff Robertson's neck. A scorpion sting near his jugular vein would most likely be fatal. He was unaware, and I did not want to panic him or cause the scorpion to sting him, so I took a stick and knocked the scorpion away.

The Panamanian jungle was wild and overgrown with vines and all sorts of foliage I had never seen before. It was so thick that the production company had to hire locals with wickedly sharp machetes to clear areas for our equipment and cast. The job paid only about 25¢ a day, considered good money in Panama in those days.

A local man took charge of the machete boys, but when the assistant director caught a couple of the boys goofing off when they were supposed to be working, he asked the local man to fire them. He refused. The assistant gave him an ultimatum to either fire the boys or be discharged. He fired them. The next day, the local man was found dead in an alley, butchered with machetes. The Panamanian jungle was a raw place in which to work. I was glad when we wrapped and made our way back to the relative quiet of the good ol' U.S.A. where drive-by shootings seem tame in comparison.

CHAPTER 11

Jimmy Stewart

Jimmy Stewart is my ultimate icon. He was the personification of what a true Hollywood movie star should be. Today you have all these punks in Hollywood who will put their dirty feet up on a talk show host's desk and give an interview with an attitude that says, "I am a megastar." Shoot, they are just legends in their own minds. Most of those would-be and never-will-be megastars cannot even spell "mega." Jimmy Stewart could not only spell "mega," but he was one of the original megastars.

I met "Mr. Stewart," which is how I always addressed him and referred to him, for the first time on the set of *Harvey* in 1950, when I was with Universal Studios. Even though it was a closed set to visitors, contract players were allowed on the set even if they were not in that particular production. For me, that was one of the great fringe benefits of being under a studio contract. Mr. Stewart let me sit next to him and study his acting. I would then go to the editing room the next day and watch the film of what he did. I was always amazed to watch how his performance came out on film.

On the set, it didn't look as though Mr. Stewart was doing anything, but on the screen, he was electrifying. I said to myself, "Boy, that's what I'd like to be able to do." I was a trained stage actor, but I realized that acting in front of the camera was a whole new set of skills and techniques. Mr. Stewart was one actor who really knew camera technique. That seed of inspiration has stuck with me throughout my career. One day, after I had the training myself, that same inspiration would also lead me to develop my camera technique school to pass along some of this essential but often ignored knowledge to other aspiring actors.

I am proud to say that, to my knowledge, I started teaching formal classes on motion picture technique before anyone else in the business.

Now every half-baked, self-proclaimed teacher who does not know a camera from a powdered doughnut is teaching some sort of camera technique, and although their teachings are absolutely of no value to a hopeful student, they take the students' money just the same.

The first of four pictures I made with Jimmy Stewart was *Winchester '73*, a 1950 release that also starred Shelley Winters, Dan Duryea, Jay C.

On the set of Hawkins *in a 1973 episode titled "Blood Feud" with Strother Martin and Jimmy Stewart.*

Flippen, and featured Rock Hudson and Tony Curtis. When they were getting ready to cast the movie, Rock came to me.

"Jimmie, I'm going to test for the Indian in the movie," he told me. "If I don't pass the test, they're going to drop my contract. How do I play an Indian?"

I said, "You don't play an Indian. Just put on the headdress and the war paint. Get on the horse and speak the dialogue without trying to do a stereotype Indian speech pattern." He did just that and got the part. He did such a good job that he was then cast in *Iron Man* with Jeff Chandler and became an instant, bona fide movie star.

In *Winchester '73*, Tony Curtis and I played two soldiers fighting the Indians. I think Tony had one line. I do not know whether I had a line or not. If I did, it was not memorable to me or the audience. My part was so small that after my character was killed, the film editor cut to Jimmy

From Winchester '73, *this is the first of my many death scenes, with Tony Curtis (left) and Jay C. Flippen fighting on.*

Stewart firing at the Indians. The action cut back to me, and there I was, alive again firing at the Indians, and millions of people who saw the movie never caught the difference.

Out on location in the desert, limousines came down to pick up Mr. Stewart, Shelley Winters, and Dan Duryea to go to lunch some distance from the set. The limo drove up a hill with the dust flying in my and Tony Curtis's faces. Tony and I had to grab a horse's tail to pull us up a big sand dune. Tony shook his fist at the retreating Cadillac.

"Someday, I'll be riding in that Cadillac," he screamed.

About a year later, he was, and the same is true for Rock Hudson. I did not get many limo rides, but they did. Instead, a year or so later, Universal threw my butt out for messing around with the wrong woman, but that is the way it goes. Some chose the limo; I chose the libido.

My second movie with Jimmy Stewart was *The Mountain Road*, which we filmed about ten years later in the Superstition Mountains near Phoenix. It was a story about an American Army demolition squad in China. For this story, I first need to point out that Jimmy Stewart had been a

Jimmy Stewart points the way in The Mountain Road *(1960). Left to right: Mike Kellin, Harry Morgan, Frank Silvera, Lisa Lu, Frank Maxwell, and me.*

pilot in World War II and flew twenty-three combat missions. He also greatly supported the war effort by promoting war bonds and doing patriotic public relations. He came back from the war as a full colonel, but he was promoted to brigadier general by an act of Congress. I believe I am correct in saying that he is the only Hollywood star to have achieved that rank.

While we were filming around Phoenix, Mr. Stewart briefly flew back to Washington to receive his promotion. We were all staying at the same hotel in Phoenix. While Mr. Stewart was in Washington, I called down to the hotel room service and imitated Mr. Stewart's voice.

"Uh, do you have any red wine?" I asked.

"Oh, yes, Mr. Stewart," the server replied.

I said, "Uh, I don't mean just any wine. Uh, I mean a…uh really good wine."

"Well, we have a very good French wine, Mr. Stewart."

I said, "Well, uh…then be so kind as to send a bottle up to Mr. Best's room, and uh…make that two bottles."

In about fifteen minutes, I had two bottles of very fine French wine

With my all-time top icon, Jimmy Stewart, in his series Hawkins.

billed to Mr. Stewart. When Mr. Stewart came back, I told him about what I had done because I do not steal.

He laughed and said in his driest, vintage deadpan, "Well, Jimmie, who's going to pay for that?"

My favorite picture with Jimmy Stewart was *Shenandoah*, a good Civil War picture that was released in 1965. I played a rebel soldier named Carter. As the star of the movie, Mr. Stewart had a lot more work to do in the film than I did. I love to fish, and there happened to be a beautiful stream flowing under a bridge where Mr. Stewart was performing an intensely dramatic, pivotal scene with a young man who had inadvertently shot his son. Mr. Stewart was acting his heart out, and nobody dared to make a stray sound.

I was fishing under the bridge, when I suddenly hooked a trout. The trout jumped and thrashed around, making all kinds of racket. I quickly stuck the pole underwater and the trout stayed quiet until Mr. Stewart finished his scene. Then, he walked down the bank to where I stood.

"Jim — " he began.

"Yes sir?"

"Come over here."

I walked to him and said, "Yes sir?"

"What the heck are you doing?"

"I'm fishing," I replied, while the trout thrashed on the end of my line.

"Yeah, well, I can see that," he said. "Uh, tell me why it is that I am up there working my tail off and uh…you're down here fishing?"

"Well, Mr. Stewart, if I ever get as rich and famous as you are, I'll go up there and act and you can come down here and fish."

"You've got a point there."

By the way, I do not know what it says about my career, but I have gotten in a lot more fishing since that day almost forty-five years ago.

In 1968, *Firecreek* was another special movie experience working with both Jimmy Stewart and Henry Fonda, another giant. After *Firecreek* wrapped, Henry Fonda had a party with "a few friends." I arrived to discover that a "few friends" meant a large crowd with valets and caterers. Big stars were everywhere — people such as Lucille Ball and Danny Kaye. I felt like a peanut in an elephant cage. I saw Jimmy Stewart across the main room talking to some bigwigs.

He saw me and said to some superstars, "Excuse me for a moment. There's Jim." He left them with their mouths hanging open and came toward me.

I thought, *"Boy, I am protected now. I am under the wing of the big boy."*

Henry Fonda was an artist and a darn good one. Henry also played poker on the *Firecreek* set with Jack Elam. That was a big mistake. Henry should have stuck to his painting. Jack proceeded to clean his clock in the card game every time. Jack was a professional gambler. He confided in me that he made more money playing cards across the country than acting in movies. I told him one time, "Jack, the reason you make so much

Above: Tough guys in Firecreek. *Left to right: Me, Jack Elam, Morgan Woodward, Gary Lockwood, and Henry Fonda. Below: Ready to fight in* Shenandoah *with Phillip Alford (middle) and Harry Carey, Jr.*

money is that your glass eye keeps them from knowing whether you're cheating." He laughed.

Jack bet on anything. If he saw two birds on a telephone line, he bet which one would be the first to fly away, and he let me pick which one. He did not care, and he usually won.

Jimmy Stewart was simply a lovely, generous man. I asked him one

In 2006, Dorothy and I visited the Jimmy Stewart Museum in Indiana, Pennsylvania, where I received the Harvey Award.

time, "You have an awful lot to say about who is in your movies, don't you?"

"Why do you ask that?"

I said, "Well, I've been in several of your movies and I've noticed other people that you regularly have in your films."

He said, "Uh…uh…well, I do have a certain amount of influence."

He will continue to have profound influence among generations of actors, moviegoers, and people everywhere who admire modesty, talent, and all-around exemplary behavior.

CHAPTER 12

Sammy Fuller

During my career, I admired the toughness I found in stuntmen and some actors and directors, such as Audie Murphy, Clint Eastwood, Budd Boetticher, and George Sherman. I have worked with some of the top minds in filmmaking, including John Huston, Alfred Hitchcock, Arthur Penn, Jerry Lewis, and Norman Lloyd. Sammy Fuller was a writer, producer, director, and actor, and one of the most brilliant men with whom I worked.

Sammy won the Silver Star during the invasion of Omaha Beach on D-Day during World War II. He pulled some of his buddies off the beach while under withering fire and saved their lives. He spent more than two years on the front lines before Germans shot him in the chest.

Sammy made several films for big studios, but many of his most cherished productions were as an independent producer and director. He directed "B" movies, but he made them look like "A" movies.

In 1958, my agent asked if I would like to go over to Sammy's office and meet him. I vaguely knew who he was, but my memory was jogged when my agent reminded me that he had directed *Steel Helmet*, a 1951 picture about the Korean War. The film should have won an Academy Award, but it was not a big enough picture to get the Hollywood machine behind it. Nevertheless, Sammy and *Steel Helmet* did win a Writers Guild Award for Best-Written American Low-Budget Film.

My agent told me that Sammy was interested in having me play the lead in *Verboten!*, a film he was writing and directing. *Verboten!* is the story of David Brent, a young Army sergeant stationed in Germany at the end of World War II. He falls in love with a German girl and gets involved with battling werewolf gangs.

I said to my agent, "Gee, that's very close to what actually happened to me."

I was eager to meet Sammy Fuller. I walked into the reception room and was greeted by a secretary who looked like she could have whipped boxer Joe Louis. She had a very strong personality, and she was surprised to see me.

"Oh, I am a big fan of yours," she said.

"That's sweet of you," I replied, but I thought, *"Where are you wrestling tonight?"*

Sammy came to the door and growled, "Send him in here."

He always had a cigar in the side of his mouth, and he talked rough and tough, much like George C. Scott in *Patton*.

I walked in and said, "Mr. Fuller, I am..."

"I know who you are," he barked. "My wife thinks you're great. So does my secretary, but I have never heard of you."

I said, "Well, I just recently heard of you."

He looked at me and grinned, "What branch of the service were you in?"

"Air Corps."

"Oh," he said. He cussed a little, and then he added, "You guys killed more of our men than the damn Germans."

That comment got my dander up. I said, "I didn't kill any of your men. I was a gunner and a radioman on a B-17. I was in the military police. The war was nearly over. I did not kill any of your men."

Somewhat appeased, he said, "Do you know what a dogface is?"

"Yes, I know what a dogface is."

He started telling me about this character in the movie. "He's a dog-face. That's infantry, the Big Red One."

"Yes sir," I answered impatiently. I glanced around his office and saw several pictures of Sammy in combat.

"This Sgt. Brent character has got to be tough," he described. "You've got to be able to kill a German any way you can."

Suddenly, he grabbed me, threw me on the couch, and grabbed a shovel—the kind that a dogface uses to dig a foxhole. "Sgt. Brent could take this and cut a man in two with it."

"Holy-moley!" I thought. *"I'm not going to take this crap."*

I spotted a bullet-ridden steel helmet on a shelf, a prop from *Steel Helmet*. I grabbed it, shoved Sammy onto the couch, and sat on him.

"And I could bash his damn brains out with this helmet!"

He looked at me calmly and said, "Yeah — I believe you could."

He got up from the couch and continued our conversation as if nothing had happened.

"Come over here," Sammy instructed.

I followed him to a desk. He sat and began to type for five minutes on an old Royal typewriter. He ripped the sheet of paper out, handed it to me, and said, "Read that."

Talking to a crowd in Verboten! *(The building behind me may look familiar to fans of* The Andy Griffith Show *because it's the same set used for the exterior of the Mayberry Courthouse.)*

I obeyed the order.

"What do you think?" he asked.

"Well, it's dialogue. I don't know what went before or what goes afterward, but this is dialogue."

"Well, then we're in agreement about that," he said.

He called in a young actress and asked the two of us to read a scene. She read the leading lady part, and I read the other. When we finished, she left the room.

"What did you think of her?" he asked.

With my usual one-track mind, I replied, "She's very pretty."

"No, what do you think of…"

"Look, Mr. Fuller," I interrupted, "I'm not passing judgment on actors."

"Oh," he answered.

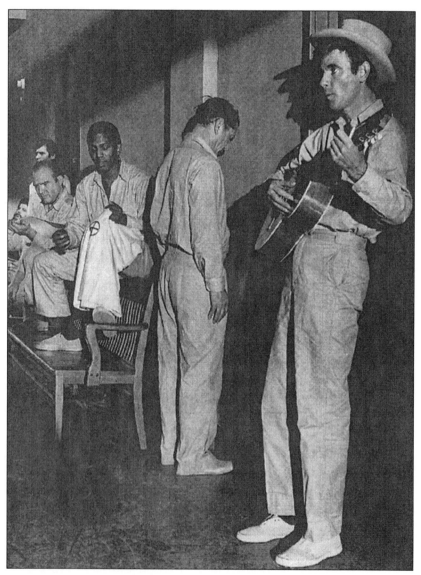

Strumming a guitar in Sammy Fuller's Shock Corridor *(1963).*

Then he called in the next actress, and I read the scene again. She was dismissed, and then for an hour and a half, I read the same scene with a parade of different actresses. Finally, I spoke up.

"Mr. Fuller, I don't know what's going on. I came in here to read for myself."

"Oh, you had the part when you walked in here. I guess I forgot to tell you."

Sammy ended up casting Susan Cummings as the leading lady. She was very pretty, and a fine and beautiful actress. I had dated her a few times in the past, but I did not want to influence the hiring decision, so I never told him. I was glad she got the part.

Our first day of filming *Verboten!* took place on the back lot at MGM. The setting was Berlin in shambles at the end of World War II. I was to do battle with a German sniper. My friend was shot, and I was to use my friend's dead body for protection like a sandbag, as I returned fire at the German. The German and I were to take turns chasing each other.

Sammy was filming a shot of me walking through a building, suddenly hearing a noise, and turning to shoot. As I was preparing for the scene, I looked at the shells in the gun and I was stunned by what I saw.

"Sam, this is live ammo!" I said.

"Yeah," he replied nonchalantly.

"But we're on a back lot. I can't shoot live ammo back here."

"Sure you can," he said. "I want to see the bullets hit."

I replied, "Well, you're the director."

I fired live ammo into buildings, and hoped that nobody was behind the walls.

Another scene in *Verboten!* called for me to ride a jeep into a crowd of rabble-rousers and werewolf gangs yelling at me. I was to yell back, "We're not here as liberators! We're here as conquerors, and don't you forget it!" A gang member was to holler back, "Go home, Yankee pig!" or something to that effect.

As we were setting up this scene, Sammy was up on an elevated camera platform. He unceremoniously called down to me, "I want you to jump off there and get in a fistfight with the crowd, who'll continue to beat you unconscious until the MPs arrive to save you."

"Okay," I called back.

Sammy rolled film. "Take one. Action!"

I jumped from the jeep into the crowd and fists were flying. I got badly beaten and received a genuine bloody nose.

"Cut!" Sammy yelled.

I held a handkerchief to my bleeding nose and approached Sammy. "Who do you have in there throwing punches like that? Have you got stunt guys in there? I'm getting the hell beat out of me!"

The crowd goes wild! Sammy Fuller wanted it real, but these guys got a little carried away.

He said, "Oh, the flyboy can't take it, eh? We're going to shoot it again."

"Sammy, tell those guys that we're supposed to be acting," I said.

"Get in there and do it, flyboy!" the old dogface barked back.

"All right then," I replied.

Take two. I got into the jeep. Cameras rolled, and I jumped down and began to deck guys left and right, putting them down one after another. Finally, I heard Sammy yell through a bullhorn, "Lie down, you son of a bitch, lie down!"

I was supposed to lie down at the end of the fight. When I finally did, it was with a little more company on the ground than Sammy intended.

"Cut!" he yelled again.

I went over to the platform and asked, "Sammy, how'd that go?"

He shot me a withering look, and then said to the cameraman, "Print take one."

Sammy enjoyed firing a .45 loaded with live ammunition into the air whenever he called "Action!" Louis B. Mayer and other movie moguls chastised him, but he continued blasting his gun into a soundstage side or wherever he desired.

"Sammy, you've got to quit doing that," officials told him. "You're shooting holes through the roof, and you're going to kill some of the grips or electricians up on the scaffolds!"

Sammy did not care. He was an excellent shot, and he could have hit the electricians if he really wanted to.

Shock Corridor, a 1963 release, was the only other movie I made for Sammy. It was an interesting whodunit involving a murder in an insane asylum. It was a low-budget but creative and compelling film with some fairly radical characters for its day.

Sammy and I became good friends through our work together and we remained so for the rest of his life. I loved the man, respected what he stood for, and admired the honesty and fresh inventiveness of his story-telling and filmmaking. I went to his house many times while he wrote *The Big Red One.* That script was actually Sammy's life story, and working on it was a labor of love. Sammy spent years pecking away on his old Royal typewriter while he wrote that script. He drank vodka all night long, but he never became drunk. I tried to keep from going to sleep, as he enthusiastically read out parts of this screenplay.

"What do you think? What do you think? What do you think?" he kept asking.

I did not see any pretty girls in the script, so it was hard for me to answer.

One day, I said to him, "Sammy, I've got an idea for a story that I think would make a very good script and it's — "

He cut me off, saying, "Wait. I don't want to hear it."

I thought that was quite rude, especially after I had spent several weeks listening to blow by blow readings from *The Big Red One.*

He added, "You didn't just hear my stuff — you *read* it. If you've got an idea, it doesn't mean anything until you put it down on paper."

I have never forgotten that advice.

Sammy eventually produced and directed *The Big Red One,* which won much acclaim. The film starred Lee Marvin and Mark Hamill, who managed to fit some World War II combat in between his second and third *Star Wars* films.

Sammy was once married to Martha Fuller. After their divorce, she married Raymond Harvey, one of Sammy's old war buddies. Harvey was a Congressional Medal of Honor recipient, one of America's most-decorated war heroes, earning medals in World War II and Korea. In 1967, Sammy married Christa, a beautiful lady, and they remained married until 1997 when Sammy passed away. His influence is still recognized and emulated by many film producers and directors around the world.

CHAPTER 13

Paul Newman

I made two pictures with Paul Newman. One was *The Rack* (1956), in which he played a Korean War P.O.W. tortured and brainwashed into giving comfort to the enemy. The screenplay was based on a Rod Serling story, and the film had an interesting cast including Walter Pidgeon, Anne Francis, Edmond O'Brien, and Cloris Leachman.

Working on *The Rack* was the first time I met Paul. When I went over to be interviewed, he walked onto the stage. At first, I thought he was Marlon Brando. At that time, they were very similar types. Paul, of course, was a hell of a lot better looking. He was very nice and very generous, but I did not get to know him very well while working on that film because I had no scenes with him. Lee Marvin and I played soldiers testifying against Paul's character in a court martial. I was on the witness stand, and Paul was just sitting in the courtroom.

Later, we became very close friends. A few years back, I was fishing on the St. John's River near my home in Florida. The fish were biting like crazy. I called Paul Newman at his home in Connecticut and said, "Paul, the fish are really biting down here. I'm catching 'em right and left. Come on down here, and I'll take you out on my boat."

Paul said, "Oh, Jimmie, I'm a terrible fisherman. I never catch anything."

I said, "Paul, you could throw your sock in the water and catch a fish."

Paul flew down in his private jet. He put his pilot up in a hotel, and then he came over to stay with Dorothy and me at our house. When he drove up to the gate, a security system with a telecom beeped.

"Jimmie, it's Paul. Buzz the gate and let me in"

"Paul who?" my voice squawked back.

"Paul Newman! Now, let me in."

I said, "Oh, sure you are. Anybody could come up to our gate and tell us he's Paul Newman. Do me a little scene from one of your pictures."

Paul was getting about half hot. I let him simmer a little longer and eventually buzzed him in.

We fished for three solid days, but all Paul caught was one mudfish. Paul's fishing prowess notwithstanding, we had a great time during that visit. One night, Paul threw Dorothy out of the kitchen and insisted on making dinner for us. He made the most marvelous meal with salad and all the fresh vegetables that he loved.

One day, I asked him if he would like to go out on an airboat. I told him I knew some folks at a honky-tonk fishing camp who had some boats they would let us use. Paul was a great racecar driver. He said, "Oh, yeah! You bet! I want to do that."

We got the boats revved up, and Paul suddenly announced, "I'm gonna drive."

I said, "Then I'm gonna walk."

He took one of the boats out for a spin. When he came back to the dock, a local driver took over, and I got on the boat with them and we rode around some more. That night, the guys at the fish camp roasted a pig for us. We had a great time. There was a pool table in the back of an old shack, and I got to play pool with "The Hustler." I will tell you this: Paul Newman may not have been much of fisherman, but he could really shoot pool.

A couple of days after he left, I was fishing on the river by myself and the fish were really biting. I could not wait to call Paul.

"Paul, you're not going to believe this," I said, "but the fish are really biting. You should come down and — " I heard a click, followed by a dial tone.

I was privileged to star with him in a Western called *The Left-Handed Gun*, which was released in 1958.

When I first moved to Laurel Canyon, Paul and Joanne Woodward lived about 500 yards from my house. We saw each other once in a while, and we always gave each other a friendly wave. That was about it. When I later got to know Paul better, I did attend a couple of parties at his house. One time, he had a big watermelon filled with either rum or vodka. We used long straws to suck the liquor from the melon. As we got less mobile, we connected straws together and finally ended up under the table —

still trying to siphon the potent juice through the string of straws to our drunken mouths.

Dennis Hopper spent a lot of time at those parties, too. Though my specific memories of such times are understandably fuzzy, I feel confident in saying that Dennis surely must have been a grandmaster when it came to melons and straws.

I dowse James Congdon and block out Paul Newman in the background during a scene in The Left-Handed Gun.

Those few such occasions were about all I saw of Paul Newman until 1957 when Arthur Penn came back into my life. Years earlier, Arthur had directed me in *My Sister Eileen* when I was in Germany, and he had advised me to go to New York. I had not seen him again until he came out to California. I heard he was going to direct a movie over at Warner Bros. I went to thank him for encouraging me to venture into a wonder-

In this scene with Paul Newman and James Congdon in The Left-Handed Gun, *I have my hand on my belly because I've been shot. Ouch!*

ful life that I otherwise would not have experienced.

"What are you doing here, Mr. Penn?" I innocently asked.

"I'm directing a picture with Paul Newman called *The Left-Handed Gun.* Do you want to be in it?"

I said, "Are you kidding?"

"No. You'd play Paul's best friend."

"I'd love that," I told him. "I worked with Paul on *The Rack.*"

"I know," Arthur said. "I've rented a house in the San Fernando Valley. We're going to rehearse there. We'll have the writers there, as well. Paul Newman, James Congdon, John Dehner, and the rest of the cast will also be there."

We went over to his rented house to rehearse. I knew very little about the script when I signed on. All I knew was that I was going to work with the man who had introduced me to the most wonderful of careers, and I was forever indebted to him. The other bonus was working with a fine cast that included Paul, my once and future old buddy Denver Pyle, Hurd Hatfield, and some of the best writers in Hollywood. Gore Vidal had a hand in writing *The Left-Handed Gun,* which was about Billy the Kid.

Historians are uncertain about whether Billy the Kid was actually left-handed, but Paul Newman played him that way. Paul had to learn to shoot left-handed, and the effort took a great deal of practice. He wore a gun during rehearsals and even when he was hanging out around his own house. He was constantly pulling that gun out to try to increase his speed. Because I had done so many Westerns, I had very fast hands and was very good with a weapon. At first, I was not sure Paul was going to be convincingly fast enough with his left hand to play a fast-draw legend like Billy the Kid, but I never should have doubted Paul's ability.

Paul worked a little differently than most actors. It is one reason that he was a great actor. We had truly great writers, and they were there with us as we rehearsed. They allowed us to improvise, even though they did not add the improvised dialogue into the script. Director Arthur Penn wanted us to have freedom and get to know our characters, what they were thinking, and the motivations behind their actions. We all loved his approach.

We rehearsed for a week or two, and then we went onto the different sets and walked through scenes. It saved a lot of time when we began actual filming, much of which took place around Santa Fe, New Mexico. The actors already knew exactly what they were going to do, and the crew knew what they were going to do. It was a wonderful way to work. Arthur also tried to shoot in sequence, which gave us the advantage of developing each character as the writers wanted.

I loved working this way, and Paul Newman thrived on that method, but our individual techniques were polar opposites. I was more spontaneous. I like to get the idea, attack it, and then see if it works. I do not preconceive what happens. I am sort of like a stick of dynamite, and I do not know whether the fuse will burn fast or slow. The ability to improvise and test what works suits me. By the same token, the more I watched Paul work, the more I came to realize that he was an actor who built his character layer by thin layer. He shellacked each layer, and then he added another. By the time he was done and ready to shoot, he had created a very solid piece of work. In *The Left-Handed Gun*, he had also developed a very sinister draw.

I was fascinated, as I watched Paul work, and I was interested to observe Arthur Penn create a working environment that allowed two entirely opposite approaches by actors to succeed. He allowed my spontaneous combustion to happen and gauge whether it stuck, while Paul was allowed room to do his mulling, building, and layering.

People often ask me, "Are you a 'Method' actor?" They refer to the Stanislavski Method of acting that Elia Kazan, Lee Strasberg, and the Actors Studio made famous. I did not know The Method, but I believed in using any method that works. I had my way, and Paul Newman had his way. There were also some actors that beat their heads against the wall in order to appear to have a headache. I thought it should be much less painful if an actor simply acted like he had a headache.

I did not see much of Paul Newman in his later years, but I am sad that he has passed away. We had some fun times, and he has left a remarkable legacy that very few will ever match in the movie industry..

CHAPTER 14

Killer Shrews

There are times when an actor *is* better off just beating his head against a wall. As Exhibit A, I present you with *The Killer Shrews*, which was sometimes billed as *Attack of the Killers Shrews*, as if the more menacing name might have made the film better.

Released just a few months after my meaty leading-man work in *Verboten!* hit theaters, *The Killer Shrews* was one of the most low-budget horror movies of its era. The film was so bad that it has become a classic. The running length is just a little over an hour, but it seems longer. It was short

Baruch Lumet and I found that reading the Killer Shrews *script didn't help make the movie any better.*

because it was released as a double feature with *The Giant Gila Monster*.

Ken Curtis, the future Festus Hagen of *Gunsmoke*, produced and acted in *The Killer Shrews*, and Ray Kellogg, a special effects legend, directed it. Ingrid Goude, Miss Sweden 1956 and second runner-up in the 1957 Miss Universe pageant, was my co-star along with Baruch Lumet, father of acclaimed director Sidney Lumet. Ingrid had beautiful eyes, among other attributes. A lot of times, I could not quite understand her, but I did not really care because I was too busy admiring her beauty.

Executive producer Gordon McClendon, who was not an actor, wanted to be in the movie. The movie cost only about 30¢ to make, but since it was Gordon's money, he had a right to be in the movie. The writers wrote a scene that had one of the shrews bite Gordon and kill him so we did not have to put up with his terrible acting anymore. Gordon was a nice guy and a legend in the radio business. He founded the Liberty Radio

Ingrid Goude tries to make peace between Ken Curtis and me in The Killer Shrews.

Network, which was a big force in radio for decades. Even so, he could not out-act a snarling, hungry shrew.

I have to confess that the only reason I made *The Killer Shrews*, other than the chance to be near the healthy Ingrid Goude, was because Sammy Fuller told me, "There's this great special effects man named Ray Kellogg who is directing his first movie. He wants you to be in it."

I told Sammy okay and appeared in the film for Ray. I did not do it for the money. The production was so cheap that we painted the sets ourselves, and actors had to walk sideways to avoid brushing against the wet paint because we did not have a double set of wardrobe. This production was so cheap. How cheap was it? It was so cheap that they strapped shaggy rugs on dogs to make them look like shrews. Special effects wizard or not, even Ray kellog couldn't make a decent-looking shrew from a dog with just 30¢.

I helped create one of the special effects. A scene called for my character to be outside the house and exposed to the killer shrews. I was

I'm about to throw Ken Curtis over the fence in The Killer Shrews.

supposed to check a boat to make sure it had not drifted away in a hurricane. The killer shrews were supposed to spot me and chase me through the woods. The crew did not know how to make sure the dogs looked like they were chasing me rather than just running through the woods for no particular reason.

"Get a raccoon and put him in a cage to keep the dogs from hurting him," I suggested. "We can drag the cage and leave a scent up where you want the dogs to go, and they'll follow the trail."

The crew followed my advice, and then the camera rolled. As I ran for my life, carpeted dogs chased after me. I did not know whether they were after the scent or whether they were really going to bite me.

The Killer Shrews was such a bad movie that it became a cult film. More people have seen it than *Verboten!* Or the other good pictures in which I appeared. Since I receive so many mentions from fans on that dang old turkey, I actually have been working with writer-director Steve Latshaw on a sequel to *The Killer Shrews*. We intend to combine new footage with stock footage from the old version, which is now in public domain.

Steve is well known in the film industry for directing little horror

In 1995, with Steve Latshaw on the set of Death Mask.

films in Florida for Fred Olen Ray. Most of Steve's films were done with a modest budget, and they earned back decent money. I first worked together with Steve when we shot a little film where I introduced some Westerns. Steve is an avid Western film buff, a walking encyclopedia with his vast knowledge of Western folklore and filmmaking. Since I have appeared in many Westerns, we have a lot in common.

Steve and I became dear friends. He also cast Dorothy in one of his classic epic horror films, *Biohazard: The Alien Force*. He even used the front yard of my home in Florida to shoot a scene for a horror movie called *Jack-O*. He later directed another little film I wrote and starred in with Linnea Quigley called *Death Mask*. It made a little money, but not much.

Steve later moved to Hollywood and bigger and better things. He has written a couple of dozen successful films, including *American Black Beauty* and *Gale Force*. I admire him, and I am flattered that he wants to collaborate with me in bringing back the shrews. Steve sometimes seems rough and gruff, but when people get to know him, they find that he is a very talented, kind, and caring man. He has been a good and faithful friend, and we both look forward to making movies together.

Steve and I have been working on the script for our new version of *The Killer Shrews*. I think the new movie will be a smash hit. With our Best Friend Films equipment and team, we will be able to shoot it for a little more than what we shot the original. I even have the dogs and shaggy rugs ready. I guess we will call it *Revenge of the Killer Shrews*. The movie's promotional tagline could be "They were a rugged menace before, but now they're a wall-to-wall terror." We are going to shoot it in 3D. Look for the movie to creep into a theater near you sooner than you dare imagine.

CHAPTER 15

Alfred Hitchcock and *The Twilight Zone*

Alfred Hitchcock once said, "Actors are like cattle." He claimed that he did not like actors, but he loved Jimmy Stewart, Cary Grant, and other high-profile stars. As far as he was concerned, lesser-known actors were peasants, and he readily admitted that. He hired good actors and then left them alone to do what they were supposed to do. That smart approach made him look good.

I think Hitchcock's real genius was that he was an extraordinarily good technical director. He knew precisely where to put the camera for the best effect. I performed in four episodes of *Alfred Hitchcock Presents* and *The Alfred Hitchcock Hour*, although none of them was personally directed by Hitchcock. In 1958, the first one in which I appeared was titled "Death Sentence," and I do not remember much about the episode. The combination of my being especially busy running from project to project during that time and the passage of about five decades has left some memories vague.

My second appearance was a 1960 episode called "Cell 227." I portrayed a character in prison with actor Brian Keith. We were depicting men on death row looking down a corridor at an electric chair. It was not a fun set on which to work on. I did not look forward to getting up in the morning and spending the rest the day sitting on death row.

In 1961, my third appearance was in "Make My Death Bed." Madeleine Sherwood, the future Mother Superior in *The Flying Nun*, played my wife, who blows me up in a car. The characters I played on the Alfred Hitchcock series seemed to have a run of bad luck.

My final appearance on the Alfred Hitchcock series was an episode called "The Jar." It was a powerful script, directed by Norman Lloyd and based on a story by Ray Bradbury. I remember that George Lindsey, soon to become well known as Goober on *The Andy Griffith Show*, did a terrific job as a mentally challenged guy. He delivered a lengthy, dramatic monologue about drowning some kittens, and George nailed it in one take. The whole cast of this episode was superb — including Oscar winner Jane Darwell, Slim Pickens, Pat Buttram, Billy Barty, Collin Wilcox, and

Working with a great cast, including George Lindsey (left) and Collin Wilcox in "The Jar," a 1964 episode of The Alfred Hitchcock Hour *directed by Norman Lloyd.*

Joceyln Brando. My character was messing around with Pat Buttram's wife, who was played by Collin Wilcox. She ended up dead, and her head was kept in The Jar.

Norman Lloyd is one of the truly great directors with whom I have been fortunate to work. He is extremely collaborative and blends well with actors. Too often in Hollywood, we work with directors who are "outside the bubble" of the filmed action. Norman was very much inside. Having that perspective is almost always a blessing to a production, and that is definitely the case with Mr. Lloyd. He did a wonderful job of casting "The Jar," especially in having the courage to go against type and cast Pat Buttram, who was known for years as Gene Autrey's comic sidekick. Pat was perfect as the dramatic, dark lead in "The Jar."

In October 2008, forty-four years after "The Jar" originally aired, Terry Pace, a faculty member at the University of North Alabama and friend of writer Ray Bradbury, put together a seminar about the episode. Dor-

In October 2008, at a happy reunion for the cast of "The Jar" at the University of North Alabama in Florence. Pictured left to right are the moderator and UNA faculty member Terry Pace, George Lindsey, Norman Lloyd, and me. PHOTO BY ANITA PACE.

othy and I were invited to attend. Norman Lloyd, George Lindsey, and I were members of the production able to be there in person, and Ray Bradbury participated from California by telephone. Collin Wilcox was unable to attend, but she sent her reflections in a letter, which was read during the evening. Several members of Pat Buttram's family were also on hand. We watched the episode on a big screen, and then Terry moderated the discussion.

Several things stick out in my mind from that experience. First, having the chance to spend a couple of days with Norman Lloyd after all those years was a real thrill. He was going to be ninety-four the next week, but he had the mental, retentive powers of a twenty-year-old. He is the living history of American movies and 20th century American theater. A seminar the night before the one for "The Jar" was devoted to Mr. Lloyd and his remarkable career. He flashed me back to some great experiences and wonderful people that I had not thought about in years.

It is always great to be with my old buddy, George Lindsey, another

A scene from "The Grave" episode of The Twilight Zone *(1961). Pictured* (left to right) *are William Challee, me, Strother Martin, and Lee Marvin.*

super talent in our business. I was also impressed by how well "The Jar" held up over time. It is an outstanding production. It was one of those occasions, so typical of any Hitchcock production, when all the right pieces were in place: Ray Bradbury's story, the teleplay by Jim Bridges, Norman Lloyd's direction, and a fantastic cast. I loved reliving some of the memories of that time working together and sharing them with an audience that included people not even born when "The Jar" was first broadcast. It was just an all-around pleasant time.

There was always top-notch writing, directing, casting, and acting on *Hitchcock.* Equally marvelous in my mind was *The Twilight Zone.* They used these beautiful sets from big motion pictures. With Rod Serling at the helm, I knew the writing would be unsurpassed. Monty Pittman wrote the first episode in which I appeared, a Western called "The Grave."

Above: A scene from the 1962 Twilight Zone *episode titled "The Last Rites of Jeff Myrtlebank" with Sherry Jackson. Below: Not quite ready for my last rites.*

It had a classic Western cast, including Lee Marvin, Lee Van Cleef, and Strother Martin. I played a guy named Johnny Rob. The story was actually based on a ghost story from my childhood in southern Indiana. I told it to Monty, and he turned it into quite an interesting script.

In 1962, the second *Twilight Zone* episode in which I appeared was "The Last Rights of Jeff Myrtlebank." I played the title character, a man waking up in his coffin after having been dead for three days. He came back to life, and from then on, strange things happen. The next season, I appeared in my final *Twilight Zone* episode called "Jess-Belle," which also starred the lovely Anne Francis as the title character bewitching me with a potion. She turned into a black leopard at night, until I stuck a silver pin through her.

In the "Jess-Belle" episode of The Twilight Zone *with Anne Francis (left) and Laura Devon.*

CHAPTER 16

A Visit to Mayberry

Appearing on *The Andy Griffith Show* was one of the great blessings of my career. It is a wonderful, wholesome family show with a perfect cast. In late summer 1960, I first appeared in the series' third episode called "The Guitar Player," which was filmed before any episodes had aired, but I was well aware of Andy Griffith and Don Knotts. I also knew Frances Bavier from her long career, which included quite a few Westerns.

The casting people asked me whether I played guitar. Because I always try not to lie, I said, "Are you kidding? I have two guitars," which was true. With that assurance, they hired me to play Jim Lindsey, a guitar player. I went over to the set at Desilu Studios.

Somebody said to me, "You'll be playing this particular song on guitar and — "

"I'm sorry," I interrupted, "but I can't play that. I don't play guitar."

"But you said that could play a guitar. You lied."

I said, "No, I said I *have* two guitars, which I do."

It was too late for them to replace me. I said, "I know enough about playing guitar that I can finger it so you'll never know the difference. That is all most performers do, anyway."

Music in films is almost always dubbed over in a sound studio to match what is shown on the screen. The producers agreed, and I got to play the guitar.

I was able to play only five or six chords, but that was enough to fake it. For a couple of scenes where my character played fancier guitar licks, they brought in a real guitar player for some close-ups. If viewers watched closely, they could tell that somebody else besides me was playing in a couple of spots, but I am sure that few noticed during the original broadcasts. During many reruns over the years, avid Mayberry fans — and believe me, they are avid — have noticed the technical detail.

Although I did not really play guitar, Andy Griffith played very well, and so did Lee Greenway, the show's makeup man. Between takes, we sang and played wonderful spirituals and old-timey country songs backstage. The crew had a hard time getting us back on the set because we

Enjoying a laugh with Andy Griffith in "The Guitar Player Returns." (Guess which one of us can actually play the guitar.) PHOTO COURTESY OF JASON M. GILMORE

were having so much fun. We worked on a pleasurable, relaxed set with Andy. He is multi-talented — adept at stand-up comedy, Broadway stage roles, television, movies, and music. When working with him, I hoped a little bit of his stardust would rub off on me.

Unfortunately, I did not have very many scenes with Don Knotts in the particular episodes in which I appeared. Don was one of our all-time comedy talents. The word "talent" often comes up when talking about the people working on *The Andy Griffith Show*.

I had only one scene with little Ronny Howard, even though he was in both episodes in which I appeared. Ron was talented and charming, and his mother and father were great parents. Rance, his father, was on the set with him while I worked. He had trained Ron to show tremendous respect. Ron was a little gentleman and very professional in his demeanor. In his continuing success in the business over his a fifty-year career, Ron has grown to become one of the giants of our industry.

My first appearance in an episode of *The Andy Griffith Show* went over

With Andy Griffith and director Bob Sweeney in "The Guitar Player Returns," my second episode of The Andy Griffith Show. PHOTO COURTESY OF JASON M. GILMORE

well with audiences and the producers. In 1961, they brought me back for a second appearance in an episode called "The Guitar Player Returns." The guitar player returned, but I still could not play more than a few chords. However, I was even better at faking it for the second go-around. Once again, the producers had a genuine guitarist doubling for me and playing some really slick licks. Together, that guitarist and I, along with a little creative dubbing, were especially sensational.

Fade out, and then fade in to almost fifty years later. *The Andy Griffith Show* is still running strong. It is not only one of television's evergreens, but since the mid-1990s, I have been invited to do personal appearances with Don Knotts and some of the other original cast members. I have been particularly honored to be included in these reunions because I did just the two episodes. My episodes are still popular enough with fans that

The 2004 dedication of the TV Land Landmark statue of Andy and Opie in Mount Airy, North Carolina, with (left to right) George Spence, Andy Griffith, Betty Lynn, LeRoy McNees, and me.

they want to include me in these reunions.

Fans often want to see me play a guitar. I bring a guitar to these reunions, and each time I have every intention of playing that guitar and Jim Lindsey's big hit, "Rock 'n' Roll Rosie from Raleigh." No one has ever heard anything like it — and probably never will.

The Andy Griffith Show and *The Dukes of Hazzard* have mutual fans. Both shows are set in the South, and they are wholesome entertainment that families can watch together. That cross-over appeal has often allowed me to work in a routine onstage in which I portray Sheriff Rosco P. Coltrane in an encounter with the "Mayberry Deputy," played by David Browning, a fine actor and tribute artist.

Above: At a Mayberry reunion appearance, I'm about to play "Rock 'n' Roll Rosie from Raleigh" any minute now. Yes sir, just any minute now. Below: "Battle of the Sheriffs" with my dear friend, David Browning (the Mayberry Deputy).

Out of tremendous respect for Don Knotts, David always refers to himself as the "Mayberry Deputy" and not as Barney Fife. We have lost Don, an incredible talent, who will always remain forever in the hearts of all of his fans as an icon. David brings back wonderful memories, and he has performed before hundreds of thousands of people who embrace the spirit of his tributes.

I have had the pleasure to work with David on many occasions when we have done personal appearances for Mayberry get-togethers and also for DukesFest. David puts on the costume of the Mayberry Deputy, and I put on the costume of Rosco P. Coltrane. We adlib a comedy routine, and it has been well received by our fans all across America. We lovingly call it the "Battle of the Sheriffs."

David is a wonderful person, along with being a marvelous talent. He, Patty, his wife, and their lovely family are a pleasure to be with. Dorothy and I consider them to be among our dearest friends.

Even though I appeared in only two episodes of *The Andy Griffith Show*, it still ranks in the top, small handful of the most enjoyable acting experiences in my career. All these years later, my connection is renewed through the reunion appearances. The high visibility of reruns likely makes those episodes two of the most-watched performances of my entire career. I am happy about that because Mayberry is certainly a nice place to be seen and remembered.

CHAPTER 17

Jerry Lewis

Jerry is an unsurpassed comic genius, inventor, humanitarian, producer, writer, and actor, and he is also my friend.

The most fun I ever had in Hollywood was working with Jerry Lewis on *Three on a Couch* in 1966. I could not wait to go to work each day.

In the film, I played Jerry's best friend, Dr. Ben Mizer, and Janet Leigh portrayed a psychiatrist. Her three beautiful, young patients were played by Mary Ann Mobley, who had been Miss America 1959, Gila Golan, who had earned the title of Miss Israel 1961, and Leslie Parrish (Miss Wow any year). Jerry played an artist engaged to Janet. He wanted to take her on a trip to Paris, but she was afraid to go because her patients had deep problems dealing with men, and she was dedicated to achieving their cure. Jerry decided to speed up their cure and expedite his trip to Paris. Posing as three different men, he courted all three patients. The set-up was perfect for showcasing Jerry's comedic and acting talents.

Long before I met Jerry, I had been a big fan. I had first met him in late 1960, when he was writer, actor, producer, and director of *The Ladies Man* at Paramount Studios. Permission was required to get on that lot, but I sneaked on the set and just stood off to the side and watched Jerry work. I was there a couple of days just watching because I had a strong desire to direct, and I loved watching him work. This particular movie was especially good to study his skills because he used a unique technology.

While directing *The Bell Boy* a year or so earlier, Jerry first used his patented innovation: a viewfinder through which he could actually see through the camera lens, as opposed to the more common, traditional parallax viewfinder mounted along side the camera. A parallax lens did not give the same accuracy as Jerry's invention, which allowed him or a camera operator to look directly through the camera lens at the action.

Video assist was another movie technology that Jerry pioneered. That technology allowed him to watch an instant replay, rather than having to wait for the filmed "dailies" to be printed. Video assist was especially useful for Jerry because he also acted in the films he directed.

Jerry is very observant. As I watched him work, he sent one of his assistants over to ask, "Can we help you?"

With Jerry Lewis in Three on a Couch.

I said, "No, no you're already helping me. I'm being helped just by getting to watch a genius. I'm an actor and I want to learn from the best."

The assistant left and I observed him speaking to Jerry. Jerry looked back at me and waved. That was it.

A few months later, I got a call to interview for a part on the television medical series *Ben Casey*, an episode called "A Little Fun to Match the Sorrow." Jerry was starring in and directing the episode. I went over to the *Ben Casey* offices at Desilu Studios to meet with Jerry.

"Mr. Lewis, I'm James Best and I — "

He stopped me. "I know who you are, and I know all the stuff that you've done." He started naming films in which I had appeared. He said, "You're a good actor."

"Thank you." I did not know what else to say. I was in complete awe.

Testing me, he said, "Say something nice about me."

I said, "Mr. Lewis, to be very honest with you, I don't laugh at a lot of the things you do because I see a lot of sorrow behind it." He looked as if I had slapped him in the face. I added, "I guess I just blew the job by saying that."

He said, "No, on the contrary. We'll talk about that later."

I got the job, and we went to work on the *Ben Casey* episode. I played a character named Dr. Sullivan. Jerry Lewis does things his way. I do not care what the circumstances are — he gets his way. Vince Edwards, who played Ben Casey, seemed more interested in betting on horses via telephone than he was in acting. He did not read "off camera" for me. He simply did not act in a professional manner. Although *Ben Casey* was a very successful series, the star certainly did not seem like a very nice person.

Jerry must have felt the same way. He threw Vince off the set and would not let him back on.

"What are you going to do?" I asked Jerry.

"You're going to play the scene at the end," he replied. "Did you ever do any comedy?"

I said, "Yeah, in summer stock and stuff like that."

He said, "Okay."

I performed the scene as Jerry had rewritten it, and although I never saw the finished episode, I was told that the alterations worked beautifully.

After we finished shooting, Jerry said to me, "By the way, I'm going to be doing a movie and I want you to be in it. Would you like to be in it?"

I said, "I'd love it."

A few months passed, and I heard nothing from him. Finally, I got a call to go see Jerry. I walked in to see him and said, "Hi, Mr. Lewis."

"Go down to my personal tailor and get four or five suits made up," he instructed.

"For what?" I asked.

"For what? You pea-pickin' so and so, didn't I tell you that you were going to do a movie with me?"

"Mr. Lewis," I replied, "do you know how many times I've been told that I'm going to do something with somebody and it didn't work out?"

He said, "Well, I don't lie."

"I'll go get the suits," I replied.

When I arrived on the set, I found out first hand what I had always heard: Jerry loves actors and he treats them with respect. He expects the same respect in return. Jerry's set for *Three on a Couch* must have had fifteen dressing rooms, each decorated with different colors and original oil paintings. Whether an actor had a one-line walk-on or was playing a lead part, each had his or her name on a dressing room door. The crew changed the nameplate the next day when somebody else came in, but that did not matter. We were treated like a star on his set. That was a typical class act for Jerry Lewis.

Jerry also wanted the set atmosphere to be light and fun. He had loud speakers placed very discreetly around the soundstage. They were hooked up to a long table with amazing, state-of-the-art sound-effects equipment, one of several devices that over the years became known as "Jerry's toys." He also had cameras and monitors covering every area of the soundstage. There was a constant stream of visitors to the set — folks from all over the world. As the visitors observed and milled around, all of a sudden there sounded a roar like a plane was diving down and crashing into the building. Other sounds were a little less discreet, and everybody wondered where those odd sounds came from and who was making them. Of course, the crew knew and became hysterical. Jerry fully embraced childish behavior with his comedy, but behind all the silliness, there was a deep understanding of comedy and a choreography to his zaniness.

One day while we were working on *Three on a Couch*, Jerry said, "Jimmie, we were talking about rehearsing. Do you know your lines?"

I said, "Yes, sir."

"Well," he said, "just go along with anything I say, but just make sure you get all those lines out."

I said, "Okay."

We began a scene and he took off on tangents that left me not knowing where in the world he was going. I just shut up and reacted to what he said until he came back to where I was supposed to say my line. It was tough but funny, and I love to laugh. I find humor in almost anything, not to mention the "king of comedy." I cannot keep a straight face around Jerry Lewis.

We had one scene where he was pretending to be a cowboy named Ringo Raintree and trying to impress a girl so she would go out with him. He wanted my character to ask for his autograph and tell the girl what a wonderful cowboy he was. We started shooting the scene, and Jerry was in there with a cigar flipping from one side of his mouth to the other and speaking in some kind of crazy Jewish-Texan accent. I walked into the scene and spoke my first line, "Ringo Raintree!"

"Cut."

"What's wrong?" I asked.

"Jimmie, I want you to really jump into the scene. Really come jumping in."

With Gila Golan and Jerry Lewis as Ringo Raintree in Three on a Couch.

I thought maybe I did not have enough energy or something, so I ramped up my energy level. The camera rolled again. I ran in there and exclaimed, "RINGO RAINTREE!"

"Cut!" Jerry again called me over. "Jimmie, I mean that I want you to jump in there. I mean physically jump in." He had someone bring over an apple box. "Now, you get up on that and you jump into the scene."

"You're kidding, aren't you?" I asked.

"No, that's what I want."

"Okay," I said.

Cameras rolled again. I shouted, "RINGO RAINTREE!" and jumped off the box and into the scene.

Jerry again yelled, "Cut! Jimmie, I want you to really jump in." He turned to an assistant and said, "Get him a ladder."

I said, "Jerry, it'll look like I am flying in there from a plane if I jump off that ladder."

"Don't argue with me," he said. "It's late at night and I don't have time to argue with you. Just do it."

I got up on the ladder, shouted "Ringo Raintree!" and jumped. I went flying into the scene. Jerry just fell on the floor laughing. It had all been a setup, and the crew was laughing hysterically.

We broke for dinner around two o'clock in the morning. Because we were shooting in an actual department store, we had to shoot at night while the store was closed.

I asked Jerry, "Were you really rolling film?"

He said, "Yeah."

"That must have cost a fortune."

"It's all right," he said. "I paid for it."

"Why?" I asked. "What are you going to use it for?"

"I won't use it for anything," he explained. "The crew gets down at this time. You've got to get the spirit of laughter going. This is a comedy."

Not everything was so high energy for Jerry. He had a low-wattage radio station in his house in Beverly Hills. I used to go over there, and he could actually broadcast through his station from his house whenever he wanted to. The little station probably reached no more than a few blocks, but what a hoot it would be to scan the radio dial and come across this hilarious station.

One room of Jerry's house was filled with recorded tapes. I saw a stack of about twenty tapes labeled "James Best." I asked, "What's this, Jerry?"

"Oh," he said, "I tape everything." It was true. I used to go down to his boat or ride around in his car, and he always turned on his tape recorder. He said, "People always want to tell me jokes and try to be funny, and sometimes they are. I've got those jokes on tape."

He also wrote down the name of every person he met and when he met him. He told me, "I keep a diary constantly of what my activity is."

I guess I will be hearing from Jerry if I have misquoted him anywhere in this book because I doubt he has any eighteen-minute gaps in his tapes like President Nixon.

After we made *Three on a Couch*, I told Jerry, "I've never seen you do a live show. I would love to do that."

"I'm going to be playing in Vegas. Come out there and see it."

I went to Vegas, and Jerry had a beautiful suite reserved for me. He said, "I've got you a great seat in the front row."

I said, "No, no, Jerry. I want to see you from backstage. I want to see you do makeup. I want to see you prepare and everything." He agreed to let me. I went back to his dressing room as he prepared to do the show, and many well-wishers came by.

There was one guy in the waiting room experiencing all kinds of spasms and making all sorts of weird expressions with his face.

"There's this guy outside waiting for you and contorting his face," I told him. "I'm concerned that maybe he's not somebody you want to see."

Jerry fell down laughing. He knew that the fellow was Charlie Callas, one of his best friends. Charlie was also one of the funniest comics I ever saw. The expressions that he can do with his face are incredibly hilarious. He soon became a fixture on *The Tonight Show* with Johnny Carson and other notable performances.

As I watched Jerry perform his act that night, I was able to see him work from start to finish, witness his utter fatigue, and then observe how he would pump himself up through sheer energy and willpower and go back refreshed.

To me, Jerry Lewis, is one of the best-known unknown geniuses in the world. He knows acting, camera work, writing, costumes, set design, and every business aspect of show business. Through all that has happened in his career, he has created and preserved his own brand. Somebody may not like Jerry Lewis's kind of humor, but as far as technically executing his accomplishments, he is absolutely the best. I am very proud to have been in a movie with him.

Around 1995, Jerry had played the Devil in *Damn Yankees* on Broadway, and he had taken the play on tour. Dorothy and I went to lunch with him in Orlando, and we reminisced about old times.

I said, "Jerry there was a serious program on television at one time called *Martin & Lewis: Their Golden Age of Comedy*. Dorothy is such a fan. Did you ever copy that?" Of course, I knew that he copied everything. About an hour later, one of his assistants came over with a whole collection of tapes to give to Dorothy.

Jerry used to invite me down to his boat, *The Pussycat*. We drove or flew down to San Diego, where the boat was docked. We used to drive to a certain point in his Rolls Royce. He drove 120 m.p.h., and cops frequently pulled us over. When they saw that the driver was Jerry, they let him off with a warning. "Mr. Lewis, we don't want to lose you. Please slow down."

Jerry agreed each time. "Will do. Thank you, officer," he said politely.

Then, there followed a squeal of tires and the smell of burned rubber, as gravel sprayed all over the officers and Jerry sped off down the road again.

When Jerry was not working, he let his beard grow, looking much like a bum. I did the same. Each time when we were out on the boat, he told me that we were going fishing, but we never fished. He was adept at backing that boat out of the slip, but we never went farther than half a mile down the harbor to a restaurant on the pier. He parked the boat right alongside the restaurant, where we got off, walked twenty feet to our table, ate, came back, and then got back on the boat to return to his slip and park again.

"Jerry, you said we were going to go fishing," I reminded him. He always made some excuse, and we never went fishing.

One day, he called me and said, "Let's go down to the boat."

"Jerry," I said, "I'm not going to go down there because you won't take me fishing. You always say you're going to take me, but you're not going to do it."

"I promise you. I'll take you fishing," he said.

"Okay then," I agreed. "I'll go." We went down to the boat. Jerry proudly showed me his fishing license, as if to prove to me that he was an avid fisherman.

"Where's your fishing tackle?" I asked.

"Here," he replied, handing me a reel that was big enough to catch Moby Dick. Not only that, but the reel was gold-plated and must have weighed fifteen pounds. He horsed around with the reel and accidentally dropped it overboard. That thing had to cost $2,000 — and back then, that was a great deal of money.

Jerry said, "Well, I guess that's that."

I said, "I'll tell you what, Jerry. If I can get it back, will you give me $100?"

He said, "Sure."

I got a triple-hook with a lead on it to see if I could snag the reel. Jerry was sure that the current had swept the reel away. I dropped the triple-hook down, jiggled it, pulled it up, and I presented him with his reel.

I said, "You owe me a $100." He never did pay me. Still, even after catching that expensive reel for him, we never did fish off that boat. I think that he just did not want to get any fish goop on the deck of his beloved *Pussycat*.

In 1967, Jerry took me on a vacation down to Rio de Janeiro. We flew down there and checked into a very fancy hotel. Jerry got a suite for himself and one for me. His suite was somewhat bigger than mine. For starters, his suite had a buffet table as big as my bed with trays filled with shrimp, caviar, and all the fixings. It was more food than anybody could think about eating in a week.

Jerry said, "I'm going to surprise you. We're going fishing tomorrow. I've rented a boat, and we're going fishing for sailfish."

I said, "That's great because I'm a very good fisherman, and also very lucky."

"I'm not," he said. "I've been fishing for sailfish for five years and haven't caught one yet."

"You'll catch one tomorrow," I promised. "I tell you — I'm very lucky. If we catch one tomorrow, then I get a suite as big yours, okay?" He agreed to the deal.

The next day, we went down to the boat. I expected one of those regular twenty-five-foot fishing boats, but he had rented what looked like a small battleship.

I said, "Jerry, we're not going out on that thing. It's fifty feet long, or more. We'll never catch anything off that. The wake will be half a mile back. The boat will be churning the water so hard that fish will have to surf and hang fin to catch the bait. There won't be any fish anywhere near us."

Jerry said, "Well, that's what we're going to fish on because I like comfort when I fish. We got aboard the Brazilian behemoth and headed out to sea. I swear to Neptune — we had no more than hit the blue water and put out our fishing poles than a sailfish hit my bait. I set the hook and handed the pole to Jerry. "There's your fish," I told him.

Jerry cranked the line in and caught his sailfish. All of a sudden, I noticed the boat was turning around. I said, "Wait a minute. What's happening?"

"We're going back," he said.

"What do you mean we're going back? I asked. "I haven't caught anything. I haven't even fished. You caught my fish. When do I get to fish?"

"No," he said. "I've got to get back while the fish is still fresh and hasn't dried out and lost any weight." We went back, weighed his fish, and got pictures taken.

Jerry Lewis poses with his sailfish.

As revenge, when I got back to the hotel, I immediately moved into a bigger suite and had a big party. I invited everybody, even unknown people from the lobby. I do not know if Jerry ever paid that hotel bill.

Jerry could get away with anything. When Jerry, Janet Leigh, and I were shooting *Three on a Couch* down at the harbor in San Francisco, he said, "Jimmie, I'm going to take you to the finest restaurants in San Francisco."

I said, "I don't know any of the restaurants."

He said, "Every night, we're going to a different restaurant, and each time, it'll be one of the finest in town."

With two Hollywood legends, Janet Leigh and Jerry Lewis, in Three on a Couch.

That night, the three of us went to a very plush, five-star restaurant with red velvet on the walls and ceiling. Waiters smothered Jerry with attention, and the staff and other patrons were stealing glances at our table.

We finally relaxed a little bit after eating dinner and we had a few drinks. Jerry proceeded to take a napkin, put a pat of butter in the center of it, and then snap the napkin sideways to propel the butter to the ceiling, where it stuck. He successfully did this three or four times with each pat sticking to the red velvet. I do not know what it costs to clean butter from velvet, but it must be expensive. Nobody said anything to Jerry because he would have simply written a check and bought the place.

"Can I try it?" I asked.

He said, "Sure." I put a pat of butter in a napkin and snapped it. It flew over two tables and landed right on a man's plate. The guy looked around, and I quickly handed the napkin back to Jerry. Not wanting to seem like an unsophisticated psycho, Janet Leigh naturally did not partake in the foolishness, but I knew that deep down, she wanted to.

Another time, we went to New York to promote *Three on a Couch* on *The Tonight Show*. Jerry was guest-hosting for Johnny Carson that night. Jerry also brought Leslie Parrish, Gila Golan, and Mary Ann Mobley

A guest spot on The Tonight Show *with guest host Jerry Lewis and Ed McMahon.*

from the cast. The show went fine and we went back to the hotel. I said, "Jerry, let's drink some tequila."

I always teased Jerry about drinking tequila because I used to go down to the bullfights in Mexico. At one time, I even considered studying to be a matador. Through Budd Boetticher, I became friends with some of the top matadors in Mexico. If the matadors did not get gored too badly on Sunday, then we went out that night. We partied, dated some of the senoritas, and drank tequila. Consequently, I developed a taste and a high tolerance for tequila and showgirls. I did not get drunk, but I did like the taste of tequila.

At the hotel in New York, Jerry said, "Best, you keep trying to get me to drink that stuff. I don't think I've ever tried tequila."

We ordered some, and after Jerry took two or three drinks, he felt no pain. He said, "Let's go for a walk."

We went downstairs and got in this big limousine. Jerry had the driver drop us off on some street where there happened to be a lot of construction work going on. There was scaffolding with plywood tunnels to protect pedestrians from falling debris. As we were walking, the limousine was following along and keeping pace. We got to the wooden pedestrian tunnel and walked in. The limo driver could not see us, but he was still trying to keep the same pace that we had been walking.

When we got about halfway through the tunnel, Jerry said, "Stop."

I said, "Jerry, we'd better keep going because the limo's going to be waiting for us to come out."

"I know," he said.

Before long, we heard honking. We knew that our limo had stopped and traffic had backed up for blocks while the driver searched for any sight of us. We finally emerged into a mad scene with traffic halted and drivers cussing Jerry's chauffeur. Jerry thought that was hysterically funny.

That same evening, Jerry bought a two-pound bag of pistachio nuts, and we returned to the hotel. We had side-by-side rooms, and as we walked down the hallway, Jerry left behind a long trail of nuts that ended at some unsuspecting guest's door. Whoever happened to follow that trail put the blame on the poor guy in that room.

Jerry Lewis has a nutty sense of humor. He is a marvelous, incomparably funny man. I learned from him so much about comedy timing. More than that, he has a heart that glows. As we all know, he has unselfishly devoted talent, money, and countless time for nearly sixty years to the Muscular Dystrophy Association (MDA), and he has raised more than $2 billion for that special cause. Jerry was the deserving recipient of the Jean Hersholt Humanitarian Award at the 2009 Academy Awards ceremony. I love the man.

CHAPTER 18

Fast Times and Settling Down in Hollywood

After Mattie and I were divorced, I was still paying alimony and also child support for Gary. Even though work was steady, there were times when I had very little money. At one point, I crawled into a garage just to find a place to sleep. Fortunately, not long after that, I got an acting job and was able to rent a place.

In 1953, I met Don Kennedy, a dear friend and fellow actor, when we both appeared in a *Hallmark Hall of Fame* drama. Don let me rent a room in the house that he was in the process of building on Rosilla Place in Laurel Canyon. To this day, Don remains one of my dearest friends. He eventually moved from the Hollywood rat race and married Carol, a lovely and loving lady. They have raised a beautiful family together in Del Mar, California.

I tried to help Don build that house on Rosilla Place, but he got tired of watching me hammer holes in the tarpaper as I tried to attach it to the roof.

"Jimmie, if you do that again, I'm going to throw you off this roof," he told me.

I guess I did not take him seriously enough. I hammered too hard and went through the tarpaper one more time. Don tossed me off the roof. Fortunately, the house was on a slope that was covered with honeysuckle vines, so Don knew that I would not get hurt when I landed. I just sort of glanced off the slope and rolled a little bit. It was not much worse than falling off a horse.

The house was partially completed, but my bedroom had no window. I got Don to come back early from a skiing trip in Aspen by threatening to install a window in my bedroom if he was not going to do it. He installed it in record time.

I lived in Don's house for quite some time, and we had some parties there that people in Hollywood are probably still talking about even today. There was drinking at the party, but it was rare for anyone to drink to extreme excess. There certainly was no dope. No one got out of hand, or

With my dear friend Don Kennedy.

he was quickly asked to leave. Don and I made a point of inviting only those people who were fun-loving and did not need the false stimulation of dope. The people that attended some of our parties were a who's who of Hollywood, as well as some hopefuls, who had not as yet built names for themselves in the industry, but would later become stars.

Don and I both loved to play guitars and sing at the parties. As I have admitted earlier, I am neither a good guitarist nor a good singer, but with a little wine, no one really cared. Everyone at the parties joined in, and at that time, most of the songs were the Harry Bellefonte type of calypso music. Everyone knew the words. Some of our guests later went on to be members of the New Christy Minstrels. A couple of our more famous guests were Jack Lemmon and Jonathan Winters.

We had some neighbors across the street from Don's house. They were getting married in Las Vegas, and Don was asked to serve as best man.

When he came back, he said, "Jimmie you have to go with me back to Vegas. I've met some of the most beautiful showgirls in the world."

I have to admit, the briefing he gave of his visit intrigued me. The next time Don went to Las Vegas, I tagged along. We saw *The Betty Grable Show* at the Desert Inn. Don was dating one of girls in the show. "See that one girl?" Don asked. "She's got the most beautiful back."

I picked three wrong ones before I got the one he meant. I was looking at legs, and he was looking at backs.

After the show, we met Don's girlfriend and some of the other dancers for coffee. We had just coffee because Don's girlfriend did not drink alcohol. The girl with the beautiful back joined us. Her face and the rest of her were very nice, too. Her name was Jobee Ayers. She was a very fine dancer and choreographer. She was to become the lead dancer for Jimmy Durante's Las Vegas stage show.

My first impression was that she was charming and sweet, but sweet was not what I was looking for in Las Vegas. I had run into a couple of the other showgirls, and when they came by our table, I asked them where they were going. They said they were going to another club for drinks. I said I would go with them. I handed Don $10 to take care of my portion of the coffee tab, and then off I went.

After I arrived at the club with the other girls, I got to thinking about how rude I had been. I told them, "I'm sorry. I have to go back." Fortunately, Don, Jobee, and the other coffee drinkers were still there. I got to know Jobee better, and she did not seem to hold it against me that I was a jerk. At least I was a jerk who could correct some of his mistakes. I'm not saying I was smitten, but I did drive my '55 T-Bird back to Las Vegas just to see Jobee a couple of weeks later. We had a good time again.

On the way back to Los Angeles, I spun out in my T-Bird and wrecked it with a big truck. It is a wonder that it was not the end of my life right there. I had the T-Bird towed back to Las Vegas. While they were fixing my car, I saw Jobee some more. I said to her, "Why don't you marry me and let me take you away from all this?"

Yes, it was the same crazy thing I had said to Mattie a few years earlier, but I was asking rhetorically this time. The next thing I knew, these showgirls are coming by and congratulating me.

"What are you congratulating me for?" I asked.

"Because you and Jobee are getting married, silly boy," one of them informed me.

Jobee and me on our wedding day in June 1958.

Top left: JoJami Best, better known as "The Tank." Top right: Janeen and an uncredited bass. "Is this a keeper, Daddy?" Bottom: Savoring a precious moment with JoJami.

Janeen. What a doll!

Jobee and I were definitely in love, so getting married was a logical step. I still was unsure if I was ready to take that step again. By that point, I had appeared in *The Naked and the Dead* and had made enough money to buy a house in Laurel Canyon. James Dean lived down Laurel Canyon from my house, and Paul Newman lived up the canyon. Instead of immediately pursuing the marriage idea, I invited Jobee to move in

Left: JoJami and me on a successful fishing trip. Right: My lovely ballerinas, Janeen, Jobee, and JoJami.

with me. She was a real lady, and to my surprise, she said no. Not only that, but the real shocker was when she took off, went back to Chicago, and left me to nurse my bruised ego.

There I was in my new Hollywood dream home, owner of a '55 fire-engine red T-Bird, and the lady turned me down. I studied the situation and realized that I was crazy to let a great woman like her get away. I went to Chicago. We were married there in 1958, and then we moved back to the beautiful house in Laurel Canyon. We were married until 1977.

In May 1960, JoJami, our first daughter, was born. I think we overfed her at first and she became a little chubby. I nicknamed her "The Tank." Little did I realize that this sweet little Buddha-faced cherub would one day grow up to win all the beauty contests in Mississippi.

The house on the hill was certainly a showplace, and we were very proud of it. Unfortunately, Jobee saw a scorpion in the kitchen where JoJami was playing. As any good mother would do, Jobee freaked. She insisted that we had to leave that house we loved. We moved to a less dangerous place in North Hollywood. We had a second daughter, Janeen. Both of our daughters have grown up to be heart-stopping, beautiful ladies like their mama, and they have always conducted themselves in a way that has made both their mother and me extremely proud.

JoJami is now in great demand as an image consultant. She lives in Delaware with her husband Eric Tyler, son Cameron, and daughter Tessa. You can find out more about her business at *www.fabulousafter40.com*.

Janeen followed in her mother's show-business footsteps, and then she followed mine. She became a professional dancer, toured with Suzanne Somers and Engelbert Humperdinck, and also was a *Solid Gold* Dancer. She is now a writer and independent film producer. She is married to actor-singer-writer-director Michael Damian, who is perhaps best-known as Danny Romalotti on *The Young and the Restless*. Together they own Riviera Films, and they have created several award-winning films, including *Moondance Alexander* and *Hot Tamale*.

Above: JoJami's family. Left to right: daughter Tessa, husband Eric, JoJami, and son Cameron. Below: Janeen, my daughter, and Michael Damian, her husband, have their own production company. Learn all about it at www.rivierafilms.com.

CHAPTER 19

The Best School of Motion Picture Technique

While we were living in North Hollywood, Jobee started teaching ballet, and I decided to start a motion picture technique school of acting to teach people what I had learned over the years about acting in front of the camera as opposed to the technique of acting on a theatrical stage.

Even with my stage training in Europe, summer stock, winter stock, and touring with a Broadway show, I had a lot to learn about acting when I worked under contract with Universal Studios. I did not know how much I had to learn until after I went down to the set

Maturing into my many cowboy roles.

that time and saw Jimmy Stewart doing *Harvey*. I had watched him on the camera, and I thought, *"He's not doing anything."* Then, I went to the editing room and found out that he knew exactly what he was doing. He knew where the camera was, what it could do, and what it could not do. He used the camera to his best advantage.

I started studying Marlon Brando, Abbott and Costello, Marjorie Main, Percy Kilbride, and all the super-talented people at the studio. I went to screenings of the daily rushes as often as possible. I went into editing rooms and learned why one person stood out and another person did not. I realized that the difference was an energy level. We are all born with what is like a fifty-watt light bulb, and a movie star needs a hundred watts in order to shine brighter than others. Being a star is a matter of turning energy up fully.

An actor has to train himself to turn his light-bulb energy up so that he drew more attention than the other light bulbs. I got to thinking about that and the technical aspect of registering a performance through a camera. Because the camera moves in close, I train for a close-up, whereas in theater, audiences are far away, essentially watching the equivalent of a motion picture wide screen that is not intimate. Consequently, actors have to enlarge their movements and project louder.

That technique is well and good, until an actor comes to Hollywood and gets in front of the cameras. Sensitive microphones hang right over his head. The camera picks up every little facial nuance. A head appears ten times bigger on a screen, and every movement of an eyebrow or eyelash is magnified. An actor has to tone a performance way down, while keeping energy way up and glowing. I started learning this through watching others, all while I was appearing in movies and television episodes during the 1950s. I had my light-bulb wattage turned way up, and so I was fortunate to stay busy.

We had a guesthouse that I made into a little theater for my new motion picture technique school. I had six or seven students when I began teaching, and one of them was Toni Basil, who later became a singer and an award-winning choreographer. She has choreographed most of Bette Midler's shows, along with those of other prominent entertainers. She has also acted in movies, including *Easy Rider*.

Word about the class spread, and demand increased. There was a stigma in Hollywood attached to theater actors. Hollywood assumed that an actor did not know enough about working in front of a camera to get the job done in one or two takes, and there is a lot of truth in that assumption. Film is a different technology and requires a different technique. It even has different terminology. Learning the different terminology was crucial.

I used simple but effective tools in my classes. I took a black and white Sony camera and mounted it on a shopping cart, which served as a dolly. I put two television sets on either side of my students so they could see what the camera was seeing, and then I took my actors and let them work in a three-minute scene.

"First do it your way, and then I'll direct you in motion picture technique," I instructed.

Students watched these kids doing it their way. Then, I told them to try it again using the correct technique. They had not realized what a difference it makes in a performance to be aware of what happens technically with the camera. They observed the new way and gasped in amazement.

For example, I taught them that in a head close-up, when the audience looks at a screen, they look at the brightest spots on the screen. Their eyes are automatically drawn to the brightest areas, which are the eyes and the teeth. A film actor has got to use those features with that in mind, and he or she has to closely control them. In a head close-up, facial features are your only assets. A slight head movement is energy, and audiences are drawn to energy, movement, the whites of the eyes, and the whites of the teeth. Add a voice and the end result is a consummate performance.

I compare head close-ups to karate. When striking an opponent, you look six inches through the other person's eyes and try to drive a fist six inches through. I had my actors study karate movements, which are strong and extremely direct. I had them look directly at their opponent/actor during their close-up and try to look six inches through the other actor's down-camera eye—the one closest to the camera. That pulled a face around slightly and allowed the camera to see three-quarters of their face rather than a profile. That is one little thing an actor can do to help build his career. More people will recognize the actor because more of the face has been photographed.

Looking six inches through a person's eye takes energy. An actor can look at the surface of a person's face, and it does not take as much energy as concentrating and looking through the one eye. The camera picks up that extra concentration and transfers it to the screen. Energy registers as exciting and interesting. A dim light bulb is always dull.

Another useful technique is being able to cry real tears. I told my students that anybody who studied with me for three months and could not cry on cue within a minute would be thrown out of class. A lot of tough guys came in there and said, "I can't cry. I haven't cried in years."

I replied, "Either you cry, or you'll get your butt thrown out of my class."

None of my students were ever known in the industry for being unable to cry on cue. Lesser-trained actors and actresses use the trick of having their eyes sprayed with glycerin to bring on fake tears. I am proud to say that I have never had an actor train with me who had to resort to this method. No matter how tough they thought they were, at the end of a month, they could cry.

Even though they were highly successful working actors, Burt Reynolds and Clint Eastwood used to sit in on my classes. I was not teaching acting per se; I was teaching what actors needed to know to produce their best performance in front of a camera. Dawn Wells, Roger Miller, Glen Campbell, Lindsay Wagner, Gary Busey, Teri Garr, and Regis Philbin were just some of my students at that time.

Lindsay Wagner was our babysitter and took dancing lessons from Jobee, who suggested that Lindsay also take acting lessons from me. One day when I was getting ready for class, in walked this lovely, doe-faced young lady. Lindsay was so sweet and natural that she became quite a good actress very quickly. In those early days, she was offered a leading part with one of the soap operas. She asked me if she should take the job. Back then, soap opera actors were not considered top-grade, but that attitude has changed considerably today.

I said, "Lindsay, I think you're going to be a big star. If you don't have to have the money, if you were my daughter, I would say don't take the job."

She did not take it. She was so grateful that she made that decision. Even today, she will do interviews and still mention that I advised her correctly.

Gary Busey was another fine, hard-working student. He had been a college football player in Oklahoma. He also played drums with the likes of Kris Kristofferson and Willie Nelson. When he started studying with me, Gary had little money. He paid for his camera technique lessons by playing the drums in a biker gang honky-tonk. In fact, it was his music that brought him to Hollywood. He said it was a little disconcerting when the only spotlight he had was the bright lights on the bikers' choppers shining in his face, and he was less than thrilled when gang members made him sing the same song over and over.

When he first started getting into acting, Gary was all energy and no discipline. One time, he became so mad at me that I had to pull him from class and out to the parking lot.

"You'd like to hit me, wouldn't you?" I asked. He was so mad that he was shaking. "Well, come on let's get it on." I was confident because I had studied karate for three and a half years and kung fu for six months with

With Lindsay Wagner at a CBS function.

Professor Lu, so I was not some old guy picking a fight willy-nilly with a rough-and-tumble football player twenty years younger than I. "I'll let you have the first swing, and if you do swing, I won't hit your face, but I'll break your arm." I never hit an actor in the face.

"I just want to be an actor so badly," he blurted.

I said, "Gary, you just need to get a little discipline. You're going to be fine. You've got it."

Everything worked out for him. I got Gary hooked up with Sid Gold, my own agent. Gary began working as an actor and progressed nicely. Then, I introduced him to Meyer Mishkin, a top Hollywood agent. Meyer had Lee Marvin and other name actors of that caliber under contract. He took Gary on, and he quickly helped make him a superstar.

I have never claimed credit for anybody's career. I just tried my best to give actors the most excellent camera technique training and advice possible. I wanted to share what had worked for me over the years. I have been thrilled with quite a few letters from former students saying that my training helped them in their careers. I can give an actor or actress a suggestion or a nudge, but ultimately, it takes that person's own talent and desire to be successful.

My motion picture technique school was so successful that people started copying it. People crawled out of the woodwork to teach so-called motion picture technique, even when they did not know one end of the camera from a peanut butter sandwich. I asked many potential students what training, if any, they had taken.

"I studied with so and so."

"What is his background in the profession?"

"I don't know."

"Has he ever acted in front of a camera?" I inquired.

Most of the time, they answered, "No. I don't think so."

"Why would you want to study with someone when you don't know if he is qualified to teach you what you need to know to be successful in such an extremely competitive industry? Would you study horseback riding taught by a guy who has never been on a horse? Why would you pay money for training by someone who hasn't made a living doing it?"

They could not argue with that, which was why I had such success. I was teaching them what I had successfully learned while earning a living acting in movies and television. More than 80% of my students went into the business and have earned a living at it. Some of them didn't make it because they either moved away or decided they didn't desire a career. They didn't actually have their hearts in it.

During that time, I was fortunate to have Renée Valente, an executive producer and head of the casting department at Screen Gems and Columbia Pictures, ask me to replace Eddie Foy, Jr., when he left the casting department. I told Renée that I would come over for one year. I wanted to see what it was like when these students came in and their jobs were on the line. I wanted to see how they conducted themselves and why they did or did not get a part, no matter how much or how little talent they had. I found it had nothing to do with their talent; it had more to do with how they came into the room. I wanted to impart this knowledge to my students.

I accepted Renée's offer and went to Columbia to head up their casting department. Columbia had about six or seven young actors under contract. The studio hoped to groom them into movie stars. I interviewed each of them. I told them I was going to use a soundstage and a video camera to teach them some motion picture technique. Half the time, they would not show up. I set up karate lessons for the guys, if they wanted them. I set up lessons in horseback riding, if they wanted to learn about that. Sometimes they showed up, sometimes they didn't. The day finally came for me to deliver to Renée my report card on the group.

"Fire all of 'em," I said.

"What?" she exclaimed.

I repeated, "Fire every last one of 'em. They'll never go anywhere. Come over to my workshop. I have Gary Busey, Lindsay Wagner, Teri Garr, and some of these people are going to be movie stars."

"We can't do that," she said. "We've got them under contract, and we've spent a lot of money on them."

I said, "You'll spend a lot more before you make them a star."

The studio never listened to me. With two exceptions, none of those actors ever made even a little dent in a successful career. One exception was David Soul, who is best known as Hutch on *Starsky and Hutch* and has continued to be successful.

The other exception was Farrah Fawcett. I put her under contract for $500 a week. Unfortunately, the studio heads followed the usual pattern and did not know the lovely lady's potential. They let her get away.

I was at Columbia for a year, and while I was there, I learned. I am still learning. I went back to the students in my school and told them, "When you go in on an interview, you've got to go in with the assurance that you know what you're doing to such an extent that there's no fear. Fear is what will lose you the job. Fear of not being able to pay your rent and fear that you've got to have this job. Don't do that. Instead, go in with the attitude that there's no one who can beat you. If they don't choose you, it's their loss. Never go on an interview even thinking about losing the part."

Of course, I have lost jobs. Everybody does, but when I did, I went to my agent and asked why I lost the job. I always told my agents never to lie to me. Tell me the good and the bad — especially the bad, so I can correct it.

When I lost jobs, my agents either told me that it was because I was too tall, too skinny, or too this and that. I said, "You're lying to me. I gave a lousy cold reading, didn't I?"

They confessed the truth.

I said, "I warned you not to lie to me. You're fired."

I got a reputation for changing my agents like socks because I did not like them to lie. I cannot learn anything from a liar except how to lie, which I do not want to learn. That same insistence on honesty was the backbone that made my motion picture technique school a success. I have looked at résumés of some supposed acting teachers and I wondered how in the world those people taught. They had never done that kind of work, and yet they earned oodles of money off those poor kids with a limited budget — under the pretext of teaching them how to act, or teaching them camera technique.

I have sat in on some of these classes by so-called motion picture tech teachers. I watched in horror, as they had the students lie down flat on the floor, hold hands, and hum. That was supposedly to get them in tune with each other. I just could not imagine actors on a working set lying down on a soundstage to hold hands and hum. I do not think it would add anything to their performances, and I am quite sure they could never get someone like Jimmy Stewart to lie down and hum with them.

One of these so-called "teachers" was a stage director — and not a particularly good one. He actually had the nerve to use the same soundstage and camera that I used when I worked at Columbia Studios. I taught during the day. He made a deal with Columbia to come and teach his class there at night. Then, UCLA and other places got motion picture technique classes. Everywhere I looked, camera technique was being taught. Even some modeling schools offered camera technique.

Students came to me and said, "Mr. Best, there's a studio doing a class. Maybe a director will come in and spot me."

I answered, "Wait a minute. Think about this. He comes there because you're a student. He's not going to hire you, a would-be actor; he's going to hire someone who's already an actor because his job depends on getting the very best. He's not going to recommend an untrained actor, unless he's got some ulterior motive."

Without fail, the students came back to me after going to that class, and they said, "You were right. The director came in and talked about what a big wheel he was and everything, all the while ogling the girl with the short skirt in the front row and asking her if she'll go out with him." I have seen that happen too many times.

CHAPTER 20

Escape to Mississippi

After about twenty years, I had seen the sordid side of Hollywood once too often, and the Los Angeles smog was suffocating. To compound it all, I got smoke-inhalation poisoning on a film set, which threatened both my health and my livelihood. I lost my car, and eventually, my home. Jobee and I had about $5,000 left to our names. On top of that, our daughters were in early elementary school. I did not want them to spend their entire childhoods growing up in that dreadful, dope-infested place, or spend their formative years breathing that awful smog.

I said to Jobee, "Let's move to Mississippi."

Both Jobee and I had been working and living comfortably in Los Angeles with our beautiful home, swimming pool, and station wagon. We owned a building for my camera technique classes and for Jobee to teach ballet and jazz. Everything was coming up gardenias, but then the poo-poo hit the fan.

Around 1968, I had accepted the role of a killer on a CBS television show. A scene called for fog, which in those days was still created by burning an oil-based solution. As we were shooting one day, the leading lady ran toward the steady-cam operator. He unexpectedly backed into a post. The actress ran into the camera at a full clip and was knocked unconscious. With smoky fog filling the soundstage, an ambulance backed up to the stage door and left its motor running, adding exhaust into the mix. The ambulance eventually took the leading lady to the hospital, leaving even more exhaust behind. Then, the soundstage doors were closed and the stage was not aired out as it should have been.

We resumed filming with my next shot, which was a fight scene. I was fighting with a man, who was forty pounds heavier than I. He kept missing his lines, and we had to do the fight sequence repeatedly. We finally finished shooting for the night. I was in my dressing room when I felt severe pain across my chest. At that moment, the wardrobe lady happened by.

"Call a paramedic!" I hollered to her. "I think I'm having a heart attack!"

"You're a funny man, Mr. Best," she laughed.

"You want to see a funny man die?" I gasped.

She realized that I was serious and rushed to call paramedics. Because of my symptoms, we all thought I was experiencing a heart attack, but it turned out to be nothing but a terrible reaction from smoke and exhaust fume inhalation. I had to sue CBS to recover my medical expenses, but all I ever received was $5,000.

A rumor soon spread that I had died, and then when my condition improved, another rumor spread that I had a heart attack. In my medical records, it looked as though that was exactly what had happened. No one would hire me. We went into foreclosure on our house. We quickly became virtually destitute. Bill collectors hounded us. We were down to our last few dollars. Since I could not earn a living in Los Angeles, I had no other reason to stay there.

Burt Reynolds — God bless him — offered me all the cash he had in the bank at the time, which he hoped would allow me to stay in town a little longer. "Jimmie, I've got $5,000 in the bank," he said. "That's all I have on hand, but it's yours."

I thanked Burt for the generous offer, but said, "No, Burt, I'll fight my way out of this."

My business manager suggested that I file for bankruptcy, but I refused.

I said, "They trusted me to pay the money back, and I will pay it back — one way or another."

My business manager abandoned me, and so did my agent. Jobee, our two girls, and I had to fight for our very existence. We had to move from our lovely home. After that, it was just a short time until we decided to move to Jackson, Mississippi. It was the best decision we ever made, and to this day, my daughters thank me for taking them out of that hell called the "City of Angels" and moving them to a heavenly place in Mississippi.

People have asked me, "How could you move to a state that was so prejudiced toward black people?"

I can only answer, "I saw more racial discrimination in one block of Los Angeles than I ever saw in the whole seven years I lived in Mississippi."

In the summer of 1970, we packed up the station wagon, said goodbye to the swimming pool and the movie star house, and moved to Jackson. We chose Mississippi because it was about as far away from life in Los

Generous praise from a generous man.

Angeles as we could get. That was a big plus. Secondly, in addition to mighty good fishing, a friend of mine assured me that Mississippi would welcome my family and me with open arms. They did! It also helped that I had somewhat of a celebrity status and was able to buy everything we needed on credit. Most of all, it was just pure, genuine, Southern hospitality that helped us ease right into our new home.

Reading to Janeen (left) and JoJami.

We bought a house, appliances, and furniture on credit. We settled in as quickly as we could. Eventually, I commuted to Hollywood when acting jobs began to come my way again. Before long, we were prospering and living pretty high off the hog. People in Mississippi were gracious to us beyond our every hope. I was immediately offered a job at the Little Theater in Jackson. The theater had been losing money, and it took me one year to put it back in the black.

I told the community leaders, "I'll teach at the Little Theater if you'll let us use the theater's big work area for a ballet school and an acting school at the same time." They enthusiastically applauded that idea, and students flocked to work with the closest thing to a Hollywood star and his professional-dancer wife that there was in their neck of the woods.

Christmas 1970 in Jackson, Mississippi, with Janeen and JoJami.

In 1972, I got the call about playing a bad sheriff in *Sounder*, which was going to be filmed in Louisiana. The film boasted a wonderful cast, including Cicely Tyson and Paul Winfield, and a child actor named Kevin Hooks. Kevin was a very good little actor, and he has become one of the film industry's top directors and a producer of outstanding works.

We had some interesting discussions about race, the South, and that sort of thing, when we were idle on the set and during our limousine rides together to and from work each day. We did not always agree with each other, but we respected each other's perspectives. Filming *Sounder* was a nice experience.

There was a little pond behind the set, where I taught Kevin Hooks how to fish for catfish. Twenty years later he was filming *Passenger 57*, one of his many hits as a director, in the Orlando area where I was living at the time. Cameron Roberts, one of my students from my Florida acting school, had a role in the film. I went over to the set to say hello. Kevin came over to hug my neck, and he said, "Oh, Jimmie, I'll never forget that you taught me how to fish."

I said, "So, are you going to put me in your picture?"

He said, "Jimmie, I would love to use you, but this picture is all about terrorists."

I guess years of playing Rosco in *The Dukes of Hazzard* blocked out the memory of how mean my sheriff was in *Sounder,* but the important thing is that Kevin remembered how I taught him how to fish. I am pleased and proud when I see his name in credits, which is often. He is a fine man and a real talent in our business.

Sounder ended up being a very good film. Both Cicely Tyson and Paul Winfield were nominated for Oscars for their roles in *Sounder,* and the film earned a nod for Best Picture and Best Screenplay Oscars. A great dog played the title character. He should have won an award, too. I was about the only white actor in the production. I played a really mean, redneck sheriff, who would not let Cicely Tyson's character visit Paul Winfield's character in jail.

In 1973, not long after making *Sounder,* my next big task was to form the Mississippi Film Commission. The governor gave me a yearly budget of $5,000. Even with that limited budget, I brought two major film projects into the state in six months — Robert Altman's *Thieves Like Us* and a musical version of *Huckleberry Finn.*

Another piece of the Mississippi puzzle fell into place in the spring of 1974 when I went to the University of Mississippi in Oxford to direct Tennessee Williams' *Orpheus Descending* for the stage.

A student asked me, "Why don't you stay and teach?"

I said, "Nobody has asked me."

Some students made a request to the dean. He asked me to become an Artist in Residence. I started in the fall of 1974 for what was to be one year. I fell in love with all the students, and I liked the experience so much that I was there for two years. I taught motion picture technique and also directed some of the student plays. We did *Bus Stop, Rainmaker,* and *Tobacco Road* during my time there.

I was the only professor that the students invited to their parties. I think they liked me because I "streaked" with them. Other than at Berkeley, I may be the only professor who ever streaked at a university. We were

During my time teaching at Ole Miss in 1975.

having a party, and after everybody drank a little too much wine, we went streaking. The campus security officers never caught me. My students loved me for having enough of a wild hair to do that.

Everybody wants to act in a play, but when the run finishes, nobody ever wants to do the work of taking down sets. To motivate the actors and crew, I hid a piece of paper on the set and told the cast that whoever found the paper would get a nice surprise. The sets would come down in a matter of minutes. They eventually found the paper, which was a ticket for a magnum of tequila. Then, we turned all the lights down except for the stage light. We sat in a big circle and passed that bottle around until we all got happy on tequila.

For the camera technique class, we brought the camera out and often worked until early in the morning. I was allowed to teach any time I wanted because I often went to California to work and was gone for two weeks at a time. I came back, and then I taught for four or five days in one week. The school and the students gave me a lot of latitude. The bottom line was that my approach worked. I had enthusiastic, talented students, and I had a ball. My students experienced the pure joy of acting, and I helped them nurture a love for it. They also learned technique and the finer points of the craft.

In the summer of 1975, actor-director Max Baer, Jr., was preparing to direct *Ode to Billy Joe*, which he was going to film entirely in Mississippi. Max was fantastic. We were on the same page about the movie business. I asked him to use some of my students in the movie, and he was delighted to do so. They had been well trained in my camera technique class, and the added incentive was that they were cheap to hire. When Max asked me what part I wanted to play, I said, "I want to play the homosexual, the man causing Billy Joe McAllister to jump off the bridge."

Max said, "Best, you've played murderers, rapists, and killers throughout your career. Nobody's going to believe you're a homosexual."

I said, "I'm an actor. I don't have to be a homosexual to play one. Besides, the other part is just a dull father."

I used university television cameras to shoot my own screen test. I sent it to Max, and after he watched it, he called me. "You're right. You can do it!"

I said, "I told you I could. I'm an actor."

"Everybody I've interviewed has tried to act like Truman Capote flitting all over the place, but you did the part in a way that works."

I said, "Well, my salary just doubled because you did not trust me."

"You can have it," he said.

Then I added, "Okay, but for every one of my students you use, my salary will go down." It ended up that I practically worked for nothing on that movie, but Max used every one of my students. They got a combined $38,000 in pay, and I gave them academic credit, too.

The crowning glory of my two years at the university was the honor of being inducted into the Ole Miss Hall of Fame. Bob Hope was also in the Hall of Fame, but he was voted in by the faculty, whereas I was voted in by both students and faculty. I got tears in my eyes when I received the award, which was like an Academy Award to me. I still have the trophy. It represents a beautiful time and place in my life that I will cherish for the rest of my life.

While we were in the process of casting *Orpheus Descending*, a drama professor sat in the theater and watched while I auditioned a shy young lady by the name of Brenda Hillhouse. She was a young country girl with a difficult family history.

The professor said to me, "Perhaps there's a better choice for the part than Brenda. We have some other students who are better actors."

"That's exactly why I want to cast Brenda," I responded. "She's paid her hard-earned money to be a student at this university. She's here to learn in the hopes of being successful at her chosen profession in the future. After all, that's what a college is supposed to do — teach students what they need to learn to make it in the tough world outside."

Brenda got the part, and much to her surprise, she was applauded by the other actors during a rehearsal. Brenda performed the role to perfection and received the Best Acting award two years in a row. I was so happy in being right about giving the shy young girl a chance to fulfill her dream. Brenda and I became very good friends and remain so to this day. Later, Brenda moved to Hollywood, became a very successful business woman, acted in several television shows, and even landed a small part in Quentin Tarantino's *Pulp Fiction*. Much to my joy, several of my students followed me to Hollywood and work in the industry today.

I worked hard for my career, and I fought hard for my students. Jobee was working hard, too. In just two years, she established the regional Mississippi Ballet Theatre. We might have worked a little too hard on our careers and not enough on our personal lives together. Jobee and I began to drift apart. She became largely active in the Jackson society scene, which was not my cup of tea. After six years or so in Jackson, we came to realize that we needed to go our separate ways, and in 1977, we were divorced.

Through necessity, I left Jackson with $500 and a suitcase, and I moved back to Hollywood. I left everything else to Jobee. I told her I would send more money as I made it so she could take care of our daughters. I adored them, and it broke my heart to be separated from them. Jobee and I loved each other, but we just could not see eye to eye or continue to live together.

CHAPTER 21

Burt Reynolds

By the time I moved to Mississippi, I had known Burt Reynolds for years. We had worked together in many television shows and movies, including two episodes of *Gunsmoke* in 1963 and 1965, when Burt portrayed Quint Asper, the blacksmith. Whenever we were shooting a picture and Burt was directing, he often looked to me to tell him where the camera set-ups should be. He had studied with me and trusted my knowledge of camera technique.

In 1966, Burt was starring in the television series *Hawk*. He called me to come to New York to help him.

"Jimmie, they're letting me direct. You gotta come back here. You know where to put the camera," he told me.

In those days, they used a camera that racked three different lenses: a 75mm, a 50mm, and either a 35mm or a 25mm. We had to know which lens to use and everything else.

Burt pointed out, "There's a part in there where you and I play against each other. It's just like a two-man show."

I asked, "What kind of money?" He told me, and then I said, "Burt, I can't do it for that kind of money."

"Please," he implored.

I replied, "Well, okay, but only if you'll take me fishing in Florida."

He agreed, and so I flew to New York. When I was on the set with Burt and his New York crew, I whispered to Burt, "Tell them to put on a 35 and set it here." I pointed to a spot on the floor.

Burt strutted around, as only he can, and he pointed with great authority to the spot I had indicated. "All right, put on the 35 millimeter and put it here," he ordered.

The crew was impressed. His direction went like that for the whole shoot. Burt was their hero because he finished early, letting the crew go home to mama, watch a football game, or whatever.

At that time, Burt was unfamiliar with the technical aspect of using that type of camera, but he was good at directing actors. He knew what he wanted from their performances, and he got it. He later learned all

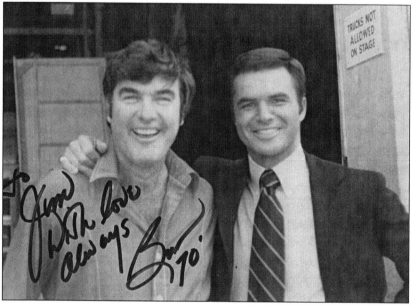

On the set with Burt Reynolds in the television series, Dan August *(1970).*

the technical aspects of directing, as well.

In 1976, while I was living in Mississippi, Burt's producer called me and said, "We're going to do a picture called *Gator* down in Valdosta and Savannah, Georgia. Burt's starring in it, and he wants you to work on the movie."

I said, "Oh, good. Send me a script."

The producer said, "No, no. Burt wants you on the picture as an acting coach. He's got Lauren Hutton and Jerry Reed, and neither one has had very much experience acting in front of a camera. Jerry's going to play a heavy, and Burt wants you to coach him how to play that kind of part."

I did not know why Burt did not just use me in the first place, but that was all right. I loved Jerry, and Burt has his favorites, too. He and Jerry were sure to make great foils for each other in the movie.

"What kind of money are we talking about?" I inquired.

The producer told me a number. I abruptly hung up the phone.

In seconds, the producer called back. "I'm sorry," he apologized, "but we were cut off."

"No, I hung up on you," I retorted. "You insulted me. Tell me again what kind of money you're talking about?"

Teasing Lauren Hutton (front) about her trademark space between her front teeth. Hairstylist Marlene D. Williams, Jerry Reed, and I display fake spaces of our own on the set of Gator *in 1976.*

He said, "Well, Mr. Best, we've got a budget — "

I quickly hung up a second time, but he called back immediately.

"Please don't hang up," he implored. "Burt says you're not going to be acting. You're just going to be more or less coaching."

I said, "No, Burt wants me to help him direct, plus coach, and God only knows what else — probably a rewrite. Tell Burt that someone has to go to the hip if he wants me."

Later, the producer called back and said, "Burt wants you."

I went down to Georgia, and we shot the picture. True to my prediction, Burt recruited me to help rewrite the script, which we did on the weekends. By the following Mondays, we had some rewritten scenes that were ready to shoot.

You cannot help but love Burt Reynolds. I took short money on a lot of Burt's movies, and I did not get billing for rewriting *Gator*, *The End*,

With Tatum O'Neal in Nickelodeon *(1976).*

or *Hooper*, but that was okay. I had not forgotten Burt's earlier generosity, the true act of friendship he offered at a time when I was in dire need.

Burt was also responsible for getting me other jobs. In 1976, he helped me get a small part in Peter Bogdonovich's *Nickelodeon*. As usual, Burt had an ulterior reason for wanting me to be around for that movie. At that time, he was suffering from hyperglycemia, but he did not know what it was. All he knew was that he felt like he was dying. We spent quite a few anxious hours during the day and at night when he called me to his room and I found him hyperventilating and breathing into a paper bag. I read the Bible to him until he calmed down. I was greatly concerned about Burt's health.

One day, he was scheduled to perform a strenuous fight with Ryan O'Neal. The director did not give a damn about Burt; he was concerned only about getting the shot. He had Burt and Ryan fight repeatedly in loose sand, which made the struggle all the more exhausting. That night, Burt ended up in the hospital.

Burt's amazing kindness and generous spirit was evident when he called me one day while we were shooting *Gator*.

"We're going to shoot some scenes at an orphans' home," he told me.

Having been an orphan myself, my ears perked up. "That's great," I told

This picture from Hooper *is one of my favorites of Burt and me.*

him, despite the fact that I had read nothing about a scene at an orphanage in the script, but it sounded very nice. *"This is going to be a really great gesture on Burt's part to add this to the movie,"* I thought.

When we arrived at the orphanage, Burt told me, "Jerry's going to sing with the kids surrounding him."

We shot the scene, and we spent the entire day at the orphanage. We even paid the kids for taking part in the film. When I got in the car to go back to our hotel, I turned to Burt and asked, "You're not gonna use that in the film, are you?"

"No," he said. "I just wanted to give those kids pleasure and have Jerry Reed sing to them." Burt's gesture was incredibly charming.

After a week of filming footage we could actually use in the movie, Burt called my room during the weekend. "Come on. You and I are going out on a date."

I reminded him, "I'm married, Burt. You know that I'm in love with my wife."

"No, no, no. It's not that kind of date," he replied. "We're just going to dress up and go out. The limousine will be here at two o'clock."

I dressed up, figuring that I would just go along and we would have lunch. We rode in a limousine to the orphanage. Burt went to the front door and gave flowers and candy to two little girls. Then, we took them to a nice restaurant, enjoyed a good meal, and returned the little girls to the orphanage. It was a sweet thing to do, and the gesture was entirely Burt's idea.

Burt can be a complete horse's butt, or he can also be the nicest guy in the world. Even though he can be a horse's patoot, he has shown me time and again that he has a heart of gold.

After eighteen years of marriage, my divorce was especially difficult for me. I found moving back to Hollywood — and the Los Angeles cesspool — equally hard. Once again, I found work, and that city was where I needed to be. I was thankful when Burt Reynolds hired me to serve as associate producer on *The End*, a 1978 film that he planned to direct.

I wrote some additional scenes for the movie, and since an acting part was not written in the original script for me, I decided to write one in so that I could later collect a residual.

The scene had Burt at a hospital, where I was swathed in bandages from head to toe and hooked up to an IV machine. I was using a telephone in the hospital hall, but Burt wanted to use it. He could not wait for me to relinquish it to him, so he shut off the IV. While he talked on the phone, I was behind him in the background, staggering down the hall and collapsing against a wall. I did this the entire time he talked on the phone. Audiences never listened to Burt's telephone conversation, but they intently watched me staggering around in the background and collapsing. The scene proved to be hilarious. The first time we shot it, a girl playing a nurse actually thought I had fainted and came over to help me. We had to shoot the scene again after we told her that I was just acting.

Jerry Belson wrote a good original script, but he had an unfortunate medical problem and was unable to spend long hours on rewrites.

Burt told me, "I am going to lock you in a room with a secretary, and I don't want you to come out until you've done the rewrites."

I ended up staying in that room and doing a lot of the rewriting on *The End.* Later, Mr. Belson came in to initial the pages I had rewritten, and that script is what we shot. It was good work and good fun. I wrote a scene in the movie that had Burt's daughter, played by Kristy McNichol,

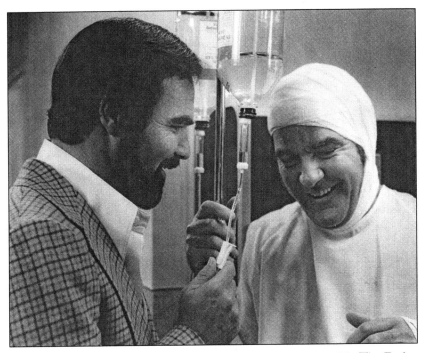

Cracking up when Burt Reynolds turned off my IV during rehearsal for The End.

in a ballet class. I did that to get JoJami and Janeen, my two daughters, jobs working in the movie.

While I was with Burt editing the closing scene of *The End,* Hal Needham called and told Burt he was having some problems with the script for *Hooper,* a movie about a Hollywood stuntman. Burt was to star in the film, Hal was to direct, and I was to play Cully, Burt's best friend.

Burt told Hal, "I've got one of the best writers in Hollywood sitting right here — James Best."

"Oh, how is Jimmie?" Hal asked.

Hal and I had known each other for years while he was a stuntman in many films. I ended up doing some of the rewrites on *Hooper,* which was based in part on the life of Jock Mahoney, Sally Field's stepfather, who was a top stuntman and a good actor. I had worked with Jock many times. He had doubled for Gene Autry, John Wayne, Gregory Peck, and many of the other big stars.

A few years earlier, Jock had suffered a stroke while appearing in a television show. When we were working on *The End*, Jock thought he was

Janeen, my younger daughter, when she was working as a dancer in Hollywood.

dying, but he wanted to do one last stunt. He suggested that we include a scene that would have him going off a bridge in a wheelchair.

"Jock, that'll kill you," I told him.

Burt brushed off my warning when I told him what Jock wanted to do.

Burt said, "Let him do it."

Jock performed the stunt, and it did not kill him. After that, he did not perform many other stunts, but for several more years, he continued to find work playing character parts.

Hooper was a nice tribute for Jock and other stuntmen. Sally Field played Burt's girlfriend. There were rewrites to make. I went to Santa

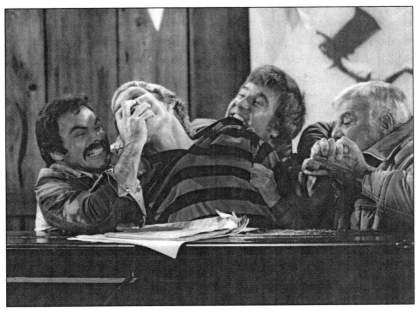

Left to right: Good ol' boys Burt Reynolds, Terry Bradshaw, me, and Brian Keith having a good ol' time in Hooper.

Barbara with Burt, Sally, and Brenda Hillhouse, my secretary (and former Ole Miss drama student). In the original script, Jan Michael Vincent played a young stuntman, who was supposedly Burt's friend, but wanted to take over the glory of being top stuntman from the old-timer, played by Burt.

I wanted more conflict between the characters. I envisioned Jan not only taking Burt's place as the top stuntman, but also taking his girl, sort of a takeoff on *All About Eve*. Jan wanted no part of that. He wanted to play a nice guy and friend of Burt's character.

I told Burt my idea. Although he liked it, he reminded me that Jan wanted to play the nice guy. I told Burt to fire his ass and get an actor who would play the part with some guts. Burt said they could not do that since they had already signed Jan to a contract. So, we let the script follow Jan playing a nice guy, but in my opinion, the story suffered from it.

In spite of a weakened script, performances from a very talented cast and stuntmen saved the film. The picture made a lot of money. Hal did a good job of directing and coordinating all the stunts. My part of Cully was originally a lot larger, but when Burt brought Brian Keith into the movie, he suggested that I give some of my part to Brian. Brian had let Burt use his home in Hawaii on several occasions, and Burt wanted to repay him. Brian had good name value to add to the movie, and he was one heck of a good actor. He later developed cancer and committed suicide, which was heartbreaking to many people in Hollywood.

I had fun on the movie. Hal even let Burt and me adlib a scene where he mimics Gabby Hayes and I imitate Jimmy Stewart. We shot the scene. The next day, the producers told us that we could not use the scene in the movie without permission from Mr. Stewart. I said I would call him and ask if we could use it in the movie. Mr. Stewart was a kind, humble, and generous man, and he happily gave his permission.

When working on some of the projects with Burt, I did not always get the official, on-screen credit that I should have. I was very faithful to Burt for a number of reasons: he was a good friend; he gave me work when I needed it most; he offered me all the money he had at a time when I most needed help. Although I paid my dues back to Burt, I will be at the head of the line for him should he ever need anything. However, if Burt needs me to work for him again, he will have to go to the hip — or take me fishing.

CHAPTER 22

Settling Back into La-La Land

After being back in Los Angeles for a little while, I became reacquainted with Dorothy Collier, a fine actress and beautiful lady. I had met Dorothy in 1967, when she was briefly a student in my camera technique class. Dorothy came from a show business family. Her parents started in Vaudeville. Dorothy worked as a child actress in television and on stage. In 1969, when I was happily married to Jobee, we hired her for a role in *George M!*, a musical that Jobee choreographed and I helped direct. Other than that, I had not known much about Dorothy.

When I moved back to Los Angeles, a mutual friend mentioned to Dorothy that I was back in town. Dorothy had just gone through a divorce herself, so our friend reunited us for dinner. After that, we continued to have dinners together—just the two of us. We hit it off right away, and although we started out as good friends, over time we grew very close and an emotional attachment developed.

During that time, Burt Reynolds had helped me get an apartment near the studio where we were getting ready to film *The End*. The apartment Burt chose for me was a building famous for its high-end escorts. I guess it was a big step up in class from my days at the Palace Hotel in New York City, but still, it was what it was. Dorothy came to visit me one time and said, "Wow, that elevator really reeks of cheap perfume!"

"You don't smell it coming from my room!" I was quick to point out.

About a year later, we decided to take the next step in our relationship. Dorothy had a cute little apartment, but I had little more than a suitcase of stuff. She said, "Why don't you just stay at my place?"

She rescued me in much the same way that I had done when I had asked Mattie to marry me and come to Los Angeles. After I moved into

Dorothy's place, I got in touch with Jobee and asked her to ship some of my personal stuff. She sent many boxes of my junk. Dorothy's father came over to visit, saw all the clutter, and said to her, "You two really must be in love."

We were in love. We ended up throwing most of my junk away. In 1986, Dorothy and I were married. We have enjoyed our life together ever

Above: During a 1969 stage production of George M!, *no one knew that we would all be family in just a few years. My daughters, Janeen and JoJami, are on either side of Dorothy Collier, my future bride.*

since. The third time has been the charm. She is my partner for life. We have spent thirty-two years together, and we continue to grow stronger as a loving couple supporting each other in every way.

Jobee also moved along with her life. She remarried to Danny Dark, a well-known voiceover announcer for many years on NBC until he

My favorite photo of my wife, Dorothy Collier Best.

Our "Best Day."

Top: In 1986, Dorothy and I enjoy our first dance at our wedding. Bottom: Best man Stan Barrett, Dorothy, me, maid of honor Linda Hart, and flower girl Brandy Collier, Dorothy's niece.

retired. He also was the "Sorry, Charlie!" voice on StarKist tuna commercials. I always tried to support JoJami and Janeen financially and in their life endeavors.

Dorothy and I bought our first house together, a storybook house on Hollywood Way in Los Angeles, just down the street from Warner Bros. Shortly after that, both of my daughters moved in with us. Dorothy and my girls have a wonderful relationship. I have always told my daughters that I love them with all my heart and that I am always just a phone call away, as I have been to this very day.

Above: Janeen, JoJami, and Dorothy clown around with me at our home in Chapin, South Carolina. Below: A bevy of beauties in my backyard. Left to right: JoJami, Dorothy, and Janeen.

CHAPTER 23

The Dukes of Hazzard

I was cast in the part of Sheriff Rosco P. Coltrane by accident. I did not want to do a television series. I had helped produce and direct *Gator* and *The End* for Burt Reynolds, and then I acted in and did rewrites for *Hooper* in 1978. At the cast party, Burt hugged me and said, "Jimmie, thank you for a good performance."

I said, "I really appreciate working with you again, Burt."

"Don't thank me," he said. "In a year or so from now, your name will be a household word."

I did not know what he meant by that, and to this day, I still do not know. All I know is that after I finished *Hooper*, my agent called me and said, "I want you to go over and see about a series called *The Dukes of Hazzard*."

"I don't want to do a gang thing," I told him. "I really don't. I've played a lot of heavies and mean guys in my career, but I really don't want to do a series where I'm doing that."

My agent said, "No, this is a good ol' boy thing. They're going to shoot the whole series down around Conyers, Georgia." I love that area because of the good fishing and the extremely nice people.

I told my agent, "My Lord, if they're going to shoot the whole thing around Conyers, I don't care if it's called *There's Doo-Doo in the Saddlebags* — I'll do it."

I went in to see the *The Dukes of Hazzard* people for the casting inquisition. There they were — producers, writers, and studio executives—lined up like a jury. All that was missing was the guillotine. They just smiled, and somebody said, "Well, we want you to play the sheriff, Rosco Coltrane, but we want it funny. Have you ever done any comedy?"

I said, "Well, I was in *Three on a Couch* with Jerry Lewis and Janet Leigh. Does that count? And I also did a lot of summer stock and winter stock."

Rosco P. Coltrane.

They asked, "Would you mind reading for us?"

I said, "Sure, I am a pro. I'll do it. I've taught camera technique for years. I guess I can read it for you."

I read the script for them, but I really did not know what to do with the part. I said to myself, *"Well, I'll do what I did with my little girls."* That is when I started doing the "kee-kee-kee" thing and "I love it, I love it"

Our first Dukes of Hazzard *publicity photo, which was taken in October 1978 just before leaving for Georgia.*

type of thing. They fell off the couch laughing and immediately signed me. Denver Pyle was being auditioned that same day and was hired immediately, too. I cannot imagine that Denver's audition involved anything more than just showing up. He was the perfect Uncle Jesse.

The next thing I knew, we were in Conyers shooting the first scenes for *The Dukes of Hazzard*. I had never met John Schneider, Tom Wopat, and Catherine Bach. I had worked with Denver in *Shenandoah*, and he shot and killed me in *The Left-Handed Gun*. He and I were friends and had known each other for years.

Sorrell Booke was a wonderful character actor. I had never worked with Sorrell, but I knew his work well. I didn't know the other kids, but that didn't matter because we all got along great. We went down to Conyers to shoot the first five episodes, and I was as happy as a June bug. When it became clear that the show was a hit, the producers moved production back to the Los Angeles cesspool. That disappointed many of us, even those who were not counting on doing lots of good Georgia fishing.

Sorrell Booke and I had plenty of physical work to do in our broad comedy as Boss Hogg and Rosco.

We shot most of the street scenes on the back lot at Warner Bros. in Burbank, California. Most of the early back-road car chases and other shots were done on the Disney Ranch, a few miles outside of Los Angeles. Disney ran us off after our chase scenes tore up the grounds too much. Then, the production company moved us out in the middle of nowhere in the desert farther up north. We spent the next six-and-a-half years shooting around Los Angeles. I could not wait to get out of there. I think John, Tom, and Cathy were young and new enough to the business that working in Los Angeles didn't faze them.

The Dukes of Hazzard began in January 1979 as a mid-season replacement, and our first season was only thirteen episodes. For the record, we shot 147 episodes over seven seasons from 1979 to 1985. We also shot two reunion movies, *The Dukes of Hazzard: Reunion!* in 1997 and *The Dukes of Hazzard: Hazzard in Hollywood* in 2000.

The television series was based on a 1974 movie called *Moonrunners*, which was written and directed by Gy Waldron, the creator of *The Dukes of Hazzard*. *Moonrunners* had a lot more edginess, but there were plenty of similarities. *Moonrunners* had an Uncle Jessie, but with a different spelling and played by veteran character actor Arthur Hunnicutt, and it had a Cooter, but he was not played by Ben Jones. Ironically, Ben was in the movie as a federal agent. Waylon Jennings played the music and narrated as the Balladeer. There was not a *General Lee* car, but the moonshine runners did have a car called *Traveller*, which was also the name of General Robert E. Lee's horse. The basic elements for the *The Dukes of Hazzard* were there. The rough edges just had to be softened up a little for the family hour on network television.

The Dukes of Hazzard was a two-edged sword for me. I thank God every day for the blessing of being part of a long-running television series that has brought laughter to the world. Reruns of the series have been shown in more than three dozen different nations. In fact, when I went to Europe, I found that *The Dukes of Hazzard* had at one point or another been the #1 show in England, France, and Germany. It also topped the ratings in Brazil, other Latin American countries, and in Japan. To be a part of something that has had that kind of an impact is a real blessing.

The other side of the sword is pretty sharp. The people who now run Hollywood are very young. They grew up with *The Dukes of Hazzard* and they know me only as Rosco. They do not want to see Rosco playing a killer or a violent person. They want me to be Rosco P. Coltrane. That is always a risk when creating a memorable character, especially on a successful television series. You can become the victim of your own success. An iconic role can stunt a career for an actor. I think that seems especially true for second bananas in comedic roles. Audiences and casting directors expect you to be the goofy character you played and they cannot see you in other types of roles.

And so it was that Don Knotts, a genius actor, earned five Emmys for his portrayal of Barney Fife, and then spent many years afterward boxing with Barney's shadow. Even Andy Griffith had trouble escaping from the career handcuffs that he put on himself with Sheriff Andy Taylor. Or more recently, Michael Richards, the enormously talented actor, created one of the most memorable comedic characters of the 1990s as Kramer on *Seinfeld*. It was an Emmy-winning, career role. It remains to be seen if audiences and casting directors will ever be able to accept him as anybody but Kramer. I hope so, but I know first hand what he is up against.

When beginning work on a new series, the last thing an actor thinks about is that it might become such a success that it will become an albatross around his neck. He dreams for success and recognition. As actors, we do not perform in hopes of toiling unnoticed for years. We want to be in the spotlight, and we will bask in every last watt. We work our entire careers for that kind of success. We do not want to back off just as we are about to grab the brass ring. We grab that ring and hope that we are prepared to deal with the good, the bad, and the ugly of any success that might follow.

When we went down to Georgia to film the first episodes, the whole cast believed that *The Dukes of Hazzard* was supposed to be a write-off for Warner Bros. At that time, the studio was in trouble. They agreed to buy just five episodes. They really did not know what they had at the time. I think they still do not know to this day, but they cash all the checks just the same. Whether or not the show matched the personal taste of network executives and self-styled elitists on both coasts, *The Dukes of Hazzard* was one of those shows that managed to put together all the right elements that appeal to a large part of America.

The combination of elements was simple. There was a grandfather figure and two very handsome boys, one blond and one brown-haired. There was Daisy Duke in a pair of shorts that would stop your heart or a covey of crows in full flight. There was Sorrell and me as a sort of modern-day Laurel and Hardy bumbling duo, and there was a magic car that could fly across a gorge, crash, and never receive a single dent. Top it off with other strong characters and Waylon Jennings singing a catchy theme song and providing the perfect tone of narration, and you had the alchemy for television gold — with or without particularly interesting scripts.

The characters on *The Dukes of Hazzard* had so much fun that our fans often assumed the actors were having the same fun. We did have fun at

John Schneider and Tom Wopat as Bo and Luke Duke, and of course, the General Lee.

first, but after a couple of years of eating dirt during car chases in the desert heat and cold, the fun began to evaporate. For example, we often had our call to be on the set in the desert at 5:30 in the morning. It was cold enough for ice to form on the little puddles of water. I had to be in just my regular blue shirt, and I nearly froze to death. Warner Bros. did not want to give me any insulated underwear because it was not in the budget. They had one of the top shows on television and they were making millions of dollars, but they had no budget for long underwear.

One day, a stuntman jumped my car into a pond for a scene. I then had to swim out for the additional takes in this dirty old water that had been there for fifty years with horses and who knows what all messing around in it. I swam out, dived down, and then popped up as if I had crashed in the water. Not even as much as an eardrop was provided.

Back on the Warner Bros. lot, things were not much better. Our dressing-room wagons were sixty years old. They were wooden framed old buildings with steel wheels on the bottom. The studio dragged them around from set to set with a tractor. The only thing worse than those dressing rooms was having no dressing room at all. Sometimes our dressing rooms would not even be delivered in the morning when we arrived. At other times, they showed up with mirrors and other things broken. Actors on other productions that did not have nearly the ranking of our show had beautiful, modern motor homes.

At the time I started work on *The Dukes of Hazzard,* I was fifty-two years old. I was falling from trees and crashing and careening around in those cars. It definitely was not all sunglasses and autographs. If I froze in the desert in the morning, I could be sure that I would be burning up by noon. As if the noonday sun was not hot enough, the crew added key lighting. They are usually big, brute lights that are about six feet in diameter. The crew cranked them about twenty feet away from us in the desert sun. You can notice in the early episodes of *The Dukes of Hazzard* that we all were sweating so badly that none of us looked as though we were wearing any makeup. The lights were so hot that they actually burned us right through our makeup. I got terrible headaches from it, and I think my eyes are still damaged.

There was no real relief from the heat to be found in the dressing rooms either. Not only that, but the same shabby old dressing rooms were used by everybody — actors, stuntmen, and extras. I do not think John and Tom minded the hard conditions as much because they were new in the business, and they were just happy to drive the *General Lee.* Cathy usually worked just a couple of days a week. She put on her little shorts and then worked mostly on the air-conditioned soundstage. If the producer had only told me, I would have gladly put on some short-shorts to get some air-conditioning. Lucky ol' Denver managed the same temperature-controlled work environment in his overalls.

That left Sorrell and me out on the battlefield most of the time with the dirt. Sorrell and I performed the chases or whatever the scene required. We did a lot of the driving ourselves for the chase scenes that were not considered dangerous or that needed close-ups of us. The crew strapped

Getting wet and falling was a weekly event for Rosco on The Dukes of Hazzard.

a camera and lights on the front of the car hood. We started and stopped the camera ourselves with a switch inside the car.

If we were not involved in a chase scene, then as likely as not, we were preparing for, or recovering from, a fight scene. I remember one episode had us in a big pie fight. Sorrell and I were covered with gobs of pie filling.

We always had visitors and spectators, including on the day of the pie fight. We were all messy from the pie fight, but the director wanted us to change quickly in order to allow him to get in another shot. Some crew members held up a couple of blankets as a shield, had us strip down, and then rinsed us with a hose while people were standing all around. Those were the sorts of conditions under which we worked.

I kept complaining to the front office about how very uncomfortable I was and how it was very hard to do comedy when I was so miserable. I told them that we were either too cold or too hot, or else members of the crew had to wash us down with a hose without being given any eardrops. I told them that every hack, would-be, cannot-be, and never-will-be actor in town had a motor home for a dressing room. I pointed out that our show was making millions of dollars for the studio, but they were underpaying us, and on top of that they were breaking us with extremely difficult working conditions. They kept saying they could not afford a motor home.

Finally, I gave them an ultimatum. "If I don't have a motor home by Friday, I quit."

The next day, there was a nice motor home, but the victory was short-lived. I knew better.

"How do you want me to stock your trailer, Mr. Best?" the caterer from craft services asked.

"Don't bother," I told him. "It'll be gone by Monday." I had a feeling that because some of the directors had fallen behind in filming their episodes, the production company was trying to finish three different episodes by Friday. I did them. Come Monday, my dressing room was no longer there. The studio executives again indicated that they simply could not afford it. I packed up for Florida.

When I quit the show, I asked Sorrell to quit with me.

"Sorrell, we'll get what we want because they can't do it without us," I told him.

Sorrell had tears in his eyes. "Jimmie, I've been a character man all these years and I've never gotten any recognition or glory. I just can't take a chance."

I said. "That's all right, Sorrell. I'll go by myself."

Trade papers reported that I had quit the show because I wanted first-class airfares for relatives and a special makeup man. I did not even use a makeup man. I let the production's makeup man put a little eyeliner on me just so that he could get a salary. I might have needed a head transplant, but I did not need makeup.

The studio tried to replace me with three different actors, sort of a sheriff of the week. They were all good actors, but what the producers had not fully realized was that I adlibbed about three-quarters of my lines. The guys writing the scripts were mostly New York boys, and they did not know the colloquial expressions that I was using on the show. I had added most of those touches myself. The writers actually got to where they wrote in the script, "Rosco and Boss adlib." If my adlibs went over and were funny, the writers took full credit. If the jokes and other material they wrote did not achieve what they intended, they were quick to accuse, "Best is adlibbing again."

Sorrell did not get a motor home either, but he was wily and subtle. He sat resolutely in his chair, and they practically had to use a crane to get him up to work.

He arrived on the set on time and in wardrobe. Somebody said, "All right, we're ready for you, Mr. Booke."

Sorrell just sat there. After quite a while, he decided to get out of the chair.

"We have liftoff," a first assistant announced.

Sorrell knew that time costs money, so he took his own sweet time gathering himself and making his way to the set. The studio should have gotten him five motor homes. It would have been cheaper. It cracked me up. I loved it. He was rebelling in his own way, but he was not a hothead like me. He rebelled with more gentility, but it worked.

On the other side of the coin, old loudmouth Best shot his mouth off about everything. There was nothing subtle about me. I warned those who were doing me wrong, "You're messing with me. Don't mess with me."

In a short time, audiences made clear that they did not cotton to the "sheriffs of the week." Those poor actors simply stood there because the writers were not writing for them. The directors did not know what to do, and poor Sorrell was about ready for a straitjacket. He was so upset that he was practically in tears. One of the vice presidents finally came to me and asked what it would take to get me to come back.

A man and his dog.

"Exactly what I told you, but now I also want a dog for Rosco, and I want to direct."

He balked.

I said, "Hey, I'm not negotiating. You don't have anybody with the intestinal fortitude to come down to Florida and dig me out of these swamps. I'll go fishing. You can sue me or do whatever you want to do, but it won't make a particle of difference because I can prove that you scuffed me."

The studio finally agreed to the motor home and to letting me direct. They said, "So, do we have a deal?"

I said, "Not yet. I want a dog."

They responded that they did not want a dog in the production because it would cost $500 a day plus another $500 a day for a trainer. I said, "I want a dog. The scripts are so much the same. This will give you a whole new angle. Rosco never gets a girl. He's stuck in a rut. At least if he has a dog, I'll be stuck with a Hogg and a dog."

I got Flash. She was a seven-year-old basset hound rescued from a dog pound. She was headed for euthanasia. I got her out and found Alvin Mears, a wonderful trainer and person. Flash became one of the biggest stars on the show, which I knew would happen. Everybody loves puppy dogs. I nicknamed her Velvet Ears. The only problem with Flash was that she weighed about sixty pounds. I think I still have back problems from lugging Flash around all those years.

I looked out for the dog, and for Alvin, too. If a scene called for Flash to be doing something that I thought was too dangerous for her, such as riding in a car at high speed, I arranged for a dummy to take her place. We called the dummy Flush. Flash also had some stunt doubles that Alvin trained, but one thing that Flash did not need was a stunt double for her close-ups. If Flash was in a scene in the car with me, Alvin put a little piece of a weenie on the visor to get her to look straight ahead as if she was paying attention to where we were driving. As soon as the director yelled "Cut," Flash knew she would get her little piece of weenie. Then, she would go back to her little doghouse dressing room for a snooze and wait for her next scene and another weenie. I never tried to convey to Flash what I knew from my experience working in a butcher shop about what weenies were made from, but I doubt that she would have cared even if she had known. She knew all that she needed to know — they tasted good.

I had to wrestle with the studio over my own treatment, and I also had to do battle for Alvin and Flash. After Flash had been on the show for about a year and was proving to be immensely popular, Warner Bros. started making various Flash products. They did not give Alvin screen credit or pay him what he deserved. That really bothered me. I told Alvin that he should go to the studio and get what he deserved. He was concerned that they would fire him, which they would ordinarily do.

Giving Flash a rub-a-dub in the tub with assistance from trainer Alvin Mears.
PHOTOGRAPH COURTESY OF ALVIN MEARS.

I told him, "If they fire you, I'll make up the difference in money to you for the rest of the series."

Alvin went to the executives, and they threatened to fire him. I went in and told the studio that if they fired Alvin and Flash and found another trainer and another Flash, then they would have to find another Rosco while they were at it. Alvin got his screen credit and also money that was more in line with what he deserved.

When I came back, the entire cast shared in the advantages gained by my walkout, but I understood why they could not quit in protest as I had done. They were all coming at the situation from different perspectives and needs.

I had one more Flash battle to tackle with the studio. I gave Alvin $1 for half ownership of Flash. I told him, "I can now legally say that I own half of Flash, and now we can really negotiate." I assured him that I would never take a dime that he made from Flash.

My faithful companion, Flash — even if she did cheat.

Then my business manager went to Warner Bros. and asked, "So where's the commodity money for all the merchandise you've been selling with Flash?" I am sure they were taken aback. Then, he added, "You see, Mr. Best owns the dog," I imagine that the Warner Bros. executives and the studio's stable of attorneys had a collective coronary.

Sorrell Booke and I made two ugly women. I thought Sorrell looked like the Queen Mother in this episode, "Targets: Daisy and Lulu."

That was nearly thirty years ago, and I am still trying to get a proper accounting from Warner Bros. about royalties earned on commodities. According to my contract, I was to earn 5% of Warner Bros.' share on all commodities with my image. The second year of the show, Warner Bros. made $180 million on *The Dukes of Hazzard* commodities alone, but I never received even a fraction of my full share. The studio has been making millions of dollars on commodities every year since then. The Screen Actors Guild is after them now. So far, the studio has been very slow to open its books. The Guild is now going to arbitration with them. I will go to the wall with the studio to get them to come clean and do what is right. Stay tuned for more about that.

If prying rightful money from the studio was difficult, getting better stories out of them was even more of a wrestling match. I would go to the writers with a story outline that I had written. One time I said, "You ought to have a story where Boss Hogg is trying to replace Rosco with a robot. Good idea, right?"

"No, no, Mr. Best, you don't have any concept of the show. You know, there's a format. You don't know the format."

I said, "I've done fifty episodes. If I don't know the format, who does?"

Two months later, a robot story was miraculously delivered from the bowels of the production office. Of course, I did not get credit for it. They changed it just enough so that I could not do anything about it.

Another time, I said, "Let's do a Big Foot thing where Boss Hogg takes a fake Big Foot foot, stamps footprints out in the swamp, and creates a tremendous bunch of people coming into the town that he can make money off of."

"Oh, no, no. We cannot do that."

Two or three months later, there's Big Foot stomping around Hazzard County.

Yet another time I said, "Let's have Boss Hogg do a scam about seeing a spaceship land with a little alien. You get a little person to play the little space critter."

"Oh, no, no. That is way out there beyond *The Dukes of Hazzard*," they said.

A little time passed, and miraculously, as if from a galaxy far, far away, a *Dukes* script called for a spaceship to land in Hazzard. Once again, the studio changed the story just enough so that there was nothing I could say about it.

When I came back after holding out for the motor home, I knew that directing some episodes would allow me to be more plugged into the show's creative decisions, at least for the episodes I directed. Of course, Sorrell and Denver had a "favored nations" clause in their contracts, which meant they got anything I got. So they got to direct, too.

Even though I was back on the set, I was not through making my point. I refused to adlib. I said, "I'm not going to adlib. If it's not in the script, then I'm not going to say it. You're paying me for what's in this script."

The studio people called Dorothy. They told her, "Jimmie's not feeling good about things again. You'd better come down here."

Dorothy came down to the set and asked them, "What's wrong?"

"Well, Jimmie won't adlib."

The writers and producers all came down to the set. They asked, "Jimmie, what do you want Rosco to say?"

"I don't want to say anything. Just send me the check. I'll say anything you write down. You hired me to say lines written for me, but you're not the ones writing my material. I am."

In making my point, I was once again embarrassing them by letting it be known that I was doing their work for them by adlibbing. While I was twisting my bayonet-sized needle in the victims with whom I was skirmishing, Dorothy saw the bigger picture.

"Jimmie, you can't do this. You can't hold out like this because you're really just hurting yourself."

As a professional, I knew she was right. I went back to work and back to adlibbing.

When I first started directing, the writers resented me because I had made it so obvious to everyone that they had not been writing for me. The writers wanted revenge. The first script they gave me to direct had an unusually high number of camera setups, which meant extra work for the director. They threw it at me thinking I would fall on my backside trying to do it. They figured I would not be able to finish my show on schedule and would probably go over budget. That did not happen — much to their chagrin.

They even sent another producer-director down to the set to sit in my hip pocket, ready to pick up the pieces when I cracked. He was there fifteen minutes, and then he told the producers, "The man knows what he's doing," and then he left.

Not only did I bring the episode in under schedule and under budget, but I also picked up about twenty minutes of footage for the director ahead of me who had not finished his show. That happened on all the shows that I directed. We had about thirty different directors on *The Dukes of Hazzard*, including some of the best, such as Don McDougall, Dick Moder, Hollingsworth Morse, and Bob Sweeney. Only two other

I loved directing episodes of The Dukes of Hazzard.

directors other than me were able to use the multi-camera system and bring an episode in under budget.

Sorrell was very happy when I came back after my holdout because we had a wonderful time working together and playing off each other. Sorrell was a great straight man, but he was also extremely funny in his own right. I could be completely off the wall in a scene. Sorrell never knew

The Dukes of Hazzard *crew loved for me to direct because they always got finished early.*

what I was going to say, but he never missed a beat.

Because the writers did not care too much for me, they did not make an effort to put me in the shots. So, I put myself near Sorrell at all times in order to get in the frame. Then, I repeated what he said. For example, if he was on the phone and asked, "Is this Charlie Locker?" then I asked, "Is that Charlie Locker? Say hello from Rosco," just to be able to be in the shot. Sorrell knew what I was doing, of course, and he went along with it. I was always hugging him and doing all this business around him just so I could get in the frame. I think the writers would have loved to have kept me completely off camera and just doing voiceovers.

Some of the things that Sorrell and I did would get the crew falling down with laughter. I acted for the crew because I was used to the theater and an audience reaction. If I could make the crew laugh, then I knew my adlibs were funny. It was common at Warner Bros. for the office staffs working on the lot to bring sack lunches over to the editing room to watch the rushes of scenes with Sorrell and me.

On a 1979 Christmas break from The Dukes of Hazzard, *JoJami, Dorothy, and Janeen joined me for a fun time in Hawaii.*

We had a tight group of writers, who resisted adding any other outside writers to their staff. They absolutely refused to even consider hiring talented writers with fine reputations for writing wonderful comedy for other successful television shows. They wanted to write for the *The Dukes of Hazzard* show. Warner Bros. writers protected their turf.

As a result of the stifled writing, we were repeatedly stuck with a lot of car chases, jumps, and crashes. There is no doubt in my mind that the producers could have saved millions of dollars by using the same stock shots. Thus they could have afforded to give the actors decent dressing rooms and eardrops. The writers thought the car was the star of the show, but I never heard the car get a laugh, except maybe when it crinkled up after a jump and then appeared straightened out in the next moment as if it was new. That was always funny to see.

I remember one particular time when I mentioned "outhouse" in an adlib. The writers came parading down to the set. One of them asked, "Isn't an outhouse an outdoor restroom?"

I said, "Yeah."

"I don't know if you can say that on television."

"Why not? You blow one up at the beginning of every show."

He said, "That's an outhouse?"

I said, "That's an outhouse." Good grief, it was like feeding shucks to a goose trying to deal with people who were not privy to the same colloquialisms as the rest of us.

CHAPTER 24

My Kind of Cast

As a lifelong fisherman, I know a great cast when I see one. The cast of *The Dukes of Hazzard* was wonderful. They all helped us hook this whopper of a show. We had a lot of fun times together.

I had worked with Denver Pyle, our beloved patriarch, Uncle Jesse, in some Westerns many years before we were reunited on *The Dukes of Hazzard*. Denver was a respected, true professional in our business, an actor's actor. Beginning long before he was forty, Denver played characters in their sixties. He required no makeup to look old because he had the rugged looks, carriage, and voice of an older man. He was a wealthy man from having appeared in several television series, as well as many movies. He owned Texas oil wells, mineral rights, and even a few head of cattle.

Denver was a patriarch to other actors, much as the character of Uncle Jesse was on *The Dukes of Hazzard*. He was very helpful as far as the other cast members were concerned. He worked more with Cathy, Tom, and John than I did because the character of Rosco generally chased after them. I played most of my scenes with Sorrell Booke's Boss Hogg character. Denver was a grandfather figure to Cathy in particular, and justifiably so because he personally took her under his wing.

Cathy, Tom, and John all have said many times that they were grateful for Denver's guidance and reassurance. They were appreciative of the advantages of working with seasoned actors like Denver, Sorrell, and me. I had a similar appreciation for legends such as Jimmy Stewart, Jerry Lewis, and Denver. Maybe a little of what I learned has been passed on down to others, and that knowledge will pass from them to others.

Watching Tom and John improve was wonderful, as far as their attitude was concerned. When we began working on *The Dukes of Hazzard*, they were young and became swept up in Hollywood glitz and glamour.

The Dukes of Hazzard *cast: (back row) Sorrell Booke, Denver Pyle, Ben Jones, Tom Wopat, and (front row) Rick Hurst, John Schneider, Catherine Bach, Flash, and me. (Note: Sonny Shroyer was doing the spin-off* Enos *at this time.)*

They became enamored of audience admiration, and their early success became evident on some of their radio and television interviews when they bordered on being cocky. They greatly enjoyed their newfound celebrity status. They were "feeling their oats," as old cowhands say, but they gathered control of the reins, mellowed, harnessed all that wonderful, naïve cockiness, and allowed their natural graciousness to take over.

Always trying to get those Duke boys. Left to right: Sonny Shroyer, John Schneider, Tom Wopat, and me.

John Schneider was underage when he interviewed for *The Dukes of Hazzard*. I think he was seventeen at the time, but he looked older. He used his brother's identification in order to lay claim to being over eighteen so he could be on the set without a parent or guardian. By the time *The Dukes of Hazzard* started shooting in October 1978, John was eighteen, but by then, his falsified age had been set. For several years after that, people thought he was older then he was.

John was a big old boy. He went in for the interview carrying a six-pack of beer and announced, "I'm Bo Duke." That is exactly the kind of thing Bo would have done. Like Bo, John had a natural, easy way with people. He has other talents also. He can sing like a bird.

Once we were all cast, we went down to Georgia to film. While we were down there, we found out that the series had been picked up for eight more episodes. CBS took little nibbles of our show — ordering just a few episodes at a time — until they finally realized that the show was going to be a smash hit.

When John came back to Hollywood, his manager came over and told the producers that John wanted to be called Bo. He did not want anybody to call him John. You had to love his robust cockiness, which I recognized right off the bat, but it did not last too long. He turned out to be one of the nicest guys in Hollywood, a very fine actor, and has gone on to star in several series, including *Dr. Quinn, Medicine Woman*, and *Smallville*. He also has appeared in several films.

Tom Wopat can be described as a good ol' farm boy from Lodi, Wisconsin. Tom was more private and self-contained than John. Like John, Tom also has a beautiful singing voice, but that talent was never used on *The Dukes of Hazzard* to the extent that it should have been. I think it would have been a wonderful addition to the mundane scripts that we sometimes had to suffer with. Tom is older than John and had considerable music credits and a couple of years on Broadway under his belt when *The Dukes of Hazzard* came along. After *Dukes*, Tom starred in the series *A Peaceable Kingdom* and *Cybill*, but I believe his true love is Broadway. He has two Tony nominations — one for *Annie Get Your Gun,* and one for *A Catered Affair*. Not long ago, Dorothy and I had the thrill of seeing Tom in the musical *Chicago*. It was on the road and we drove over to Raleigh, North Carolina, to see him. He was brilliant. I was so proud of him.

Probably more than any other actors on the show, Tom and John really bonded. Part of that had to do with their relatively young ages and also the fact that they were in so many scenes together. Tom and John were learning to catch their first rabbits together. I remembered what that was like. A lot of people probably do not know this, but when John and Tom left the show, Sorrell and I quit at the same time. The studio settled with Sorrell and me within twenty-four hours. They thought they could replace John and Tom, but they quickly realized that Boss and Rosco's adlibbing could not be replaced.

We all appeared together in personal appearances on the weekend, and we quietly did a great deal of charitable work. Warner Bros. wanted publicity about our charitable appearances, but we always shut them out.

Publicity was not what it was about. I was very fortunate to be with a group who were all on the same page about that.

I remember when Cathy, Sorrell, Rick Hurst, and I flew in for the Black Gold Festival in Hazard, Kentucky, in 1981. Hazard is right in the middle of the coalmine region in the mountains of eastern Kentucky. Flying into that area is dangerous. We were in a small plane, and the short landing strip was uphill.

"My Lord, it's not long enough," I told the pilot.

The pilot replied, "Well, the runway's going uphill. That'll slow us down."

His assurances were not very comforting. I knew there was more than one way a hill could slow you down. It was a hair-raising experience, but we landed safely.

We went in there not realizing the popularity of *The Dukes of Hazzard* with folks in and around Hazard. The town had one main road, and we arrived to find that people had parked in their cars for two and three days waiting for us. We raised over $1.5 million for the coal miners' families there. Warner Bros. did not want us to go back the second year because of the danger of arriving by airplane. The studio honchos were afraid they would lose their cash cow in a hillside crash.

It was on that trip that Cathy ripped the back seam in her well-fitted jeans, as we were getting into a car. When we arrived at a little makeshift stage, she emerged, and I saw the rip. I placed my hand over the torn fabric, and I am sure the gesture looked like I was doing something naughty, but actually all I was doing was just trying to protect Cathy's modesty. I greatly enjoyed covering for Cathy.

Sorrell Booke was a wonderful character to study. He was born in Buffalo, New York, and served in counterintelligence during the Korean War. I did not know until years after working with him on *The Dukes of Hazzard* that Sorrell could speak five languages.

Our set at Warner Bros. was open for anybody and everybody. One time, there was a contingency of Japanese gentlemen visiting to observe us filming. The members of the Japanese group came in and were standing off to the side. I saw Sorrell walk over to them and start talking. I was sure he was talking some sort of put-on, Asian gibberish, so I pulled him aside.

"Sorrell, don't do that," I cautioned.

"Don't do what?"

"All that fake Japanese stuff. That's insulting."

"What are you talking about? I'm speaking Japanese."

"Are you kidding me?"

"No. I can speak Japanese."

"Where did you learn how?"

"I was over there for about six months," he explained. I learned that the intelligence agency had recruited him for his natural skill with lan-

Rosco takes a liking to his Rolls Royce patrol car in the "Ten Million Dollar Sheriff"
episode of The Dukes of Hazzard.

guages. He had such an ear for sound that he could hear anyone from the United States talk, tell where they were from, and even narrow the location down to a specific city.

Sorrell and I bonded, just as John and Tom had bonded. We had great rapport doing our scenes with all the adlibbing, but we were more like two old hunting dogs working a familiar trail. I never saw the inside of

I was so pleased to be able to take Sorrell Booke on a fishing trip. Here we are admiring his catch.

Sorrell's house. In fact, I do not believe any of the cast did. We saw each other so much during the day that there was not much time left for more relaxed socializing.

Sorrell had a heart of gold. In 1983, Dorothy and I had bought a home in Chapin, South Carolina, and the local hospital came to me for help with a fundraiser for children with special needs. I immediately agreed and told the organizers that perhaps I could get Sorrell to appear so that Boss Hogg and Rosco could do the fundraiser together. A wealthy man offered his big ranch for a picnic for the kids. The local television station supplied a helicopter, and we flew in and dropped down right in the

With my daughter, Janeen, during filming of her episode, "A Baby for the Dukes."

middle of the kids. It was thrilling for all of us. Sorrell was like that. He tried to help out whenever he could.

Sorrell loved to do just about any kind of personal appearance. He loved the adoration, but more than that, he just loved meeting and being with the people who adored Boss Hogg. When we did personal appearances together, I automatically fell into doing Rosco and treating him

JoJami appearing in The Dukes of Hazzard *episode, "The Hack of Hazzard."*

like Boss Hogg. I opened doors for him and that kind of thing, and he expected it because he was Boss Hogg.

Even with all his worldly experience, Sorrell had never been fishing, so I invited him to come down to Florida. I love any kind of fishing. I promised Sorrell that I would take him fishing for sailfish. We headed out on a professional fishing boat and we hit choppy waters. Poor Sorrell began getting seasick right away, but he tried to ride it out. We baited and cast our lines. We had not had our lines set for even fifteen minutes when a sailfish hit my lure. I set the hook, handed the pole to Sorrell, and said, "Sorrell, there's your sail." Sorrell cranked him in, even as he got sicker by the minute. He finally got the sailfish in. He had never caught one before. He proudly held it while I filmed him with my video camera. Fortunately, we got the footage we needed in one take, because as I stopped shooting, Sorrell leaned over the railing and lost his lunch.

Later on, Sorrell became critically ill with cancer. We never knew because he never complained. A friend of his visited him while he was sick, and later he told us that Sorrell was so proud of the sailfish he caught that he had it mounted over his fireplace. It was one of his greatest pride-and-joys among all his career awards. When we lost Sorrell in 1994, I lost my true little buddy. I still really miss him.

I was sitting in a restaurant in Los Angeles when a man walked in who looked so much like Sorrell that I nearly choked on my food. He could have been Sorrell's twin. I knew the man was not him, but I could not fight back the tears. I just wanted to see my little fat buddy again. I missed him so much.

When we filmed *The Dukes of Hazzard: Reunion!* in 1997, Denver Pyle was also battling cancer. He had lost his hair and had to put on a fake beard and fake hair. I was very sad about his condition. We lost Denver on Christmas Day later that year.

When we were on an outdoors location in Georgia filming an early episode of *The Dukes of Hazzard*, a makeup man was putting makeup on my face. I did not care about makeup. I agreed to have it put on mostly just to make sure the makeup man kept his job. As I sat, I was bad about moving my head around and talking to whoever walked by. The makeup man held his hat up to block the sun. As a gag, he pinned a *Playboy* centerfold inside his hat to give me something to lock in on and keep my head still while he made me up. That worked just as well on me as putting a piece of weenie on the visor worked to hold Flash's attention in those car scenes.

Laughing, I asked, "That photo works great for me, but what have you got for poor Cathy to look at?"

"Well, nothing," he said.

I went back to the hotel and got a Polaroid camera. I took off all my clothes except my boots, gun belt, and hat. I set the timer on the camera, snapped a picture, and then gave the print to the makeup man to put in his hat. I was about thirty yards away one day when Cathy was getting made up. All of a sudden, I heard this tremendous shriek, and then Cathy ran toward me screaming. She jumped in my arms.

"I'm in love!" she screamed.

Funny that Flash never reacted like that about the weenie over the visor.

Cathy was so sweet, but she seemed quite shy when we first met. I believe she was sometimes a little self-conscious. She was fairly new to acting when we started work on the series, and like John Schneider and Tom Wopat, she was quite young — only twenty-four years old when we started. Her vitality and freshness, a look of natural innocence, and legs that few women have and every woman would die for were a big part of what made her perfect as Daisy Duke. It was simply impossible to miss the obvious fact of how attractive she looked in short shorts — or anything else for that matter.

Cathy got so into her character and the scene that sometimes she forgot we were filming. There were times when a director yelled, "Cut," and Cathy asked, "Did they shoot that? I wasn't ready yet." That kind of immersion in a scene is rare among actors. Cathy had little acting training, so it was not as if she fell back on "Method" acting. She was just "in the moment" and did not always realize when the filming started.

For whatever reason, writers did not give Cathy much dialogue. They tended to write just a line or two to keep her active in a scene. Wardrobe people were instructed by the front office to keep her in shorts as much as possible. One script titled "Diamonds in the Rough" had substantial scenes for Cathy, and I was directing that episode.

I went to Cathy and said, "You know, I've been teaching camera technique for many years. I'm going to have you really do some good acting in this one. I love you and I'm going to protect you. You're going to look really great in this episode — I promise."

She just beamed and welcomed the chance. She did a beautiful, professional job in the episode, and she showed her latent acting ability. Studio executives were flabbergasted. They never realized her capabilities. They called for another script that again gave her some meatier things to do and more extensive dialogue. I did not direct that one, and whoever directed it did not protect and nurture her performance the way she needed. It showed, but she always looked great, so there was no real worry.

Fans love Cathy. She is a tremendously kind person and a doting mother to her two beautiful daughters. She is always on hand for deserving charitable events, and someone I have been glad to see at our personal appearances.

Another cast favorite was Sonny Shroyer, one of the most loving and charitable guys I have ever known. He would do anything for me, and I love him as a brother. He was wonderful as Rosco's deputy, Enos Strate. Sonny

Sonny Shroyer as Enos Strate.

was two different people: a twelve-year-old boy in a grownup body, and a "Method" actor. He liked to pretend that his roles were real life, and he went to great lengths to prove it to himself. For a man his age, Sonny managed to maintain a refreshing naïveté. He lives in Valdosta, Georgia, with his wife, Paula. Our personal appearances together have been delightful.

Sonny actually studied acting with me while we were shooting *The Dukes of Hazzard*. He came to my acting classes carrying little dialogue cards in his hip pocket.

"Sonny, you don't need those," I told him. "You know that dialogue inside and out." Despite my advice, he insisted on looking at the cards. "Sonny, you've got only three lines in this particular scene," I said. Knowing that he had memorized his lines, I grabbed the cards and tore them up. He threw a fit, but performed fine without the cards.

Sonny did some fine work in other movies, and he often played a wonderfully bad "heavy." The first time I met Sonny, he played a Federal Agent in *Gator*. He had played football in Florida with Burt Reynolds. He was wonderful in *Forrest Gump* as legendary coach Paul "Bear" Bryant, and he was brilliant as Governor Jimmie Davis in *Ray*.

One time on *The Dukes of Hazzard*, I told Sonny, "We do an awful lot of physical stuff in our scenes — falling over furniture, sliding down stairs on a door, and falling out of trees. It's much funnier if Rosco falls on top of you." Sonny bought that malarkey all through the show, and he invariably found me falling on top of him for a cushion.

In one episode, Sonny stood behind me, as we left Boss's office. The Duke boys were in the midst of a brawl, and Boss Hogg wanted Rosco and Enos to stop the fight. I fired my gun into the air and the chandelier fell. Sonny was very goosey. If I pointed my finger at him and shouted, "Goo-goo," he jumped halfway across the room. As we prepared for the scene, Sonny asked the prop person for a hot cup of coffee.

"Don't get hot coffee," I advised. "Get some cold coffee. When that gun goes off, I know for sure that you'll spill it on me.

He said, "No, Jimmie, I won't spill it on you."

"Why does it have to be hot?" I persisted.

Like a good Method actor, he replied, "I want to see the steam. I hate seeing movies where there's a coffee-drinking scene that has actors slurping cold coffee with no steam."

I knew he was set on having hot coffee, so I pleaded one more time, "Sonny, don't you spill that coffee on me."

Sonny Shroyer's star always shined in Dukes of Hazzard *scenes.*

"I won't spill it," he promised.

"I'm going to shoot my gun off and the chandelier is going to fall," I warned.

"I know."

They rolled the camera. I walked out and shouted, "Freeze! Freeze! Freeze!" and shot the gun off. Sonny reacted, threw coffee all over me, and I suddenly felt a cool wetness that turned into a fiery burn. My gun had no bullets, but it was real. Still stinging from the blistering coffee bath, I tried to pistol whip Sonny. I chased him all around the stage, but I could not catch the big old boy. He was afraid of me, but not half as afraid as I was of hot coffee. For years, Sonny denied that he spilled hot coffee on me. I finally showed him the clip from the show verifying that he spilled coffee on me, but he steadfastly remained in denial that it was *hot* coffee.

Sonny also never admitted to being a lousy driver, but everyone in the cast and crew will attest that he often ran over the cameras, props, or furniture in his path. We were shooting a scene where Enos and Rosco screeched their patrol cars to a stop in front of Boss Hogg's courthouse office.

"Sonny, I'm going to slide into the curb, and you're to come in behind me. Now, if you hit me, make sure I'm either in the car, or completely out of the car. Don't hit me when I'm halfway in or out."

The scene called for me to slide into the curb, followed by Sonny careening to a halt just behind me in his patrol car. I pulled up first, and then waited as he cruised near the curb. I began to climb out — and *blam!* He nailed me from behind with a rear-end collision so hard that the impact drove the door jam into my back. I whipped out my pistol, as Sonny hot-footed it toward the courthouse — screaming and yelling the whole way. Intent on killing him, I hollered and chased him down the street, as all the while the cameras rolled.

Whenever new directors came to our show, the producers told them, "Never stop filming when the scene is over because we've discovered that we get some of the best stuff out of what happens next." I adlibbed every chance I could, and the directors kept the cameras rolling until I said something naughty that they could not use. That made them cut the camera.

Directors often came and asked, "What do you want to do here?"

On one episode, I told the director, "Let's have a popcorn machine explode and blow the popcorn up in the air. I'll try to salt it on the way down while I try to grab kernels to my mouth." That was in the episode

"Miz Tisdale on the Lam." I did stupid, silly stuff like that, but it often worked. In "Diamonds in the Rough," the first episode I directed, there was a scene where Boss and Rosco were eating spaghetti across the table from each other. I told the prop man, "Get the longest strings of spaghetti you can and tie them so they are one great big long piece."

Sorrell took one end in his mouth and I chewed on the other. It was like the two dogs in *The Lady and the Tramp* slurping one piece of spaghetti. We kept chomping on it until we got down close to each other and Sorrell took a pair of scissors and cut the spaghetti in half. That was not in the script, but we tried it, and it worked. Sorrell played along with my wild ideas.

In the episode "Ransom of Hazzard County," Rosco was supposed to light Boss Hogg's cigar. I said, "Sorrell, why don't I set your hat on fire when I'm trying to light your cigar?"

"Can we do that?" he asked, a little more worried than usual.

I said, "Oh, sure."

The producer said, "No, no, no. Those are Stetson hats that cost $250. We can't afford that."

They were making millions of dollars a year off the show, so I said, "Just don't film a new car jump. Use stock footage of one of the Charger jumps, and then we can afford the hat."

The producer thought that was a good idea. "Okay," he said. "You've got one hat to burn."

I began to plot exactly how to execute the little stunt. After a while, I said to Sorrell, "I'm going to soak the front of your hat with lighter fluid." Sorrell was game for that. I added, "I don't know how big that flame's going to shoot up, but if it starts to roar or something, just knock it off, or I'll knock it off for you. We'll just adlib until something funny happens."

The set was filled wall to wall with crew watching us set up the scene because they did not know what was going to happen either. We said our dialogue. I got the lighter and flicked it. A tiny blue flame about a quarter of an inch high caught the brim of his hat. We adlibbed lines, and I thought, *"This isn't working worth a darn."* Then, while we adlibbed some more, the flame began to grow bigger, and soon flames like a brushfire danced atop Sorrell's head. The crew cracked up, and the cameraman laughed so hard that tears ran down his face and he could not see through the viewfinder.

"Cut!" the director yelled, doubled over with laughter.

Sorrell never flinched, and we got a funny scene out of the stunt.

Ben Jones was another cast favorite. He was professional and conscientious about his approach to his character, Cooter Davenport. With the possible exception of Mayberry's Goober Pyle, Cooter's probably the best-known mechanic ever created for a television series. Warner Bros. never treated Ben and Cooter with the respect they should have, and the writers did not compose good material for that character.

Ben also butted heads with producers over how his character was to look. They wanted him to be unshaven and dirty. Ben did not want that kind of image, and he thought the character would be just as effective cleaned up. In the end, Ben cleaned up with Cooter. Right after appearing in *The Dukes of Hazzard*, he ran for Congress in his district in Georgia — and won. He was elected to serve two terms. He lost in his effort to win a third term because he was a Democrat, and the Republicans won back many of the House seats during the 1990s with Newt Gingrich leading a Republican charge.

In recent years, Ben has done more than anyone to promote *The Dukes of Hazzard*, stay connected with fans, and emphasize the show's appeal as down-home, wholesome family entertainment. After serving in Washington, Ben moved to Sperryville, Virginia, a fairly isolated town. He opened Cooter's Place, a roadside store on the Shenandoah Parkway near the national forest.

In 2000, I went to Cooter's Place for a personal appearance, and we drew 6,000 people to an event that I thought would attract only a few hundred. We stayed in Ben's house, and then rode in a *General Lee* to the store, where throngs of people lined the highway.

"There must have been a big accident or something," I said, when I saw police directing traffic. I soon discovered that they had simply run out of parking places in the designated fields, and traffic was backed up, as folks parked along the road wherever they could.

At Cooter's Place, the local high school band played during our arrival. I immediately got out of the car, took the band director's baton, and started acting like a fool. The band kids started hitting sour notes because they were laughing while playing their instruments, and we all had a great time. Ben and Alma Viator, his lovely wife, have since expanded the Cooter's franchise and have museum/stores in Nashville and Gatlinburg, Tennessee.

Ben and Alma were the original promoters of DukesFest. The festival began at the store in Sperryville, but the event quickly outgrew that venue.

It moved to the Bristol Motor Speedway in Bristol, Tennessee, and then moved to Nashville. In 2008, John and Elly Schneider took over the festival and held DukesFest in Atlanta. At DukesFest, tens of thousands of fans from all over the United States and several foreign countries converge to meet most of the living cast members and see dozens of *General Lee* cars and other *Dukes of Hazzard* vehicles.

In 2005, I played to the crowd at the CMT Music Awards in Nashville. A bunch of The Dukes of Hazzard *cast appeared, and the audience went crazy.*

Ben has been just tremendous in his efforts to keep the series alive and exciting for fans. He has accomplished much in his life. He is a very no-nonsense, intelligent, self-made man. He has truly lived up to the title of his recent book *Redneck Boy in the Promised Land*.

Rick Hurst joined *The Dukes of Hazzard* cast in the second season to play Deputy Cletus Hogg, when Sonny's character was spun off to his own series, *Enos*. Rick more or less took the part Sonny had vacated. Rick had good credentials when he joined us. He had worked for seven years in film and television. He also has a Master's in Fine Arts from Temple University. I like Rick because he is a fine gentleman and has a talent for comedy that few actors have. His comedy timing is impeccable, and he added much to the show.

When *Enos* ended, Sonny came back to rejoin *The Dukes of Hazzard* cast, and Rick was let go. The producers did not know what they had in Rick's talent, and their way of letting him know about the cast change was shameful. The whole cast was lined up on the soundstage to have some publicity photos taken. Rick was told to step out of the shot, and we all wondered why. They informed him that he would not be returning as a regular cast member. We all stood there in shock. All of us were well aware of the past heartlessness of the producers, but this was beyond wrong. Rick had appeared in forty-five episodes, and he did not deserve that kind of disrespect.

We were all delighted when we shot the two reunion movies and Rick was called back to rejoin us. I was thrilled to work with Rick again. He is a dear friend, and he has worked extremely hard for the entire cast in trying to get Warner Bros. to step up to the plate and give us the contractual monies that they owe us. He has submitted the problem to the Screen Actors Guild, as we wait to see how the studio tries to squirm out of its obligations this time.

The great thing about *The Dukes of Hazzard* is that it is a family show with three generations of faithful audiences enjoying the many reruns. The entire cast feels great pride for the show's reputation for good clean fun. Fans loved the show from the get-go. When the series first came out, more than 200 television critics reviewed the episodes, and only about three were favorable, which just goes to show the truth about critics' tastes.

The Dukes of Hazzard never won any awards. We were a Top Ten show for three solid years, and only two award nominations were ever bestowed on our cast and crew. One nomination went to Flash, my basset hound buddy, who was nominated one year for a Patsy, the Emmy Award for animal acting. She lost to Benji. The other nomination went to our costume people, who earned an Emmy nomination one year — no doubt in large part thanks to Cathy Bach and the way she dazzled audiences in her Daisy Duke outfit.

As I have mentioned, Flash had her own dressing room, which was actually a big doghouse. I had it built and decorated with a Rebel flag that matched the flag on the *General Lee*. It was entirely politically correct.

I must make it clear that no human or hound in the cast had disregard for any race, creed, color, or ethnicity. None of us would have sanctioned the use of the Rebel flag if its intent had anything whatsoever to do with a racial problem. Folks have tried to stir some controversy about it from time to time over the years, but disrespect was the furthest thing from our minds.

I researched the Civil War and learned that the Rebel flag was a battle flag used during battles between the North and the South. Young soldiers from the South were so poor that they picked up parts of whatever uniforms were handy on the battlefield and put them on. Union soldiers complained that they could not tell a friend from a foe. Since soldiers needed a battle flag, three or four Rebel flags were created. One of them had so much white on it that Union soldiers thought Confederate soldiers were surrendering when they waved it — that is, until shooting resumed while they waved the flag.

The South finally ended up with the battle flag colored in blue stripes and white stars against a red background, but it had never implied any racial statement. Many brave black men fought and died under that flag. Through the years, certain repugnant groups, such as the Ku Klux Klan, and some individuals have adopted the flag as one of their symbols for negative thinking and actions. That unfortunate use of the Rebel flag has nothing to do with the original intent, and we saw nothing wrong with using the battle flag in *The Dukes of Hazzard.*

When we went on personal appearances for CBS and Warner Bros., some of the greatest reactions we ever had came from black audiences. I am proud to find this to be true everywhere I am recognized. Black fans of our show recognize the show's intent and the nature of our use of the Rebel flag. Red, white, blue, or black, fans have embraced *The Dukes of Hazzard* and all of its good-natured and good-intentioned elements. The only place I ever saw negativity about the flag on the *General Lee* was with a handful of rabble-rousers who were looking for an angle or cause to get their faces on television. Their attempts were grandstanding, plain and simple, and I have no patience for that. It does nothing but interfere with the good clean fun that the rest of us try to enjoy.

The *General Lee,* that wonderful Dodge Charger, was as much a character on the show as the actors. Some might say that the car was the true star. I never heard the *General Lee* tell a joke, but it went fast and jumped, jumped, and jumped. Of course, I cannot talk too much about the *General Lee* because all I ever saw of the vehicle was its back end.

A lot of people asked me if I ever drove the *General Lee.* They would not let me drive it. John and Tom had many lively "discussions" about who was going to drive the car in particular scenes. Both were excellent drivers, and both loved to drive. That said, it is surprising they did not wreck more of them. Tom wiped out several cameras and crashed the car several times. One time, he rammed the front end of an eighteen-wheeler. We could not understand why he was having difficulty. He was coordinated and he had a motorcycle, so it was clear that he knew how to handle a vehicle. Then, we learned that Tom could not see well without glasses. He was fitted with contact lenses, and he stopped wiping out the cameramen.

John was actually a professional driver. He lived, breathed, and collected cars. He also bought a bunch of *General Lees*, restored them, and then sold them at a handsome price.

The *General Lee* was a magic car with beautiful lines. A few years back, there was a contest in England to rank the ten top cars that had ever been used around the world in television. The *General Lee* won top honors, beating out the Batmobile and KITT, the *Knight Rider* car.

CHAPTER 25

Ham Actors
(Honey Baked, That Is)

I was shooting *The Dukes of Hazzard* in Georgia, and an actress named Jeannie Wilson was guest starring in the episode "Mary Kaye's Baby." Jeannie had read somewhere that I had taught Gary Busey. She kept after me about teaching again when I returned to Los Angeles.

I really did not have any interest in doing that, but I agreed to meet her acting group when they got together to do scene work. I was so impressed with the group's passion that I agreed to start a class if they found a space.

I hit it off with Jack Lucarelli, Jeannie's boyfriend and later, her husband. He agreed to help run the school. They immediately found a space in Toluca Lake that was close to Warner Bros. The school was located upstairs above a Honey Baked Ham store.

Jack was a good student and a fine actor, and he had a wonderful way with his fellow students. He learned camera technique quicker than anyone I have ever had in my classes. I was still working on *The Dukes of Hazzard* and could not devote as much time as I needed to my acting school, so I trusted Jack's ability to teach my technique.

I asked him if he would like a half partnership, and he accepted my offer. He performed wonderfully, and he was responsible for training some of the actors, many of whom went on to work professionally. Students studying with me included Jeannie Wilson (*Simon & Simon* and *Street Hawk*), Tim Reid (*WKRP in Cincinnati* and *Sister, Sister*), Robert Woods (Bo Buchanan on *One Life to Live*), Dennis Haskins (*Saved by the Bell*), Jenilee Harrison (*Three's Company* and *Dallas*), Tracy Scoggins (*Dynasty* and *Babylon 5*), Gary Grubbs (numerous films), Newell Alexan-

In 1981, I tried to look cool with my good buddy Jack Lucarelli.

der (numerous films), Linda Hart (Broadway, television, and film actress), and Rosemary Lovell (*Sordid Lives*).

Jack went on to be a producer and director in feature pictures *(Jackals* and *A Gift from Heaven)*. His wife Jeannie is a beautiful lady and was Miss Texas in the 1968 Miss USA Pageant. Both she and Jack diversified their careers. Jeannie became a nutritionist, and they have collaborated on books, including a recent one on James B. Lile, the Arkansas knifesmith who designed the "Rambo knife" for the *Rambo* movies.

CHAPTER 26

Quentin Tarantino

One of the most famous students from my camera technique school was not known for his acting ability. His name was Quentin Tarantino.

Quentin walked into my class one day and said, "Mr. Best, I want to meet you. You worked in my favorite movie of all time."

"Really? What's that?" I asked.

"*Rolling Thunder.*"

"*Rolling Thunder?*" I asked. I had played such a mean person in that film. I turned the part down three times before I finally accepted it. They kept raising the money to where I finally rationalized that it was okay to prostitute my integrity for that much money, so I did it. Tommy Lee Jones and William Devane also were given enough reasons to appear in the film.

Quentin started quoting lines from the picture. Then, he mentioned other movies that I made and quoted dialogue from them, too. What a memory he had. It helped that he had managed a video store. He obviously liked movies of all kinds.

When Quentin got onstage in class, he was less than adequate. I told Jack Lucarelli, "Throw him out. Get him out of the school. He's a terrible actor."

Jack said, "The poor guy hasn't got any money. He sleeps in the theater once in a while because he doesn't even have enough money for bus fare."

"Oh. Well, hell. Let him stay."

I went to Quentin and told him, "You're a lousy actor. You should take up writing."

This incident happened when Jack was teaching the class. Quentin wanted to use some of his original writings in the class.

"Why do you want to do that?" Jack asked. "Why don't you use some written material from professionals who really know how to write?"

It just goes to show that nobody at any time can predict what is good or bad. It seems that the material that Jack finally let Quentin do in that acting class was a scene that was later used in *Reservoir Dogs*, a successful film that Quentin wrote and directed.

In 1996, Quentin was the executive producer on a film called *Curdled*, which was about a serial killer. I read the gory, blood-soaked script, and I concluded that it was absolute trash, and I presumed that it would never make any money. When I was asked to accept a part in it, I asked my agent, "What kind of money are we talking about?"

He said, "We're not talking any money. It's for scale, and you'll be working with Quentin Tarantino."

"You've got to be kidding me!" I said. "I haven't worked for minimum in fifty years, and I'm not about to start again, especially with a guy who doesn't know diddley squat about directing. The fact that Quentin had been nominated two years earlier for an Academy Award as Best Director and had won an Academy Award for writing *Pulp Fiction* did not make me change my mind. I was so amazed by his success that I scratched my head and wondered, *"Where the hell did he learn to direct?"*

Quentin has an amazing ability to hire people that can do their jobs exceptionally well. John Travolta is a perfect example of that in *Pulp Fiction*. Even so, I was not about to take part in Quentin's bloody movie, and as I predicted, the movie died at the box office. It was a gory story about a group of people whose job was to clean up the blood left all over walls and floors by people who had been brutally murdered or had committed suicide. No one could have saved that piece of bloody trash.

I am also correct about stating that Quentin cannot act. He proved this by winning a 1996 Razzie award for Worst Actor for his work in a supporting role in *From Dusk Till Dawn*. Aside from acting, Quentin is unquestionably a major talent and a keen creative force who has helped keep the edges sharp in filmmaking. Like his work or hate it — and I have done both — I have to admit he is one of a kind. Thank goodness our planet has room for only one of him.

CHAPTER 27

Sunny Times in Florida

It was never my intention to continue living in Los Angeles, but when *The Dukes of Hazzard* moved from Georgia to Warner Bros., I was stuck in the city for seven years. I kept my sanity by running away to Florida and South Carolina whenever I had a break from shooting. When the series ended in 1985, Dorothy and I were living in South Carolina. We had a beautiful home on Lake Murray, and the fishing was great, but we missed the Florida sunshine. In 1987, we moved back to the Orlando area.

In the late 1980s, Orlando was touted as the "new Hollywood," or "Hollywood East," as the film commission had coined the phrase. Universal and Disney had built studios there, and it seemed promising that Dorothy and I could enjoy the best of both worlds. We could live in a beautiful city with great fishing and keep our hand in the industry we both loved.

In 1988, Dorothy and I saw a need for trained, local actors to compete in the growing Florida film industry. We opened the James Best Film Acting Workshop in Longwood, and it operated for about five years. We had around 700 students pass through our doors during that time. We had a lot of fun at that school. We had showcases, musical reviews, and we made wonderful friends we love to this day. Gary Busey even sent Jake, his son, to study with me. I believe Jake has the distinction of being my only second-generation student. Jake has wonderful acting instincts, and he has had success in such films as *Starship Troopers*, *Enemy of the State*, and *Identity*.

After a few years of running the school, Dorothy and I realized that we were working way too hard and had no time to spend on our own projects. We closed the school down. I decided to teach at the University of Central Florida for a year because I wanted to build my credentials in

Florida. I did not want folks in the acting and film business to think I was coming into the state and then leaving the minute I had taken all I could. Too much of that had been going on. That is why Florida film production lagged behind and why other states were pulling ahead.

Before long, some of the same sort of sleazy snakes that were a problem in Los Angeles slithered into the Eden of the so-called "Hollywood

Dorothy in Florida with our first beagle, Freckles Anne. This little puppy started our love of beagles.

East." The Governor appointed several film and music professionals from around the state to an advisory board, but then he brought in the head honchos from Universal and Disney Studios. The big studios only wanted their interests taken care of and did not care about anything else. They just wanted cheap labor and tax savings.

The film commission had a plan to spend $150,000 for a party out in California that was supposed to entice directors and producers to bring their productions to Florida.

"That isn't going to work," I bluntly said. "You're going to have this party down there on the beach. The only people you're going to get are

Dorothy, my Florida backyard beauty.

Hell's Angels and would-be actors seeking a free drink. Aaron Spelling, Steven Spielberg, and folks like that aren't going to come down there for a glass of cheap California wine."

I knew that building a solid, lasting film business was more about nuts and bolts and dollars and cents than wining and dining. The State of Florida needed to provide a creative setting with competitive tax incentives that made business sense. Unfortunately, the governor did not listen to the professional staff, which actually had the correct input to make Florida a successful production state, and so the old-time Commission members quit.

The big boys from Disney and Universal took advantage of the Florida talent by utilizing them as glorified extras at very little compensation, or sometimes, no compensation at all. They still brought in the main stars and key crew members from Los Angeles, and Florida became just a location state. Government officials have taken out most tax breaks and other incentives, so I fear that Florida will fall even further back in future productions. Florida has some beautiful locations and trained crews that are as good as or better than many from Los Angeles. Even the studios have become basically tourist attractions. The potential for Hollywood East has fallen by the wayside

In 1995, Dorothy and I fought against the current and started our Best Friend Films production company in Florida. With multitalented Steve Latshaw directing a script I had written, we produced *Death Mask*, which was released on video. We were able to make it for only about $100,000. We were lucky to catch part of the wave in the horror-film resurgence that was beginning at that time.

While shooting *Death Mask*, we met a young man named Kevin Lang. Kevin was originally from Lowell, Michigan, where he had produced live concerts and opened Pyramid Recording Studios at the age of seventeen. He had moved to Orlando to attend Full Sail, a media production school. He had just graduated, and he was working as a camera loader on our film. We liked Kevin immediately. He had what it took to be successful in the film business. His easygoing personality, wit, and dry sense of humor were a great combination. He was just getting started in Orlando, and jobs were a little scarce at first, so we invited him to stay with us until he got on his feet. He quickly became in high demand with Orlando film crews. That was good, because he was eating us out of house and home. Anybody who knows Kevin knows never to ask him if he is hungry. We

In 2008, Dorothy and I traveled with (left) Ken and Sharon Smith, buddies and business partners, during a Mediterranean cruise.

just take his hunger for granted. Kevin is as honest as the day is long, and we love him like a son.

In 2002, Kevin became a partner in Best Friend Films. With the onset of high-definition digital technology, we realized that was the future for our independent production company and the industry. That technology enabled low-budget film projects to compete with the studio-dominated film industry. Kevin brings to his partnership with our company a vast knowledge of the new digital world. His technical knowledge and creative energy continue to be a strong driving force.

Best Friend Films has continued to be on the cutting edge of HD digital production. We were one of the first production companies in the southeast to obtain the Panasonic Varicam. We were the first to add the Pro 35 lens adapter, which allowed us to use Panavision prime film lenses on a digital camera. This exciting technology has enabled us to build an impressive client list, but our true goal is to shoot more of our own projects for theatrical and DVD release.

In 2007, our good friends, Ken and Sharon Smith, joined the team as partners. We had met Ken and Sharon in 1995 at a Western film festival that they were sponsoring. They were such a fun-loving couple that we became instant friends. We love to travel together, and we have gone to Europe on three fabulous cruises. Ken owned an Automotive Chemical distributorship. He and Sharon built it up to where it was the parent company's largest distributorship in sales and annual growth. In 2006, after twenty-one years, they decided to sell their business to the parent company.

Ken and Sharon have always been there for Dorothy and me, so it was a natural decision for them to join our production company. They have brought entrepreneurship and a business background that are hard to beat. We are developing several exciting projects, and we have upgraded our HD camera to two Panasonic HDX 900s with all the bells and whistles. We have also added two of the revolutionary RED 4K HD cameras and extensive lenses and accessories. By using in-house equipment for our productions, we keep budgets down and increase our production quality on the screen.

With our great team in place, we truly believe our company slogan: "Magic Happens Amongst Best Friends."

In 2004, on the set of the Best Friend Films production of House of Forever *with (left to right) Michael Damian, Dorothy Best, Kevin Lang, and Dan Tomlinson.*

CHAPTER 28

Dukes Reunions and Remodels — More or Less

There had been talk off and on for years about doing a *Dukes of Hazzard* reunion movie, but the idea became serious around 1996. The studio sent a script over to my agent for me to read. It was not great, and I was not thrilled, but as always, I asked my agent what kind of money they were talking about.

He told me.

I said, "I'm not doing it for that."

My agent and the producers went back and forth in negotiations, but the money still was not right.

My agent finally told me, "That is their final offer. If we don't take it, they're going to replace you."

"So be it," I said. "Go to the wall. I've read the script. They can't do it without me."

The studio had tried that before when they replaced me on the original series, and that did not work out for them. Sure enough, four or five days before they were scheduled to start shooting the reunion movie, the studio sent word to fly me in to Los Angeles. I got my money.

In April 1997, *The Dukes of Hazzard: Reunion!*, the first reunion movie, was broadcast. By that time, Sorrell Booke, my old buddy, had passed away. Denver was in the movie, but he was not in good health. Singer Don Williams replaced Waylon Jennings as the Balladeer, but the rest of us were back. The best that can be said is that it was a reunion. It was good to be working together again.

That first reunion did well enough in the ratings that Warner Bros. wanted to put together another reunion movie. The script for *The Dukes of*

Hazzard: Hazzard in Hollywood was even worse than for the first movie. The story followed the characters going to Hollywood to sell country music songs and raise money for a hospital back in Hazzard. As before, I did not want to appear in this one, but it was a job and the money was there. In May 2000, it was broadcast with all the principal cast members back, except for Denver, who had passed away in 1997. Mac Davis was the new Balladeer.

Paying tribute to Sorrell Booke during the first reunion movie are (standing behind me, left to right) writer Gy Waldron, Rick Hurst, Denver Pyle, Ben Jones, Catherine Bach, Sorrell's daughter Alexandra, Tom Wopat, John Schneider, producer Skip Ward, and Sonny Shroyer.

There were lots of things that did not work about the second movie, but it was palatable. Fans were nice about it, and once again, it did well in the ratings.

After that success and with the growing popularity of the show in reruns, the movie moguls and young guns in Hollywood decided they wanted their shot at the *Dukes of Hazzard* franchise. They decided to make an updated version with an all-new cast. I knew they would mess it up. I heard from Ben Jones, who had seen the script. He told me it was just awful. They were using bad language, dope, and all kinds of stuff.

Ben went on a public campaign to protest how the new movie was trashing the wholesomeness of the original series and characters. I have never seen the movie and do not plan to. I have seen just little snippets in trailers, read reviews, and heard fans talk about it. It was universally panned. This old dog could smell that stinker a mile away. I was really disappointed that Willie Nelson agreed to play Uncle Jesse, and Burt Reynolds, of all people, played a skinny Boss Hogg. I am sure the money was right, so I cannot criticize my friend for taking what I am sure was a good payday for him. But I was personally disappointed to think of

Back in the saddle again as "Boss Rosco" in the second reunion movie.

my old friend, one of the all-time, movie titans, in such a sorry movie. The film was ranked as the worst movie of the year by several critics and organizations.

In 2007, Warner Bros. produced *The Dukes of Hazzard: The Beginning*, a prequel to the other stories. It had yet another new cast, except that Willie Nelson was back as Uncle Jesse. The film apparently was so bad that even the studio bosses knew they could not release it in the-aters. It went straight to DVD, and from what I hear, bombed there, too. I was sad that a whole slice of Americana like the original series could be exploited at will. I was not so much bothered that the studio sought ways to extend the franchise and make money. That was their right. How-ever, they could have been creative enough to do it with integrity and keep it wholesome, family entertainment. I sugarcoat my opinion about these two movies because my publisher cannot print words that express my true feelings.

CHAPTER 29

Off Camera and On Vinyl and Canvas

I cannot sing or really play a guitar, but when I was acting with Gene Autry's company, I got friendly with Dave Burgess, one of the producers for Gene's record companies, Challenge Records and 4 Star Records. Dave is a great songwriter and guitar player. He was a founding member of The Champs, who produced "Tequila" and other song hits from the late 1950s to the mid-1960s. A young Glen Campbell played rhythm guitar with the group for a little while in the late 1950s. Jimmy Seals and Dash Crofts (later Seals and Crofts) were also in the group for a few years.

Dave Burgess and I were fishing buddies, and we were out fishing one time when I said, "Dave, I write a little bit of poetry now and then."

Dave said, "Well, let me see some of it."

So, I showed him some of my poems. He found some that he liked and set them to music. I knew nothing about music, but I went down to the recording studio and watched Jerry Wallace cut my song. Then lo and behold, Dave got one of my songs cut by Lefty Frizzell, and then Ricky Nelson used a couple for one of his albums, which tickled me to death.

At music recording sessions, I was unaccustomed to the different talents at work. Musicians sat there and called out numbers, and the next thing I knew, they were playing the tune. I do not know how musicians do that. I am not sure I would understand it even if someone explained it to me. I was amazed to see them play instruments that blended so beautifully without even a real rehearsal. That is a talent I wish I had.

Dave and Deon, his wife, made me godfather to David, their son. Deon was an accomplished dancer in Hollywood. She appeared in several movies with Elvis Presley, and she performed in *The Music Man*. She and Jobee were good friends. Later, she became a fine, Native American subject artist. In 2001, she and I staged a successful art show in Nashville, and I was honored to show my paintings with her.

I am sorry that Dave no longer speaks to me. He listened to someone with a drinking problem tell untrue stories about me, claiming untruthfully that I had bypassed Dave for my own selfish desires. The man totally misinterpreted a phrase I had used, and I have never been able to convince Dave to hear my side of the story. I hope he reads this book and reconsiders our friendship, which should be renewed. Life is too short to hold grudges — especially those based on a false claim.

I guess I always wanted to draw or paint, even as a young boy in grade school. I never had lessons or the opportunity to take them during the Depression when money was better spent on food and clothing. In grade school, during some of my more boring classes, I had a tendency to draw cars, airplanes, and shapely girls not unlike some of the famous "Vargas Girls" pinups. Teachers discouraged that sort of activity and strongly encouraged me to put my mind to more productive activities.

When I was in high school, we chose some of our subjects. I liked pretty girls, and since there were some pretty girls in the art class, I took art. I did not know anything about art and did not really care much about it except for all the pretty girls. The art teacher threw me out of the class when she found out that I was insincere about learning how to draw and paint. My philosophy is that the Good Lord does not put limitations on people when they are a little bitty baby. In other words, we all have the necessary equipment — with some obvious and sometimes unfortunate exceptions — to be successful at the same tasks. We start out on basically equal footing. Along the way, some of us learn how to walk forward, but some of us try to do everything backwards and fall on our butts.

In 1964, I was fortunate to be walking the right way along a street in North Hollywood. I passed an art gallery, dropped in, and immediately noticed some people painting in the back of the gallery.

"What's going on?" I asked.

The gallery owner said, "We rent easels here for $3 a night. You can slop as much paint as you want and you won't stink up your own house with turpentine."

I got to thinking about what he said, and I recalled the art teacher throwing me out of class. I knew I could paint if I wanted to, and by golly, pretty girls or not, I wanted to. I went in there, bought a canvas and some cheap brushes and cheap paint, and I started slinging paint. The gallery owners, a husband and wife, were both professional painters, and they patiently observed my efforts.

After I had been slinging paint there regularly for about a month, the owner told me, "Mr. Best, you're either going to be one of the best painters in the world, or the worst because you have absolutely no discipline."

I said, "I don't even know what you're talking about. What discipline? I've had no instruction, so I can't be disciplined one way or another."

He began to show me a few little brushstrokes. Before long, I started to develop some actual technique. After about four or five months, I completed a fairly large painting, a landscape of an old house back in the South. That was great with the gallery because they got to sell me the paint. All of us burgeoning artists thought our paintings were special, so we had our paintings framed. It took me a while to get to that point, but I finally thought this one painting was not too bad. I left it there to dry and I told the gallery owner, "When it dries, please frame it for me."

A few days later, he came to me and said, "Do you want to sell that painting?"

"Are you kidding?" I asked, totally shocked.

He assured me he was not kidding. A woman had been by the gallery and liked the painting. "I can get $500 for it," he said.

I said, "I don't know. My little girls love the painting. They've already told me they want to keep it. I'm sorry, but I can't sell it."

He said, "Do you mind if I paint a copy of it to sell?"

I didn't know anything about such things, so I just said, "Sure, go ahead." I didn't think anything about it.

I was painting quite a bit, and I took a class from a Japanese artist. Unfortunately for me, he went back to Japan, and I never got to study any more with him. At least I got to see what watercolor could do on a piece of paper. I continued to paint and experiment with different styles and media. One day, Jobee and I drove by a parking lot in front of a drugstore where there were four or five artists showing their paintings.

Jobee said, "Jimmie, your paintings are as good as those."

I said, "You've got to be kidding. Those are professional artists."

When we got home, she grabbed three of my paintings and took them back down to the parking lot. About a half an hour later, she came back with money in her hand. I said, "Whoa!"

I immediately went down and talked to those people. They said I could show my work with them and told me where they were going to be showing next. All I had to do was give them a percentage of whatever I sold. That sounded fine to me. Not entirely believing that folks would pay for one of my paintings — and still hearing echoes from my boyhood art teacher — I sold paintings for $35 to $50. It was gratify-

With Firecreek, *one of my personal favorites of my original oil paintings.*

ing that somebody wanted to buy something into which I put my heart and soul, but I've come to wish that I had those paintings back.

I developed a genuine interest in becoming an artist. I started painting with serious intention. I sold paintings to friends and celebrities, including Jerry Lewis, Burt Reynolds, Lucie Arnaz, who has three of them, and a lot of folks associated with *The Dukes of Hazzard*.

I visited my hometown a few years after I started painting and sold one of my paintings to the very art teacher who tossed me out of her class back in high school. That was sort of a sweet revenge. The real reason I started painting was to prove that I could draw and paint, as well as to contentiously demonstrate to my art teacher that she was right at the time, but ultimately wrong.

The Internet has become the world's largest art gallery, and my Internet sales to customers from all over the world are great. I met Scott Romine when he was a police officer during one of my personal appearances. He is an ardent *Dukes of Hazzard* fan, and we became immediate friends. He is always full of fun and has a personality that few can resist. He is married to a lovely lady named Kori. Scott is talented in many different ways,

Hanging out in the hood with my friend Scott Romine.

including painting. He and I collaborate on paintings of the *General Lee* that have been quite popular at *Dukes of Hazzard* events and on eBay. I paint the landscapes, and Scott paints the portrait of the *General Lee*. They have become collector's items for many fans.

Scott also designs and maintains my web sites. I am proud to say that I get nothing but compliments from the fans all over the world. Scott is a remarkable man, and I am proud to call him a true friend.

Few people doubt that I am a twelve-year-old in an eighty-two-year-old body. I refuse to act old. I play combat games with young gamers all over the world, but the most fun I have is when Scott and I team up against any and all comers in the *Battlefield 2* game. Scott professionally flies the helicopters in the game, and I am his gunner. I have tried to fly the helicopters, but I am constantly going upside down and crashing. I stick to what I know best. If anybody is interested in playing, you will find

Scott and me playing under the battle name "GrimReaper2226." Bring it on! When I finish playing an extremely competitive game online with a bunch of young gamers, I always type, "Thank you for letting this old man kick your butt."

They invariably type back to me, "How old are you?

I laugh and type back, "82 and counting."

Then, they type back, "There isn't any way an eighty-two-year-old man can kick our butts like that."

I type back, "Not only did I do it, but I am also Rosco P. Coltrane from *The Dukes of Hazzard*."

They type back something like, "Sure you are, and I'm Daisy Duke." Scott gets a real kick out of that.

We made a DVD on a trip down to Conyers, Georgia, where we shot the first five episodes of *The Dukes of Hazzard* series. I drove my patrol car and dressed just like Rosco. We had a ball and did some crazy things that only Rosco could get away with. It is a funny DVD. It also has some footage of our home and life in Hickory, North Carolina.

In 2006, we moved to Hickory after having lived in Florida for twenty years. After experiencing four hurricanes in a row, all while I was having excruciating pain from a kidney stone, Dorothy and I decided that the Good Lord was telling us to get the hell out of Dodge. Dorothy designed a beautiful new home, which has an art studio where I create my paintings.

More than any other subject matter, I seem to be drawn to rural landscapes. I paint ponds, streams, forests, and mountains, and I often include an old barn or shack in there somewhere. I try to capture on canvas part of my childhood when I was raised in a small town surrounded by trees and clear, sparkling creeks and springs. I find inspiration in those rural settings.

I also paint scenes where I think the fish might like to hang out. I remember the fishing trips with my father when we waded in the streams in the fall with all the splendor of colored leaves washing about our feet. I have painted those memories many times, and I guess I am never happier than when I face a chalk-white canvas and fill it with the brilliant colors of those memories.

Painting takes me home again.

CHAPTER 30

Write and Wrong in Hollywood

In the mid-1980s, after leaving Hollywood again, I began concentrating more on writing. I had been writing quite a few years, but had not pushed it. One of the themes of some of my writing was the old chain gangs that I had heard stories about years earlier when I was jailed for vagrancy and starting a fire in the Georgia city park. My fellow prisoners had told me all those horror stories about the old chain gangs, and those stories stuck with me.

Back in the 1960s, I wrote *The Heaviest Chain,* a one-act play created for my acting class. The story followed a guy trying to escape from a chain gang. The warden's wife was enamored of him and tried to help him escape.

Burt Reynolds happened to be sitting in on my class, and he later told me, "Jimmie, you ought to write that into a screenplay."

I wrote a full script called *Sweatin' Blood and Doin' Time.* I was very happy with it, and I still think it is one of the best scripts I have ever written. That sounds conceited, but I honestly think it is good. I put an offer on the front page of the script. The offer was $1,000 to anybody who read twenty pages and put it down. Nobody has ever asked me for a dime.

I took *Sweatin' Blood and Doin' Time* to people I knew at Warner Bros. One producer friend read it and said, "Oh my."

Hearing the concern in his voice, I asked, "What?"

He said, "I wish we had read this script several months ago."

"Why is that? I asked with concern in my own voice.

He said, "Well, we just signed Paul Newman to do a movie called *Cool Hand Luke,* and yours is a better script.

I said, "Well, can you do mine later?"

He said he could not. Meanwhile, the writer of *Cool Hand Luke* somehow heard about my script and I was barred from the *Cool Hand Luke* set.

I had no intention of crying to Paul and saying, "They won't let me on the set." I did not do that sort of thing, but I knew that I had something good with that script, and other people did, too.

Around 1971, I was working on a television show for Four Star, at the old Republic Pictures studio, where producer Marty Rackin had his production office. He was with Four Star Productions and also was head of the production department at Paramount for several years. He had produced, written, or directed some portion of over a hundred movies during his career. He knew his way around the movie business, and he knew what worked.

I boldly went up to Mr. Rackin's office, and he welcomed me. I said, "Mr. Rackin, listen…"

He cut me off, "You got the part, didn't you?"

I said, "Oh, yes sir, I got the part. Thank you. But I'm not here about that." As the words came from my mouth, I looked at his desk and saw that he had a stack of about two dozen scripts. I thought, *"Good grief. Well, I'm into the fat now, so I'll just go ahead and talk about it."*

I said, "Mr. Rackin, I want to ask a favor. I know you're a very busy man, but you'd be doing me a great favor if you'd get somebody whose opinion you trust to read a script that I have written. I think it's a good script, and I'd love for them to give you a comment on it."

He said, "Jimmie, you've done good acting jobs for me for many years. I'm a very prolific reader. I read about three scripts a week. I tell you what — I'll read it myself."

Stunned by his generosity, I thanked him profusely and floated from his office on a cloud. An hour and a half later, my agent called me and said, "Mr. Rackin wants to option your script with his own money."

I was astounded. Marty Rackin never optioned any script with his own money. He always used other people's money. That was his rule, but he told my agent that this was one of the finest scripts he had read in five years. He said, "I want to do this movie." He said that he was tied up working on *The Revengers* with William Holden and Ernest Borgnine and was spending a lot of time in England, where the film was being scored. It was less expensive to shoot and score films outside the United States, and Marty's job as producer was to find ways to make money on his films.

He said, "When I get back, I'm going to get this on the boards." He optioned my script for six months for $5,000.

He came back to Los Angeles and told me, "Jimmie, I'm still tied up on some other projects, so I can't get to yours yet. I want another six months."

I said, "That's fine." I knew he really wanted to do the picture. He gave me another $5,000, which was a fortune to me at that time. When the second option was about to expire, Mr. Rackin had a heart attack. He called me and said, "I've had a heart attack and I need another option."

I said, "Mr. Rackin, I'm not going to charge you any more money for an option. You can't help that you had a heart attack."

He said, "No, Jimmie, don't worry about it. I want an option for another six months."

He paid another $5,000, but with his heart condition, Mr. Rackin was never able to produce my script. *Sweatin' Blood and Doin' Time* reverted back to me. He passed away a few years later.

There I was with an admired script that I could not get anyone to read. I was still confident about the script. If a man like Marty Rackin, who had read all those scripts through the years and had written and produced countless movies, liked my script so much, then that was a good indication that I really had something.

A little while later, I was back home in Mississippi, when I got a phone call from a producer. He said, "We've heard about *Sweatin' Blood and Doin' Time*. We want to buy it."

I said, "What kind of money are we talking about?"

He said, "$75,000."

I said, "I'm sorry, but no."

Two or three days later, he called back and said, "We'll give you $100,000."

I said, "No. The thing is that I still believe that someday this script will set me free." I still own *Sweatin' Blood and Doin' Time*.

In *Sweatin' Blood and Doin' Time*, I have a scene about a chain gang. The lead man in the chain gang is a big black gentleman. He is the chanter, the one who calls out the cadence for the guys to swing those picks and drive the steel spikes into railroad ties. They do it all day in the blistering sun. If one does not have a time to expel his breath in a grunt, his body locks up and he dies from exhaustion, so exhaling in a cadence relaxes his muscles for a few seconds in between strokes. It was a great privilege to be a chanter. He makes up the lyrics that are not unlike modern-day rap. I think chain gang music was the original rap because the gang told news about their loved ones, or how the system treated them badly, or how they wanted to get off the chain someday.

In my script, I include the chant for the chanter. I open the scene with darkness, and then follow with a swinging sledgehammer driving a spike into some wood and the cry of the chanter.

> *No use to cry, no use to beg;*
> *They'll snap the chain and break your leg.*
> *Ain't no escape, the men all say,*
> *So turn that gun another way.*
> *Five men tried and five men died;*
> *No buckshot'll tear this poor man's hide.*
> *Your back is festered from the lash;*
> *You're whipped and cursed and called just trash.*
> *Hear that cry on down the line.*
> *I am sweatin' blood and doin' time."*
> *You want a drink of water, you fall to your knees,*
> *Sayin' boss man, just a drop if you please.*
> *Then you feel a whip burn deep into your side,*
> *'Cause a price of a drink is a piece of your hide.*
> *Hear that cry on down the line;*
> *We're sweatin' blood and doin' time.*

It is that type of thing, but it is all chanted in a rhythm pattern. When he chants, "No use to cry, no use to beg; they'll snap the chain and break your leg," the reference is to the guards. They run a master chain through the leg irons of the prisoners when they are sleeping in their bunks. In the morning, a guard comes in and yanks that chain to pull the prisoners out of the bed. If a prisoner does not hit the floor quick enough and is still in his bunk, that chain pulls him out of the bunk and likely breaks his leg. I did not remember anybody telling me about that, and yet after I wrote it, I found out that was an actual fact.

Another script I have written is called *High as the Willow*. Tennessee Williams wrote a one-act play called *This Property Is Condemned* about a little girl walking along the railroad tracks. She is dressed up in her older sister's dress and is wearing fake beads. She is carrying a Raggedy Ann doll and a rotten banana. This little boy comes along, and they get to talking. The little girl says, "I'm going to be just like my sister."

The little boy asks what the girl's sister did. The little girl says, "She entertained the railroad men until she died."

I always wondered what happened to that little girl when she grew up. At the end of the play, the little girl just walks down the tracks. In my movie, I named her Bess after a girl I knew who was a lady of the night back when I lived at that fleabag hotel in New York. I found out that this little girl in my play grows up and has an illegitimate child when she is fifteen years old. She is run out of town, and her baby is put up for adoption.

The girl finds her way to New Orleans. She wants to be a dancer, but she ends up being a stripper-hooker. She finally decides that she does not want to live that life anymore. She goes back home to her small town and encounters her son, but of course she does not know he is her son. It turns out the boy has been adopted by a man who owns a bar where Bess was a waitress when she was teenager. All sorts of complications unfold. It is really a very good story. It would make a star out of a young actress. Getting it made — that is another story.

I also wrote a play called *Hell-Bent for Good Times* that takes place during the Great Depression. It is about a crotchety old guy and his wife raising their grandchildren, who are just coming of age. I called it *Hell-Bent for Good Times* because the family is really trying to get through the Depression with laughter instead of tears. We toured the play in several theaters, including the University of Central Florida, a well-known theater near Orlando called The Ice House Theater, and then in Jacksonville, Florida, and Columbia, South Carolina.

We also took it to Atlanta and Los Angeles against the big boys. We got standing ovations all the time with the play. I played the old guy, which was not a stretch, and the wonderful Peggy Stewart played my wife in the Los Angeles production. Peggy is a great actress. She was under contract to Republic Pictures and did a ton of Westerns. She is still known as Queen of the B Westerns. Unfortunately, Peg was typecast at Republic and rarely got the chance to show the full range of just how superb she is. If I ever get *Hell-Bent for Good Times* made, she will have that chance. She is marvelous in the role.

After touring the play, I adapted the story into a screenplay. Our Best Friend Films production company shot about half an hour of it as a promotional piece with our high-definition cameras. We submitted it to some film festivals, where it was always well received. It won best dramatic short at Florida's Melbourne Independent Film Festival. We eventually hope to shoot the whole film, now titled *Back Door to Heaven,* and we are working toward that goal. Of course, making a film takes lots of money, but it is a labor of love for me. If I eventually get to make the movie, what is going to happen is that the big shots who know everything there is to know about the picture business in California are going to ask me, "So what else have you got for us, old man?"

I will pull out *Sweatin' Blood and Doin' Time,* and maybe they will read some of my other scripts and say, "Where've you been all this time?" as if I have been hiding under a rock or something. That is the way they always do. It is like John Travolta. After *Saturday Night Fever* and *Grease,* he could not get anywhere. Then, he blew the doors off with *Pulp Fiction,* and all of a sudden, he was a star and they thought they discovered him all over again. A talent like Travolta was never lost, but those fools looking for lost talent sometimes just get lost in the woods while searching for it, when all the time, that great talent was right under their noses.

I would love to make Hell-Bent for Good Times *into a movie with the amazing Peggy Stewart.*

As we all know, Hollywood today is not like the old days where they listened to talent or at least respected talent. Agents and lawyers now run the town. They get a known writer who has won an Academy Award, they get a producer who has produced an award-winning picture, and then they shoot a picture for $80 million. The agent does not care whether it makes a dime. He has received 10% from the actors, the writer, and the producer. I do not believe that an agent will spend his time reading a script where he might earn only $50,000.

Dorothy cringes every time I say that Hollywood worked better when it was run by people who knew how to pick and appreciate talent. Back then, there was not so much nepotism and simply chasing after quick dollars. I am not naïve enough to think that Hollywood has not always involved money and business, but it has not always been so crass and closed. It is just a heck of a lot tougher today.

In Hell-Bent for Good Times, *I am either acting or just really tired.*

Maybe they will rediscover me as they did John Travolta. It would be nice not to go to my grave with Rosco P. Coltrane having the last word and my tombstone reading "Kee-kee-kee." I would like for it to say, "Here lies an actor," and not add, "who was overlooked when he got old."

CHAPTER 31

Family Ties

As I mentioned at the top, my birth name was Jewel Franklin Guy. My mother was an Everly. When I was a teenager, my adopted parents told me that my birth father was having a reunion with some of the family. They asked me if I wanted to go. I told them, "No, they're not my parents. You're my parents. You raised me. I have no other mother and father."

Many years later, when I got on *The Dukes of Hazzard,* I became more curious about my birth family. In 1978, I was down in Conyers, Georgia, working on *Dukes.* I had breakfast one morning with the man who owned the motel where all the cast and crew were staying. At one point, he mentioned that he was originally from Kentucky.

I said, "Really? So am I."

"We're going back there next week on a vacation trip," he told me.

"Really? Where are you going?" I asked.

He replied, "We're going to Central City."

"I was born in Powderly."

He said, "That's right where we're going."

"When you get back there, ask if anybody remembers a Guy family".

A week later, he came back and found me. He said, "Jimmie, we not only found the Guys, but we found a lady who held your mother when she died. And we found out that you have a sister in Chicago."

I got a hold of Maudie, my sister in Chicago. She told me that I had two living brothers that had never been adopted. Later, I found out that they had left the orphanage when they became too old to stay there. One of my brothers had been killed in World War II, when a sniper shot him crossing the Rhine River.

I met my sister and we had a small reunion with her family back in Kentucky. I found out that Don and Phil Everly, the Everly Brothers, are my first cousins. In 1992, the Everly Brothers were doing a big benefit concert back in Central City, and I was invited to go onstage with them. They graciously, lovingly introduced me back into the family. I have forgotten how many thousands of people were there, but they raised a lot of money. The payoff for me was that I was able to reunite with a lot of my blood relatives.

In 2004, Dorothy, Powderly Mayor Don Hancock, and I dedicated James Best Way in Powderly, Kentucky.

As nice as it was to meet my relatives, it was not quite what I had envisioned. Many of my cousins approached me with cameras and autograph books. They treated me like a celebrity, rather than like a relative. I don't know what I expected. As I reflected on the experience later, I realized that what they did was understandable. They knew me as Rosco and perhaps other roles long before they knew me as their relative.

Dukes Of Hazzard reunites show's star with family he lost at age 3

James Best with his brother John Paul Guy, who he had not seen for more than 50 years. The Dukes Of Hazzard star says a psychic experience reunited him with his long-lost family.

It was a strange experience to pick my brother out of a crowd after fifty years.

A few years before that, in 1981 at the same Black Gold Festival in Hazard, Kentucky, that I mentioned earlier, we had a parade. There was such a crowd that they called out the National Guard to walk alongside our car. Cathy Bach and I were sitting on the top of the backseat of a white convertible, as we slowly moved toward a makeshift stage that was set up as an observation area and surrounded by cameras. In a scene almost out of *This Is Your Life*, one of the officials said, "Mr. Best, would you come up here please?" They stuck cameras in my face, and then the official added, "We want you to meet your brother."

Sure enough, one of my brothers was standing there. It was the first time I ever met him. There I was in front of the cameras unsure of what to say. I was delighted and stunned. My brother and I embraced, but that was about it. I had to get back in the car because the convoy had to keep going. I met up with him again at a gathering that night. We talked for about twenty minutes. It was a nice, slightly overwhelming visit, but I never saw him again.

I had yet another first encounter with one of my brothers. This story is strange but true, as I am too old to lie. I cannot remember exactly where I was during a personal appearance, but I believe it was Memphis. Cast members from *The Dukes of Hazzard* were gathered on an outdoor stage, as we listened to a band and waited for our cue to go on. There was a fence around the backstage area because thousands of people were on the hillside and the whole area surrounding the stage.

The police had warned us not to go near the fence because people wanting autographs would lean against the fence and somebody might get hurt if the fence gave way. People could have gotten crushed. We agreed that we would stay away from the fence and the sea of faces. I looked out into that crowd and spotted a man. I walked toward him, not all the way to the fence, but fairly close.

I pointed to him and asked, "Who are you?"

"I'm your brother," he responded.

"What was my name?"

"Jewel Guy," he immediately replied.

I had the police go get him and his family and bring them backstage. Out of that whole throng of people, something inside me caused me to zero in on that one man — my brother. We talked and he got autographs and pictures. That was it.

My sister and two brothers have all since passed on, as have the brothers I never knew. It was good to make a connection, and to have a chance to acknowledge each other. Our lives were not shared lives. If not a bond, we had at least made a connection. I have seen the Everly Brothers on several occasions over the years. It's funny — I was always a big fan of them and their music. They also became big fans of *The Dukes of Hazzard.* I doubt we ever would have met if it had not been for the series. That was the thing that put me in an arena where we could cross paths and make a connection.

I'm very proud of my son, Gary.

I have also tried to mend fences with Gary, my son from my first marriage. We had become reacquainted during *The Dukes of Hazzard*. By that time, he was curious to find out what his father was really like. For my part, I wanted to show him that I was not as bad a person as he might have been led to believe. I had not been a good father to him on a personal level — as far as being a part of his daily life — but I had tried to

My beautiful granddaughter Lauren, daughter of my son, Gary, and his wife, Angela.

be the best father I could, and I had supported him financially while he was growing up.

Many years later, we both wanted a true father-son relationship that we had missed. One day in the early 1990s, I called him and told him that I wanted to take him to Canada to go fishing. He was up for a reunion trip. So, we went on this fishing trip, and we had a wonderful time together — just laughing, giggling, and having a ball. We then proceeded to get into a political discussion. We were polar opposites, and we soon realized that we were never going to have a meeting of the minds in that area. I convinced him that we should not talk about politics anymore because we might come to blows. It was that intense. We stopped talking politics and enjoyed the rest of our vacation together.

A few years later, Dorothy and I went to visit Gary, his wife Angela, and Lauren, my granddaughter, at their home in Redmond, Washington. Gary told me that he had agreed to stop talking politics with me not because he feared I might beat the crap out of him, which I could not have done, and which we both know, but out of respect. We had a good laugh about that, but we still steer clear of politics.

With or without politics, Gary and I have never quite been able to find the father-son relationship we both tried to capture. It is because we seldom have been in close enough proximity with one another for a long enough time to establish that really close bond of a father and son. We stay in touch and have a mutual love and respect for each other. He turned out to be a fine husband and father. I am very proud of him. I am fortunate to have been able to have a relationship with my son and his family, and I am truly grateful for that.

CHAPTER 32

All in the Family Business

My favorite actor on *The Dukes of Hazzard* was Dorothy Collier, who has become known as Dorothy Best. She appeared early in our second season in an episode called "The Rustlers." She was born in Beaver Dam, Wisconsin, but at age seven, she moved with her family to Los Angeles. Her parents had been a dance team in Vaudeville and later had their own show in Wisconsin. Dorothy and her brother, John, started as child actors in Los Angeles. She appeared in television shows ranging from *Leave It to Beaver* and *GE Theatre* to singing "High Hopes" in a Frank Sinatra special.

Dorothy studied theater at the acclaimed Los Angeles City College, where she received a Best Actress award. She was involved in the first Kennedy Center American College Theater Festival in 1969. She performed at Ford's Theatre in a production of *The Way of the World*. As an adult, most of her acting was in the theater. She performed in numerous productions, mostly around the Los Angeles area, which was rich with talent and competition. She received excellent reviews and was recognized with acting awards.

Dorothy eventually found that she likes producing even more than acting. She has a special talent for it. She has been a producer on virtually all of our Best Friend Films projects, and has produced theater productions. Dorothy also manages the financial side of our enterprises.

Dorothy and I are partners in all aspects of our lives together. She likes to fish, and we both are crazy about animals, especially dogs. We have raised three generations of beagles and are the proud owners of two Cavalier King Charles spaniels, Peaches 'n' Cream and Li'l Toby, and a precious beagle named Daisy Mae, who is better known as Daisy Doozy. Dorothy and I collect donations from every *General Lee* that I autograph

Above: Dorothy Collier, my future wife, appeared in the Dukes of Hazzard *episode entitled "The Rustlers" with Catherine Bach (left), Denver Pyle, and Mel Tillis (far right). Below: Dorothy and me fishing in Alaska in 1981.*

Above: In 2002, we renewed our vows on a Rhine River cruise. Below: The Best family: Dorothy and me with Peaches 'n' Cream, Li'l Toby, and Daisy Mae.

at personal appearances all across the country. We give the money to the Humane Society in Hickory. I am happy to say that those donations have so far amounted to thousands of dollars. All the animals are kept as comfortable and happy as possible until loving owners adopt them.

CHAPTER 33

Curtain Call

As I reach a ripe old age, I am unafraid to think about how little time I might have left. Folks my age start thinking, *"Maybe I've got another year or two,"* which is something I never thought about when I was young and healthy. I might die tomorrow, or I might live another twenty years, and none of us knows.

Death starts to take little bites out of all of us the moment we are born. He just nibbles a little faster on some of us than others, but the prospect of little time left does not frighten me. I do not fear death. I

In 2008, Dorothy and I appeared at a Western film festival in Winston-Salem, North Carolina.

With the Magnolia Award at the Dixie Film Festival in October 2006.

just do not want to die in pain, if I can help it. That sure would be nice to avoid. The only thing that makes me sad about having so little time left is leaving the people I love and those who love me. There are also films and other projects I still want to get done, and there are always fish that need catching.

I truly hope that you have enjoyed reading this book and journeying through my life and my experiences in Hollywood. If so, I hope you will recommend this book to your friends. If I have overlooked some people and experiences, the slights are unintended.

I can be blunt and even a bit raw in the way I express things, but I have earnestly tried to entertain and enlighten people about glorious Hollywood in its heyday. I lived it, and I loved it, but now I neither live nor love it. Hope springs eternal, and perhaps Hollywood will someday return to her rightful glory with great stories, talent, and leaders that rely on decent, well-written, and well-acted movies that the world craves and certainly deserves.

Even if only my dearest friends and relatives read this book, it has fulfilled a very important dream of mine. I have written this with the hope that it might encourage some young or aging hopefuls who strongly wish to participate in the entertainment business. They should give it a try as a full-time occupation. Even though a career in show business is one of the most rewarding a person can follow, it is also one of the most merciless businesses. It takes immense courage to survive. I hope Dorothy and I will continue to find that courage as we work to make movies that are well received by those desiring quality entertainment without the necessity of excessive violence, special effects, and vulgarity. We know there is a large audience starved for wholesome movies, and Hollywood has ignored them far too long.

I will also continue to thank God every day for the opportunity to have been a small part of an often glorious industry that has brought laughter and tears of joy to this troubled old world. I have recently received three lifetime achievement awards: The Jimmy Stewart Museum's "Harvey" Award, The Magnolia Award from the Dixie Film Festival, and the Crystal Reel Award from the Florida Motion Picture and Television Association (FMPTA). I am appreciative of those honors, but I have no intention of hanging it up. I do not want to rest on laurels of any kind just because I am getting old.

While I have never been a regular church-going person, I have always tried to remember the Ten Commandments and the Golden Rule, and to live a Christian life. I know there is Someone greater than us in this old universe. While I may never fully grasp God, I strive for that understanding and I am grateful for the life I have been given. Not understanding something, but still believing in it — I suppose that is called faith.

Thinking along those lines led me to write the following poem in about ten minutes. I think it is a good way to end this book. It is my version of an exclamation point. Here it is with my thanks for reading what I have had to say. God be willing, maybe I will touch my rainbow just one more time before He takes my hand and leads me into eternity.

The Breath of God

The warm and gentle breeze
That shakes the brilliant autumn leaves—
Could this be the breath of God?
And the wind that blows and causes
The breaking waves of the Emerald Sea,
I just wonder sometimes, could it be?
The breath of God?
A little child's kite against the bright blue sky.
I just wonder, what really makes it fly?
Could it be the breath of God?
And what holds up my plane so it can fly?
What could it be? I wonder why.
Could it be the breath of God?
We all have felt the touch of a gentle breeze,
And seen its strength against the trees.
But we cannot see or smell the wind,
But know its strength when strong trees bend.
It is a simple faith we all can share
To know that God is always there.
For so many times, He tries to say,
Just follow me. I know the way.

I show that I've still got my quick-draw at the Sonora Western Film Festival.

A Few of My Favorite Poems
I Have Written

Summer Storm A-Comin'

There's a summer storm a-comin',
But it doesn't mean a thing.
Been quite a few these past few months,
But it never brings no rain.

Summer storm a-comin'.
You can always tell,
When the hot wind starts to blowin'
Like it's comin' up from hell.

The old sun beats down on my dry land,
With its hot and fiery breath.
It's doin' its best to burn us out,
And starve us half to death.

It's been many and many a month
Since this county has had some rain.
My farm is parched and plum bone dry,
Where once stood rich, ripe grain.

I just don't know which way to turn;
My land's all cracked and dry.
And all we own is a rusty old plow,
Since the mule, he up and died.

It sure does make a man feel helpless
When there ain't nothin' he can do right now.
Ain't no use plantin' the fields again;
There ain't nothin' goin' grow no how.

Summer storm a-comin';
It ain't goin' to bring no rain.
Only thing a-fallin' are my children's tears,
Makin' streaks down a dusty window pane.

I lie awake most every night,
And no matter how they try,
My children, they cannot fool me;
They're hungry — that's why they cry.

I don't mind goin' hungry,
'Cause I been hungry many times before.
But it's sure hard to tell the little ones
There just ain't no food no more.

Summer storm a-comin',
But its just passin' time.
And I just cannot help but wonder,
If heaven's forsaken this land of mine.

But my little ones, they stand and watch it,
And always pray a might.
God have mercy on us below,
And bring us rain tonight.

Summer storm is a-leavin' now;
It's going to pass us right on by.
I got to turn my head away;
Children shouldn't see their Daddy cry.

But God in all his mercy,
Saw the tears I could not hide.
And he touched my cheeks with raindrops,
And they never knew I cried.

I'll never forget that summer storm,
And the lesson I learned that day,
Taught me by my little children,
When they taught me how to pray.

Crown of Thorns

The cross you carry may seem to get heavier,
With every step you take.
And your eye is dry from the tears you cry,
When you thought your heart would break.

Something deep inside of you,
A restless feeling warns,
To be a king among humble men,
You must first wear the Crown of Thorns.

While the cold wind blows about you,
And you stand alone in tattered rags,
Let your love be the warmth for others,
When the faltering spirit sags.

Don't let the burden bend your back;
Grab this old world by the horns,
And join the very few who have
The courage to wear the Crown of Thorns.

Blind Greed

I had heard it said so many times,
That money rules the earth,
And I was in complete
Accord until my baby's birth,

It was then that my attitude changed,
About my greed and hate and strife,
And looking about me, I was soon to learn,
I was missing half of life.

My eyes were blinded by my greed,
And the material things I sought —
Judging my friends and foes alike,
By their money and what it bought.

But now I have learned a lesson,
For many wealthy men I have known,
Who never really lived at all
And left this old earth alone.

How many rich folks are there,
When upon their sick bed lie,
And plead for another chance at life,
And cannot bribe death, and die.

This last poem is a very special gift for all my loving family and friends.

Do Not Weep

I stand at the door to eternity,
And like so very many of my friends
and loved ones,
Soon I too must pass through those dark portals.

My passing is but a moment of
God's heavenly plan,
So I do not fear, for it is the passage
To another experience and a door that
All must pass through at some time
in this mortal existence.

But all must walk through it alone.
Although my life has been a journey
of love and laughter,
Do not stand at my grave and weep,
For I am not there; I do not sleep.

I am with you in the bright sunny days
And flaming orange sunsets,
The white bellows of foam that crash
Against the ragged shores.

And I am with you as you walk
In the soft white sands of time.
I ride the wind that shakes the trees,
And cools the fevered brow.

I am the diamond's glint
on fresh fallen snow,
I am the sunlight on golden ripe grain.
I am the flash of red on "Old Glory,"
I am the high clear note of a whippoorwill
calling to its mate.

Do not weep for I do not sleep,
For I am always with you.
Now and forever. And with my love
and memory,
You will never walk alone.

Selected Filmography

Compiled by Nel Williams

Movies

Year	Title	Character
2007	*Moondance Alexander*	McClancy
2006	*Hot Tamale*	Hank Larson
2006	*Once Not Far From Home*	The Doctor
2004	*House of Forever*	William Clancy
1998	*Death Mask*	Wilbur Johnson
1998	*Finders Keepers*	John Massey
1997	*Raney*	Uncle Nate
1978	*Hooper*	Cully
1978	*The End*	Pacemaker patient
1977	*Rolling Thunder*	Texan
1977	*The Brain Machine*	Rev. Emory Neill
1976	*Gator*	(Uncredited)
1976	*Nickelodeon*	Jim
1976	*Ode to Billy Joe*	Dewey Barksdale
1972	*Sounder*	Sheriff Young
1968	*Firecreek*	Drew
1967	*First to Fight*	Sgt. Carnavan
1966	*Three on a Couch*	Dr. Ben Mizer
1965	*Black Spurs*	Sheriff Elkins
1965	*Shenandoah*	Carter (Rebel soldier)
1964	*The Quick Gun*	Sheriff Scotty Wade
1963	*Shock Corridor*	Stuart
1962	*Black Gold*	Jericho Larkin

1960 *The Mountain Road* .... Niergaard

1959 *Cast A Long Shadow* .... Sam Mullen

1959 *Ride Lonesome* .... Billy John

1959 *The Killer Shrews* .... Thorne Sherman

1959 *Verboten!* .... Sgt. David Brent

1958 *Cole Younger, Gunfighter* .... Kit Caswell

1958 *The Left-Handed Gun* .... Tom Folliard

1958 *The Naked and the Dead* .... Rhidges

1957 *Hot Summer Night* .... Kermit

1957 *Last of the Badmen* .... Ted Hamilton

1957 *Man on the Prowl* .... Doug Gerhardt

1956 *Calling Homicide* .... Det. Arnie Arnhoff

1956 *Come Next Spring* .... Bill Jackson

1956 *Forbidden Planet* .... Crewman *(Uncredited)*

1956 *Gaby* .... Jim

1956 *The Rack* .... Millard Chilson Cassidy

1956 *When Gangland Strikes* .... Jerry Ames *(Uncredited)*

1955 *A Man Called Peter* .... Man with Jane at youth rally *(Uncredited)*

1955 *Seven Angry Men* .... Jason Brown

1955 *The Eternal Sea* .... Student

1955 *Top of the World* .... Major French's Orderly *(Uncredited)*

1954 *Return From the Sea* .... Barr

1954 *Riders to the Stars* .... Sidney K. Fuller

1954 *The Caine Mutiny* .... Lt. J.G. Jorgensen *(Uncredited)*

1954 *The Raid* .... Lt. Robinson

1954 *The Yellow Tomahawk* .... Private Bliss

1954 *They Rode West* .... Lt. Finlay *(Uncredited)*

1953 *City of Bad Men* .... Gig *(Uncredited)*

1953 *Column South* .... Primrose

1953 *Seminole* .... Cpl. Gerard

1953 *The Beast from 20,000 Fathoms* ..... Charlie — Radar man *(Uncredited)*

1953 *The President's Lady* .... Samuel Donaldson *(Uncredited)*

1952 *About Face* .... Hal's Roommate

1952 *Flat Top* .... Radio Operator *(Uncredited)*

1952 *Francis Goes to West Point* .... Cpl. Ransom

1952 *Ma and Pa Kettle at the Fair* .... Marvin Johnson

1952 *Steel Town* .... Joe Rakich

1952 *The Battle at Apache Pass* .... Cpl. Hassett

1952 *The Cimarron Kid*............................Bittercreek Dalton
1951 *Air Cadet* ....Jerry Connell
1951 *Apache Drums*.......................................Bert Keon
1951 *Target Unknown*............................ Sgt. Ralph Phelps
1950 *Comanche Territory*..Sam
1950 *I Was a Shoplifter* ... Police broadcaster in surveillance plane *(Uncredited)*
1950 *Kansas Raiders*................................... Cole Younger
1950 *One Way Street* .... Driver *(Uncredited)*
1950 *Peggy*..Frank Addison
1950 *Winchester '73*...Crater

Television

Year	Title, Episode	Character

2000 *The Dukes of Hazzard: Hazzard In Hollywood* (TV movie)
....Rosco P. Coltrane
1997 *The Dukes of Hazzard: Reunion!* (TV movie) ....Rosco P. Coltrane
1991 *In the Heat of the Night* "Sweet, Sweet Blue".........Nathan Bedford
1990 *B.L. Stryker* "Night Train"....................................
1983 *The Dukes* .... Sheriff Rosco P. Coltrane *(voice)*
1980 *Enos* "Grits and Greens Strike Again"........Sheriff Rosco P. Coltrane
1979-1985 *The Dukes of Hazzard* (141 episodes)...Sheriff Rosco P. Coltrane
1979 *Centennial* "The Scream of Eagles"................... Hank Garvey
1979 *How the West Was Won* "Luke"..................... Sheriff Gruner
1977 *McLaren's Riders* (TV Movie)...................... Lamarr Skinner
1976 *The Savage Bees* (TV Movie) .... Deputy Mayor Pelligrino
1975 *The Runaway Barge* (TV Movie) .... Bingo Washington
1974 *Savages* (TV Movie) .... Sheriff Bert Hamilton
1973 *Hawkins* "Blood Feud" ....
1970 *Dan August* "In the Eyes of God".........................Wiley
1970 *Lancer* "Goodbye, Lizzie" ....Clayt
1970 *Run, Simon, Run* (TV Movie) ....Henry Burroughs
1969 *The Guns of Will Sonnett* "Robber's Roost".............. Harley Bass
1969 *Gunsmoke* "Charlie Noon".........................Charlie Noon
1968 *Bonanza* "The Price of Salt" .... Sheriff Vern Schaler
1968 *Felony Squad* "The Distant Shore"...........George 'Lucky' Collins
1968 *I Spy* "Suitable For Framing".........................The Doctor
1968 *The Mod Squad* "The Price of Terror".................Frank Lynch
1967 *The Guns of Will Sonnett* "Meeting at Devil's Fork".......Rake Hanley

1966 *Felony Squad* "Flame Out" . . . . Arnold Wyatt

1966 *The Green Hornet* "Deadline for Death". . . . . Yale Barton

1966 *Hawk* "Blind Man's Bluff" . . . . Emile

1966 *I Spy* "Lisa" . . . . Sam

1966 *The Iron Horse* "High Devil" . . . . Chico

1966 *Perry Mason* "The Case of the Unwelcome Well" . . . . . . Allan Winford

1965 *Ben Casey* "A Little Fun to Match the Sorrow". . . . . . . Dr. Joe Sullivan

1965 *Amos Burke, Secret Agent* "Steam Heat". . . . . Tucson, "The Cowboy"

1965 *Daniel Boone* "The Devil's Four" . . . . Jethroe Wyatt

1965 *Flipper* "The Call of the Dolphin". . . . . Dr. Peter Kellwin

1965 *Honey West* "A Matter of Wife and Death". . . . . Vince Zale

1965 *The Men from Shiloh* "Letter of the Law". . . . . Curt Westley

1964 *The Alfred Hitchcock Hour* "The Jar" . . . . Tom Carmody

1964 *Combat!* "Mail Call" . . . . Trenton

1964 *Death Valley Days* "Hero of Fort Halleck". . . . . Jim Campbell

1964 *Death Valley Days* "Sixty-Seven Miles of Gold" . . . . Jimmy Burns

1964 *Destry* "Go Away, Little Sheba". . . . . Curly Beamer

1964 *Gunsmoke* "The Glory and the Mud". . . . . Sam Beal

1964 *Rawhide* "Incident at El Toro" . . . .

1963 *Ben Casey* "Six Impossible Things Before Breakfast". . . . . Simon Waller

1963 *Bonanza* "The Legacy" . . . . Page

1963 *The Fugitive* "Terror at High Point" . . . . Dan

1963 *The Gallant Men* "The Warriors" . . . . Pvt. Hook

1963 *G.E. True* "Open Season" . . . . Ernie Swift

1963 *Gunsmoke* "With a Smile". . . . . Dal Creed

1963 *Perry Mason* "The Case of the Surplus Suitor" . . . . Martin Potter

1963 *Rawhide* "Incident of the Rawhiders". . . . . Brock Quade

1963 *Rawhide* "Incident at Spider Rock". . . . . Willie Cain

1963 *Redigo* "Little Angel Blue Eyes" . . . . Les Fay

1963 *Temple Houston*. . . . . Gotch

1963 *Twilight Zone* "Jess-Belle". Billy-Ben Turner

1962 *Bronco* "Then the Mountains" . . . . Banton

1962 *Cheyenne* "Sweet Sam". . . . .

1962 *Cheyenne* "Satonka". . . . . Ernie Riggins

1962 *Death Valley Days* "The $275,000 Sack of Flour". . . . . . . Ruel Gridley

1962 *Hawaiian Eye* "Day in the Sun" . . . . Johnny Olin

1962 *Laramie* "The Runaway" . . . . Johnny Best

1962 *The Rifleman* "The Day a Town Slept". . . . . Bob Barrett

1962 *77 Sunset Strip* "The Long Shot Caper" . . . . Babe Mackie

1962 *The Twilight Zone* "The Last Rites of Jeff Myrtlebank" . . Jeff Myrtlebank

1961 *Alfred Hitchcock Presents* "Make My Death Bed". . . . . Bish Darby

1961 *The Andy Griffith Show* "The Guitar Player Returns". . . . . . Jim Lindsey

1961 *The Barbara Stanwyck Show* "The Choice". . . . . Joe

1961 *Bonanza* "The Fugitive". . . . . Carl Reagan

1961 *Have Gun, Will Travel* "Quiet Night in Town: Pt. 1 & 2" . . . Roy Smith

1961 *Michael Shayne* "Strike Out". . . . . Danny

1961 *Stagecoach West* "The Dead Don't Cry" . . . . .Mike Pardee

1961 *Stagecoach West* "The Arsonist". . . . . .Jack Craig

1961 *Surfside 6* "One for the Road". . . . . .Ernie Jordan

1961 *The Twilight Zone* "The Grave" . . . . Johnny Rob

1961 *Whispering Smith* "The Hemp Reeger Case". . . . . .Hemp Reeger

1960 *Alfred Hitchcock Presents* "Cell 227" . . . . Hennessy

1960 *The Andy Griffith Show* "The Guitar Player" . . . . Jim Lindsey

1960 *Bat Masterson* "Dakota Showdown" . . . . Danny Dakota

1960 *G.E. True Theater* "Aftermath". . . . . .Hardy Couter

1960 *Laramie* "Company Man". . . . . Ben Leach

1960 *Lock Up* "The Beau and Arrow Case" . . . . .Roy

1960 *Men Into Space* "Beyond the Stars" . . . . Lt. John Leonard

1960 *Overland Trail* "Escort Detail" . . . . Frank Cullen

1960 *Pony Express* "The Story of Julesberg". . . . . Bart Gentry

1960 *The DuPont Show with June Allyson* "Love on Credit" . . Jovan Wilanskov

1960 *The Rebel* "Death Watch". . . . . Waares

1960 *The Rebel* "Night on a Rainbow" . . . . Ted Evans

1960 *Stagecoach West* "High Lonesome". . . . . .Les Hardeen

1960 *The Texan* "Killer's Road". . . . . Clay Kirby

1960 *Wagon Train* "The Clayton Tucker Story". . . . . Art Bernard

1960 *Wagon Train* "The Colonel Harris Story" . . . . Bowman Lewis

1959 *Black Saddle* "Client: Nelson". . . . . Ben Travers

1959 *The David Niven Show* "Good Deed" . . . . Frank Simms

1959 *The David Niven Show* "Portrait" . . . . Private Boland

1959 *Laramie* "The Lawbreakers". . . . . .Dallas

1959 *The Lineup* "Lonesome as Midnight" .Rhodes

1959 *The Man and the Challenge* "Maximum Capacity". . . . . . David Mallory

1959 *Rescue 8* "Trail By Fire". . . . . Chad Kern

1959 *Startime* "Cindy's Fella". . . . . Duke

1959 *Wagon Train* "The Andrew Hale Story" . . . . Garth English

1959 *Wanted: Dead or Alive* "Six-Up to Bannach" . . . . Luke Perry

1958 *Alfred Hitchcock Presents* "Death Sentence" . . . . Norman Frayne

1958 *Bat Masterson* "Stampede at Tent City". . . . . Joe Best

1958 *Behind Closed Doors* "The Enemy on the Flank" . . . . Webb

1958 *Climax Mystery Theater* "The Secret Love of Johnny Spain" . . . . . . Shag

1958 *The Millionaire* "The Fred Morgan Story". . . . . Fred Morgan

1958 *The Restless Gun* "Jebediah Bonner". . . . . Jim Kenyon

1958 *Schlitz Playhouse of Stars* "Guys Like O'Malley" . . . .

1958 *Target* "Assassin" . . . .

1958 *Trackdown* "Sunday's Child". . . . . Joe Sunday

1958 *Trackdown* "The Mistake". . . . . .Bob Ahler

1958 *Tombstone Territory* "Guilt of a Town". . . . . Matt Porter

1958 *Wanted: Dead or Alive* "Sheriff of Red Rock". . . . . .Stoner

1957 *Code 3* "Death in an Alley" . . . . Arkansas Trueblood

1957 *Have Gun, Will Travel* "The Long Night". . . . . Andy Fisher

1957 *Richard Diamond, Private Detective* "Merry-Go-Round Case"

. . . . Jack Milhoan

1957 *Sheriff of Cochise* "Lynching Party" . . . . Mike Norris

1957 *Trackdown* "Marple Brothers" . . . . Rand Marple

1957 *West Point* "Dragoon Patrol" . . . . William Purdom

1957 *Zane Grey Theater* "Three Graves". . . . . Pyke Dillon

1956 *The Adventures of Champion* "Andrew and the Deadly Double". . . . .

1956 *Cavalcade of America* "Women's Work" . . . . .Slate Morley

1956 *Crossroads* "Anatole of the Bayous" . . . .

1956 *Frontier* "Out From Texas" . . . . Jason Cartwright

1956 *Frontier* "The Texicans". . . . . Ben Reed

1956 *Red Ryder* "Gun Trouble Valley". . . . . Perry Cochran

1956 *Telephone Time* "The Gingerbread Man". . . . . .American Soldier

1955 *The Adventures of Champion* "The Stone Heart" . . . . .Paul Kenyon

1955 *The Adventures of Kit Carson* "The Phantom Uprising" . . . .

1955 *Buffalo Bill, Jr.* "The Death of Johnny Ringo" Telegrapher Larry Martin

1955 *Cavalcade of America* "One Day at a Time". . . . .

1955 *Death Valley Days* "Million Dollar Wedding" . . . . Tiny Stoker

1955 *The Lineup* "The Casino Case". . . . . .Jim Kasino

1955 *The Lineup* "San Francisco Playboy" . . . .

1955 *The Lone Ranger* "Framed for Murder" . . . . Jim Blake

1954 *The Adventures of Kit Carson* "Frontier Empire". . . . . Henry Jordan

1954 *Annie Oakley* "Annie and the Outlaw's Son". . . . .

1954 *Annie Oakley* "Outlaw Mesa". . . . . Scott Warren

1954 *The Gene Autry Show* "Hoodoo Canyon". . . . . Ray Saunders

1954 *The Gene Autry Show* "Holdup". . . . . .Bank Teller

1954 *Hopalong Cassidy* "Silent Testimony". . . . . Rick Alston

1954 *Stories of the Century* "Little Britches". . . . . Dave Ridley

1953 *Cavalcade of America* "Night Strike" . . . .

1953 *Hallmark Hall of Fame* "McCoy of Abilene". . . . .

1953 *Skip Taylor* (TV Movie). . . . .

Director

Year	Title	Episode
1984	*The Dukes of Hazzard*. . . . ."Cale Yarborough Comes to Hazzard"
1984	*The Dukes of Hazzard*. . . . . "Dead and Alive"
1981	*The Dukes of Hazzard*. . . . . "Diamonds in the Rough"
1978	*The End* (Movie) . . . . *(Uncredited)*
1976	*Gator* (Movie) . . . . *(Uncredited)*

Writer

Year	Title
1998	*Death Mask* (Movie) . . . .

Producer

Year	Title
1978	*The End* (Movie) . . . . (assistant producer)

Self

Year	Title	Episode
2006	*CMT Insider*. . . . . "Special Edition: *The Dukes of Hazzard*"
2005	*After They Were Famous* . . . ."Crime-fighters"
2005	*Inside Fame*. . . . . "*The Dukes of Hazzard*"
2004	*The 20th Anniversary Hazzard County BBQ* . . . .(2004 video documentary short)
2002	*TV Road Trip*. . . . .
1981	*The Midnight Special* . . . .
1981	*Family Feud* . . . . "Heroes vs. Villains 2"
1980	*Family Feud* . . . . "*The Dukes of Hazzard* vs. *The Waltons*"
1980	*Family Feud* . . . ."*The Dukes of Hazzard* vs. *Angie*"

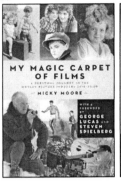

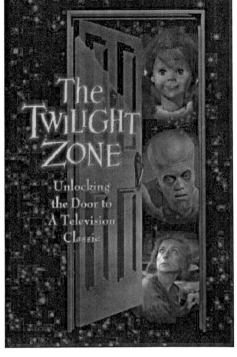
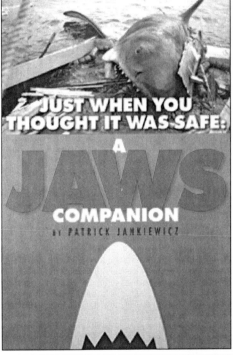

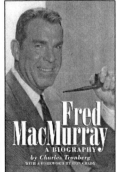

Printed in the United States
221668BV00003B/1/P

9 781593 934606